Intersecting Inequalities

Intersecting Inequalities

Women and Social Policy
in Peru, 1990–2000

JELKE BOESTEN

The Pennsylvania State University Press
University Park, Pennsylvania

An earlier version of chapter 3 was published in 2003 as "Poor Women in Peru: Reproducers of Poverty and Poverty Relievers," in "Women and Development: Rethinking Policy and Reconceptualizing Practice," special issue, *Women's Studies Quarterly* 31, nos. 3 and 4 (2003): 113–28. Chapter 4 was previously published as "Free Choice or Poverty Alleviation? Population Policies in Peru Under Alberto Fujimori," *European Review of Latin American and Caribbean Studies* 82 (April 2007): 3–20. An earlier version of chapter 5 was published as "Pushing Back the Boundaries: Social Policy, Domestic Violence, and Women's Organisations in Peru," *Journal of Latin American Studies* 38, no. 2 (2006): 355–78.

Library of Congress Cataloging-in-Publication Data

Boesten, Jelke.
    Inequalities : women and social policy in Peru, 1990–2000 / Jelke Boesten.
        p.   cm.
    Includes bibliographical references and index.
    Summary: "Examines how food aid, population policies and policy against domestic violence reflected and reproduced existing inequalities based on race, class and gender in 1990s Peru"—Provided by publisher.
    ISBN 978-0-271-03670-0 (cloth : alk. paper)
    ISBN 978-0-271-03671-7 (pbk. : alk. paper)
    1. Poor women—Government policy—Peru.
    2. Poor women—Services for—Peru.
    3. Poor women—Peru—Social conditions.
    4. Equality—Peru.
    5. Peru—Social policy.
    I. Title.

HV1448.P4B64 2009
362.5'5610820985—dc22
                                                2009046441

Copyright © 2010 The Pennsylvania State University
All rights reserved
Printed in the United States of America
Published by The Pennsylvania State University Press,
University Park, PA 16802-1003

It is the policy of The Pennsylvania State University Press to use acid-free paper. Publications on uncoated stock satisfy the minimum requirements of American National Standard for Information Sciences—Permanence of Paper for Printed Library Material, ANSI Z39.48–1992.

CONTENTS

List of Illustrations vii
Preface and Acknowledgments ix
List of Abbreviations xv
Glossary xvii

1 Introduction: Intersecting Inequalities 1
2 The Peruvian State and (Poor) Women 19
3 Food Aid, Motherhood, and Women's Work 44
4 Population Policies, Poverty, and Women's Bodies 74
5 Violence, Democracy, and Resistance 107
6 Revisiting Women 137

References 155
Index 171

ILLUSTRATIONS

1 Commemoration poster for Vilma Ortega Quispe, president of the Departmental Federation of Clubes de Madres of Ayacucho. © Jelke Boesten 2006. 139

2 Teodomira de la Cruz runs for congress with Avanza País. © Jelke Boesten 2006. 142

PREFACE AND ACKNOWLEDGMENTS

Candelaria Ascona Salgado lives in one of the urban squatter settlements near the center of Lima. Her adobe house is tiny. She lives there with her partner as well as with one grown-up daughter and an adolescent grandson left behind by another daughter. I got to know Candelaria and her family in the spring of 2000 through this last daughter, who had migrated to Amsterdam, where we became friends. Candelaria, to whom I represented a lifeline to her long-gone daughter, opened her house to me. She also made time to talk about her activist past and the social networks she maintained in the neighborhood. Candelaria and her family gave me a first insight into the lives of millions of Peruvians living on the fringes of cities in self-built homes and neighborhoods.

The neighborhood in which Candelaria lives is a typical migrant settlement, illegally built in the late 1960s and early 1970s. In 1970, Candelaria came to Lima from her rural hometown in the Andean province of Huancavelica together with her first child and her first husband. Like many other migrants, this young family searched for a better life in the city but found nothing but wasteland on the desert-like hills surrounding Lima. Optimistic and determined, Candelaria "occupied" a piece of land on one of these hills and built her house. She also helped make a neighborhood that today boasts a health care center, a school, and garbage collection and transport services. People still respect her because of her involvement in building and organizing the settlement during the 1970s. Back then, she brought together some of the other young women to organize an all-women's committee. Candelaria took the initiative to organize activities such as the nurturing of children; she mobilized support when she needed to confront governmental or nongovernmental institutions concerning licenses, building materials, donations or charity, and social services; and she was dedicated to the creation of social unity in a new neighborhood that was largely neglected by the state.[1] Her organization was a result of social and material needs that were crucial to family survival and that demanded the communal activism of women in the neighborhood in order for their families to survive.

Her *comité de damas* (ladies committee), founded in 1973 among *vecinas* neighbors, is today a *comedor popular*, a community kitchen, a phenomenon that has become widespread in Peru since the political and economic crises of the late 1970s. At my request, one day Candelaria invited the *junta directiva* (executive committee) of this *comedor popular* to her home to talk about their current issues and worries. Because Candelaria herself no longer participated in the local women's organizations, she appeared to be as interested as I was to listen to these three younger women who were her neighbors. The women told us that the government, still under the leadership of President Fujimori at the time of the meeting, provided the major material support to their, and other, organizations, much more than Church-based charities and international agencies did, as was common in Candelaria's day. The *comedor popular* had received money to pay for the rent of a building they used; they had received kitchen utensils, and monthly rations of foodstuffs. Moreover, nongovernmental organizations offered courses on nutrition and hygiene, and organized poetry contests. In Candelaria's day there also had been courses, she explained, but those were literacy courses offered by student volunteers. It had been difficult to attend them, she told me, because many husbands did not approve of their wives learning to read and write. The present-day *comedor popular* was apparently well supplied, and the women were enthusiastic about the additional social activities they performed. However, the conversation soon uncovered many disagreements and doubts. Was it not true that other *comedores* received more resources? Did other children not receive food at school instead? Was it not true that some *comedores* had even been given a car? Did some *comedores* not misuse the supplies by using them to make money? What had happened to the initial basis of solidarity that underpinned the organization? The women seemed to disagree on many issues.

After about an hour, a loud knock on the door interrupted our increasingly interesting conversation. Candelaria mumbled something like "There is the policeman." The man, who did not enter, but shouted from the doorway, was the "policing" husband of one of the women present, Marcela, and demanded her immediate return home. The meeting thus ended in an unsatisfied mood, as we did not get the spirit of the conversation back after Marcela had left. As this had been my first conversation with organized women in Peru, the dynamics of the meeting and the wealth of

1. Interview with Candelaria Ascona Salgado, Lima, April 2000.

information left me with much to ponder. After the other women had left, Candelaria confused me further by suggesting that she did not want to participate in the *comedor* because all those women were receiving too much money and were probably corrupt. It was April 2000, and Fujimori was on the verge of being re-reelected by dubious means. This partly explained the government's generosity towards the women's organizations, and the resulting conflicts and accusations. These elections were showing the extent of electoral clientelism that existed in the country, which jeopardized, in Candelaria's opinion, the basis of solidarity and community support that had been central to the women's organizations.[2]

I began to investigate the relation between grassroots women's organizations and other entities: Why did these organizations, initially set up as part of a series of strategies that sought to improve the daily life of their members, still exist under the tutelage of the state? What were the interests of the state in maintaining these organizations? Would the organizations survive without outside support? Why did the state direct certain social policies at women and not at other groups? To what extent did the image of these organizations—and their members—influence state policies? Why did husbands still police their wives when these women seemed to be such prominent members of their community through their organizations? These questions led me to ask a series of other, complementary, questions. Considering the widespread presence of grassroots women's organizations in Peru, these questions, further discussed in the introduction, led me to believe that it was worthwhile to examine how hegemonic perceptions and representations of women from the lower socioeconomic sectors helped shape policy-making and implementation and how the women at whom policies were aimed dealt with responsibilities that were embedded in the intersecting inequalities of class, race, and gender.

The study that followed became interdisciplinary, drawing not only upon history, which I read for my first degree, but also upon anthropological methodologies, political theory, and sociological analysis. Although this interdisciplinary approach runs the risk of not satisfying all "true" historians, anthropologists, sociologists, or political scientists, I believe that the chosen theme, the period studied, and the questions asked demand an interdisciplinary and flexible approach. Fortunately, the subject centers of which I have been part in my academic life—gender studies, Latin American studies, peace studies, and development studies—affirm the benefits of interdisciplinary study and encourage its practice. This book was influenced and supported by many people. Michiel Baud, at the Centre for Latin

---

2. Interview with Candelaria, Felia, Marcela, and Ruth, Lima, April 2000.

American Research and Documentation in Amsterdam, has supported my ideas critically, constructively, and generously, and I cannot thank him enough for doing so. The former Belle van Zuylen Research Institute for Gender Studies at the University of Amsterdam, at that point directed by Selma Leydesdorff, gave me the opportunity to undertake my project. I thank all the participants of the Institute for their collective and interdisciplinary commitment to question the assumptions that often sustain inequality. I was lucky to find a welcoming and encouraging supervisor in Frances Gouda, and I am very grateful for the trust she showed in me and my work. Sybille Lammes, Marie-Louise Janssen, Margriet van Heesch, and Sonja van Wichelen were fun and constructive workmates. Astrit Blommestijn and Marjolein Denslagen helped with administrative confusions. The Netherlands Institute for Scientific Research funded two of four fieldwork periods, for which I am grateful.

In Lima, I thank the historians Carlos and Marina Contreras, who, since my first journey to Peru in 1998, invited me into their home and gave me the feeling of finding a safe haven in a turbulent city. Margarita Zegarra, apart from guiding me through the archives and people in the world of gender history in Peru, invited me to her pleasant and constructive history workshops, which, unintended, changed my life forever. The work she and her colleagues do at the institute for documentation related to women's history, CENDOC-Mujer, deserves all the future support it needs. I thank Candelaria Ascona Salgado and her daughter Beatriz, who introduced me into their lives and, in doing so, gave me a first glimpse of a neglected and often invisible social group. If there is one social group in Peru that is transforming society with energy and imagination, then it is probably to be found among urban migrants such as Candelaria. I also thank Candelaria's *vecinas* and all the other women in Lima, Huancavelica and Ayacucho, who generously told me about (parts of) their lives and who gave direction and body to this book. The Manuela Ramos *promotoras* of the Casa de Bienestar in Pamplona Alta, Huancavelica, and Ayacucho and the grassroots women's organizations FECMA and FEDECMA in Ayacucho and FEMOCCPAALC in Lima have all been central to this study. I cannot thank them enough for their generosity in sharing their views and ideas with me. The feminist organizations Flora Tristan and Manuela Ramos-Lima and the women of the Movimiento Amplio de Mujeres have been welcoming and helpful. In addition, and for distinct reasons, I would like to thank Carlos Aramburú, Maruja Barrig, Cecilia Blondet, Betsy Flores, Maria Emma Mannarelli, Nelly Mejia, Vilma Ortega†, Kelly Alanya, Virginia Vargas, Alicia Villanueva, Victoria Villanueva, and Delia Zamudio.

In Britain, I thank the Latin America Centre at the University of Oxford for their friendly welcome in 2002. At different stages of research, writing, and beyond, Nikki Craske, Temma Kaplan, Fiona Macaulay, Lorraine Nencel, Jacobijn Olthoff, and Annelou Ypeij have been invaluable for the development of the ideas here exposed. The librarians of CENDOC-Mujer, Flora Tristan, and the Catholic University of Peru, all in Lima, of the Centre for Latin American Research and Documentation in Amsterdam, and of the Latin American Centre at the University of Oxford have been of great help. The Bradford Centre for International Development at the University of Bradford gave me the opportunity to continue working on this book and develop new ideas while also doing research in Tanzania. The Centre for International Participation Studies, Department of Peace Studies, at the same university facilitated a stimulating work environment during 2006–7, while friends and colleagues in Manchester were always there for good discussions while enjoying food and wine. The School of Politics and International Studies at the University of Leeds and its Centre for Development Studies gave me a warm welcome in 2007–8. During the summer of 2008, I found Polly Wilding willing to read the entire manuscript, for which I am very grateful. Her critical eye and cheerful comments greatly improved the book.

Chapters 3, 4, and 5 are partly based on papers earlier published in the *Women's Studies Quarterly,* the *European Review of Latin American and Caribbean Studies,* and the *Journal of Latin American Studies,* respectively. I thank the reviewers and editors of these journals for their helpful comments.

Annick Manrique and Guillermo Castrillon were the friends who distracted me from "fieldwork" and took me up in their own, specific, *Limeño* city sites. Their friendship made me more participant than observer, which was an invaluable experience. In Amsterdam, I could always count on a very warm welcome home, and many friends have supported me by cooking, offering somewhere to stay, hanging out, helping out, and coming over to the places where I chose to be. I want to thank them for a friendship that is truly irreplaceable. I thank my family for their trust and for the patience with which they accept my traveling, my absence, and my homecomings. Meeting Paulo Drinot midway through this project has been the real life-changing event. I feel very lucky that it turned out this way. Not only daily life but also this book would have been different without him. Paulo's attention and patience in reading several versions of the manuscript and his tireless capacity for constructive criticism have made this project a rich and exciting endeavor. I can only add that the result is entirely my own responsibility.

ABBREVIATIONS

CEM	Centro Emergencia Mujer, Emergency Center for Women
CONAMUP	Comisión Nacional de la Mujer Peruana (National Commission of the Peruvian Woman), 1970–76
CNC	Comisión Nacional de Comedores Autogestionarios (National Committee of Self-Managed Communal Kitchens)
CVR	Comisión de la Verdad y Reconciliación (Truth and Reconciliation Commission), 2001–3
FECCPALC	Federación de Centrales de Comedores Populares Autogestionarios de Lima y Callao (Federation of Self-Managed Communal Kitchen Centrals of Lima and Callao), founded in 1991
FECMA	Federación de Clubes de Madres de la Provincia de Ayacucho (Provincial Federation of Mothers Clubs of Ayacucho), founded in 1988
FEDECMA	Federación Departamental de Clubes de Madres de Ayacucho, (Departmental Federation of Mother's Clubs of Ayacucho), founded in 1991
FEMOCCPAALC	Federación de Mujeres Organizadas de Centrales de Comedores Populares Autogestionarios y Afines de Lima y Callao (Federation of Organized Women Pertaining to Self-Managed Communal Kitchen Centrals and Related Issues of Lima and Callao), 1999
INABIF	Instituto Nacional para el Bienestar Familiar (National Institute for the Well-Being of the Family)
MIMDES	Ministerio de la Mujer y Desarrollo Social (Ministry for Women and Social Development), 2002–
NGO	Nongovernmental organization

PROMUDEH	Ministerio para la Promoción de la Mujer y el Desarrollo Humano (Ministry for the Advancement of Women and Human Development), 1996–2002
PRONAA	Programa Nacional de Asistencia Alimentaria (National Program for Foodstuff Support), 1992
PRONAMACHCS	Proyecto Nacional de Manejo de Cuencas Hidrográficas y Conservación de Suelos (National Project for the Management of Hydrographic Basins and the Conservation of Soils)
USAID	United States Agency for International Development

GLOSSARY

Asistencialismo	Assistentialist; giving assistance to people without transforming the structures that created the necessity for that assistance
Autodiagnóstico	Self-assessment
Autogolpe	Self-coup, staged by President Fujimori in 1992
Capacitaciones	Training/workshops
Club de madres	Mothers' club
Clases populares	The poorer sectors, the urban "masses"
Comedores populares	Communal kitchens
Comité de damas	Ladies' committee
Criollo	Person of Hispanic-Peruvian decent
Engaño	Deceit
Feministas	Feminists
Fujimoristas	Supporters of Fujimori
Fuji-shock	The economic adjustment measures implemented in 1990 by President Fujimori to stabilize the economy
Hacienda	Large farm, plantation
Junta directiva	Executive Committee
Líderes	Leaders (here of women's organizations)
Limeño	Person from Lima
Médicos legistas	Forensic doctors; physicians who report back to judicial authorities
Mestizo/a	Person of mixed-race descent
Mancha India	Indian stain
Orientadores legales	Paralegal consultants
Populares	Grassroots; in this context, organized women at the grassroots

Políticas	Politicians; in this context, feminists in political parties and/or government
Posta de salud	Local health care center
Promotoras	Facilitators, people who go into the field to give information and support on particular themes
Pueblos jóvenes	Literally "young villages"; urban squatter settlements
Rondas campesinas	Peasant defense forces
Socias	Members of a women's organization
Tecnócratas	Technocrats
Vaso de Leche	Glass of Milk Program, 1984
Vecinas/os	Neighbors

1

INTRODUCTION:
INTERSECTING INEQUALITIES

In December 2002, I approached the Comisaría de la Mujer, a special police station for women in the Andean city of Ayacucho. The officer in charge that day was willing to talk about the problems of women who came to the Comisaría, and the problems he had in finding solutions. At first, my impression was that the officer was a dedicated man who believed in the rights of women. The police station, which had opened in 1999 and was a huge success if measured by the number of women who came to report aggressions, was filled with women sitting on the two benches placed against the walls. Although the facilities were poor and the police officers could barely deal with the number of women they encountered on a daily basis, the women patiently waited their turn. I had come with Kelly, a Quechua-speaking anthropology student at the local university. Because many women in Ayacucho speak Quechua, and I do not, Kelly's help was vital. In general, it seemed, these women had come to seek compensation in the form of a divorce, maintenance allowance, and money to pay the hospital bills that they had incurred as a result of the beatings that they had suffered. Some women sought protection. One of them was Dori. Her left eye was bandaged and she sat on one buttock, as the other was too painful to put weight on. Dori had a baby on her back, and she was pregnant with the next. The local governor of her district, also present at the scene, had taken her to the police station because, he said, Dori could not take care of herself or her children any longer; she lived on the donations of her neighbors while the father of her children did nothing to help out. Kelly approached her to ask if she wanted to talk to us. Before she had the chance to answer, the police officer in charge intervened. He started to speak to her in Spanish with a raised voice so that everyone in the office—and probably anyone outside the office, where the aggressor was waiting—could hear that Dori had been beaten up by her husband for many years very severely and that she had come to the police station only because the local governor had brought her. We all learned that Dori had been stupid enough to have stayed with this abusive man and that he made her pregnant all the time but never helped out financially. We also learned that the husband was not her husband, as he had a legal family with someone else. Dori, who could not defend herself in Spanish against the officer, sobbed quietly in her corner. When Kelly and I went out of the office in the hope that the public humiliation of Dori would then stop, the policeman drew up Dori's accusations in Quechua and proceeded to talk to the aggressor, who was waiting outside. The man bribed the police officer so that he would not be charged.

Personal history and circumstance notwithstanding, the intersection of gender, race, and class contributed to this woman's marginalization, and not only in relation to the elites in Lima: she was an outcast in her own town, her neighborhood, and even her own home. How was it possible that a special police office for women could treat Dori like this? Knowing the racism and sexism of police officers, what did she expect from her denunciation? Would she have come if the local governor had not brought her? Why did the policeman not speak Quechua to this woman, if Quechua was also his first language? How could he be bribed over such a sad case? What are people's stakes or benefits in humiliating this woman? Why did Dori not run away from her partner?[1] This book examines such questions by focusing on the intersecting inequalities of race, gender, and class in the constitution, reproduction, and maintenance of marginality in Peru. My main argument is that despite efforts to improve the position of women through prodevelopment and emancipation policies that directly target poor women, these policies are often severely obstructed by existing inequalities. I concentrate mainly on the 1990s, when the government of Alberto Fujimori implemented a series of projects directed at poverty alleviation and gender equity in an international context of neoliberal restructuring and UN conferences and treaties that sought to address women's rights. The national context of violent authoritarianism and inequality, however, seriously hampered attempts to transform society and improve the social and economic position of marginalized groups, in particular poor women.

To examine the workings of intersecting inequalities and governmental projects of emancipation and development, I study three policies in detail—poverty relief, population programs, and policies against domestic violence.

---

1. This particular case is further analyzed in chapter 5.

These case studies unveil some of the tensions inherent in the juxtaposition of development and emancipation during the 1990s, and show how, in the design and implementation of social policy, existing hegemonic inequalities based on race, gender, and class are both challenged and reproduced. The examination of the three cases of social policy also focuses our attention on the role of grassroots women's organizations and their middle-class allies such as feminist organizations and NGOs in challenging the prevailing racism and sexism in Peru's institutions. I first look at food distribution to women's organizations such as *comedores populares* (communal kitchens), *vaso de leche* committees (glass-of-milk committees), and *clubes de madres* (mothers' clubs), practices that started as soon as urban women organized themselves in the 1960s, expanded rapidly during the 1980s, and became institutionalized—and supported by legislation—during the 1990s. Such large-scale and institutionalized food distribution appealed directly to women's roles as carers in the community and not to women's actual capabilities as independent and productive citizens. In addition, the political interests attached to food aid, on both the international and national levels, often hamper actual poverty reduction. A look at the experiences of women's organizations in poor neighborhoods in Lima and in highland Ayacucho, the center of violence during the war between Shining Path and the counter-insurgency of the Peruvian armed forces, shows how women negotiate their roles as mothers and caregivers, their struggles for survival, and the discrimination and abuse they encounter.

In a second case study, I examine population policies that were uncovered as highly damaging and discriminative. Internationally, population control was an important and long-standing concern dominated by Malthusian notions that emphasized a strong correlation between social, economic, and environmental problems and the number of children women have. In Peru, from the 1960 until the 1980s, population policies received considerable opposition from both the Christian Right and the anti-imperialist Left. One of the consequences of this opposition was an increase in the gap between middle-class women, who had access to contraceptive methods (albeit a limited number) and reproductive health services, and poor women, who had little or no access. During the 1990s, poor women were targeted through an aggressive national "family planning" program. In 1997, allegations of coercive sterilization methods in rural and poor urban areas were proven (CLADEM 1998, CLADEM 1999, Defensoria del Pueblo n.d). These policies reveal the tension between instrumental uses of women's bodies as a mechanism of poverty reduction and the necessity to improve access to reproductive health care among poor and rural people. A study of women's

4   Intersecting Inequalities

experiences of reproductive health in rural communities in the Andean province of Huancavelica adds to understanding of the sterilization program by showing how existing inequalities made abuse in health services possible.

In a third case study, I explore attempts to combat violence against women through support programs for battered women. The high prevalence of domestic violence in Peru suggests that authoritarian forms of patriarchy are fostered in and reproduced by the family, making this more than metaphorically the "breeding place" of a nation trapped in racialized and gendered inequalities.[2] During the 1990s, much-awaited legislation against domestic violence was adopted and programs to support abused women were set up. However, as we will see, the design and implementation of the policies were at best halfhearted, and show how everyday violence finds resonance in Peru's institutions. Racist and sexist notions of citizenship and rights are articulated not only in the slow process of developing legislation and measures against domestic violence, but in the response of the professionals who are subsequently supposed to enforce such measures. What happened to Dori at the police station in Ayacucho will be further analyzed, as will the personal experiences of other women in urban and rural Ayacucho. These women's own interpretation of everyday violence and their struggles to stop it will be central to this chapter.

By focusing my study on the design and implementation of three social policies directed at poor Peruvian women, I expose mechanisms with which inequality based on gender, race, and class is, on a daily basis, maintained, reproduced, and, although often less visibly, challenged. These mechanisms are not only available to and used by authoritarian leaders such as Fujimori, but embedded in society and mimicked at all institutional levels, creating a myriad of hierarchies sustained through daily forms of violence and humiliation. Not only is racism institutionalized in Peru (Drinot 2006), but so is sexism. As a result, class relations are gendered as well as racialized, for example through domestic service. These parameters of hierarchy—race, class, and gender—intersect, especially in the lives of poor women.[3]

---

    2. Family, or kinship, is intertwined with ideas about nation, race, sex, and gender and can often be encountered in images of the nation (e.g., Wade 2003). Of course, the domestic nature of many racialized nation-building projects is the subject of many studies of colonialism and postcolonialism (e.g., Clancy-Smith and Gouda 1998; Stoler 1995 and 2002; R. Young 1995).
    3. Other parameters might play a role in perceptions of hierarchy and authority as well, particularly age. Sexuality and religion are also factors for differentiation with social consequences. However, race, gender, and class are the main pillars of institutionalized differentiation in Peru. For a further theoretical discussion of the illimited number of "signifiers," see Butler (1990); for a discussion of the potential importance of certain social divisions over others, see Yuval Davis (2006).

The idea that categories of differentiation overlap and intertwine, that racial differentiation influences gender and vice versa, that class positions are often racialized, and that gendered discrimination differs according to class positions became a political and analytical topic among feminists after bell hooks criticized the idea of a "global sisterhood" in *Ain't I a Woman* (1981). Since the 1980s, the fragmentation of the "category woman" and the relationship between social divisions have been extensively debated in feminist forums in the United States and beyond (Brah and Phoenix 2004; Phoenix and Pattynama 2006; Yuval-Davis 2006). These debates have led to increased awareness of the particularities of forms of discrimination, and the fluidity and historicity of race, class, gender, ethnicity, and other social divisions. The term "intersectionality," introduced by Kimberlé Crenshaw in 1989, serves to help us understand the dynamics and productivity of such overlapping and mutually constitutive divisions and "aims to make visible the multiple positioning that constitutes everyday life and the power relations that are central to it" (Phoenix and Pattynama 2006, 187). These (hierarchical) power relations are hegemonic and normalized in daily life, and, as Yuval-Davis observes (2006, 198), "they are expressed in specific institutions and organizations, such as state laws and state agencies, trade unions, voluntary organizations and the family. In addition, they involve specific power and affective relationships between actual people, acting informally and/or in their roles as agents of specific social institutions and organizations." The need to study women's positions from an intersectional perspective is therefore evident if we are to understand both women's position in society and their relationship with the state.

To analyze women's position in society and their relationship with the state, we need to look at the ways in which citizenship is differentiated. Maxine Molyneux argues that citizenship provides the framework for "problematizing the changing relations between state and society" (2000b, 35). The study of citizenship has been dominated by the influential work of T. H. Marshall, who viewed citizenship as entailing "membership of and participation in the community" (Marshall 1973, cited in Held 1989, 190). Debate around Marshall's theory of citizenship highlighted the necessity for looking beyond class in order to include race, ethnicity, and gender as differentiating categories in state-society relations (Held 1989; Pateman 1988; Yuval-Davis 1997; Squires 1999). Bryan Turner's argument that the "evolution of citizenship was a contingent and variable process . . . in constant flux" (Molyneux 2000b, 35) showed that citizenship and the civil, political, and social rights associated with it are not self-evident and that citizenship is not a stable status that one acquires only once. In Latin America, as Abel and Lewis observe (2002, 9), "social citizenship is deferred as the substance of social rights is acted upon unequally or is denied, rights are subverted by fraud, and regimes play lip service to forms of citizenship for the sake of international recognition, aid or loans." As such, Abel and Lewis continue, there is a "yawning gap" between rights-in-principle and rights-in-practice, perpetuated by the use of many Latin American governments of social rights to maintain a network of clients. Citizenship, and levels of inclusion and exclusion, are mediated through political choices and public policy and are, of course, highly gendered (Dietz 1998, 378–400; I. Young 2001, 401–29; Squires 1999). Policy is not a technical instrument that solves problems, but is embedded in and a reflection of the state-society relationship and the changes politicians and policy makers pursue in that relationship (Shore and Wright 1997, 5). At the same time, policy is often deployed as if it were solely a technical instrument and consequently often collides with the nontechnicality and nonrationality of the problems it intends to solve. Studies in the state-society relationship in Latin America show that expanding citizenship by liberalizing policy and legislation in relation to gender often runs up against existing social inequalities (Molyneux 2000b, 40). In exploring the particularities of the evolution of gendered citizenship in Peru, this book contributes to the literature on gender and the state. In particular, it links up to the literature that examines Latin American processes that expand women's citizenship while remaining enmeshed in often conservative racist and sexist social and political structures (Lievesley and Rai 1996; Waylen 1998; Jaquette and Wolchik 1998; Craske 1998, 1999; Matear 1999; Dore and Molyneux 2000; Schild 2000; Craske and Molyneux 2002).

Recently, the study of gender and the state in Latin America has received increasing scholarly attention. *Hidden Histories of Gender and the State* (2000), edited by Elizabeth Dore and Maxine Molyneux, looks at two centuries of independent history and takes a comparative perspective, with chapters on Costa Rica, Colombia, Nicaragua, Argentina, Mexico, Brazil, Bolivia, Cuba, and Chile. *Hidden Histories* is a landmark in the study of state-society relations and the gendered nature of state formation. Since its publication, several in-depth country studies of gendered state-society relations in Latin America have addressed how women's organizations formulate demands and negotiate a space within an often deficient and prejudiced state and its institutions; the nature of the relationship between feminist activism and grassroots activism; and how different ethnic and class positions influence the relation between women and the state and between each other. Such questions are addressed in, for example, the works of, Patricia Richards (2004) on Chile, Amy Lind (2005) on Ecuador, Fiona Macaulay (2006) on Brazil and Chile, and, with an emphasis on social movement theory, Carol Ann Drogus and Hannah Stewart-Gambino (2005) on antimilitary and religiously influenced activism in Brazil and Chile. These studies show how grassroots activism is often intertwined with the activities of NGOs and feminist organizations, while at the same time being in constant negotiation in order to maintain a minimum of autonomy. These studies also highlight how governments, especially during the 1990s, have not necessarily resisted widening women's participation and, under the influence of global political trends such as neoliberalism and the formulation of universal women's rights, are often keen to address women's issues both in legislation and policy. However, these efforts are often constrained by existing inequalities and prejudices. Peru is one of the most unequal countries in Latin America, but during the last decades of the twentieth century it followed the international trend in which women's issues and gender equity were increasingly addressed using legislation and policy. Therefore, this country study will contribute to our understanding of state-society relations and gender in Latin America by offering valuable case studies that enrich comparative perspectives on these processes.

The study of state-society relations in Peru has long focused on class (Cotler 1992; Stokes 1995; Graham 1991), or on particular regimes (Collier 1976; Stepan 1978; McClintock and Lowenthal 1983; Kruijt 1994; Crabtree 1992; Crabtree and Thomas 1999; Carrión 2006; Degregori 2000). In an important 1998 paper, Jeanine Anderson discussed the contemporary history of the relationship between the state and Peruvian women. Anderson concluded that women were never really approached as citizens in their own right, with legitimate claims on the state; rather, Peruvian women "possess entitlements but they cannot be sure of being able to exercise them" (Anderson 1998, 94). Anderson did not look at how race, class, and gender intersected in women's differentiated marginalization, but she recognized that political alliances between "disenfranchised groups" might be a way forward (ibid.). Anderson's paper was written perhaps too early for a critical reflection on the gender politics of the Fujimori regime, but since then several scholars have evaluated the 1990s in this respect (Blondet 1999, 2002; Schmidt 2006). Both Schmidt and Blondet emphasize that political interests and personalized politics underpinned gender policies, creating an often contradictory and always ambiguous meaning embedded in Fujimori's gender politics. Recently, Stephanie Rousseau (2006) has unpacked how these politics of gender have impacted on women's citizenship, while Christine Ewig (2006a, 2006b) has looked at health sector reform during the same period. Both Rousseau and Ewig emphasize the neoliberal and increasingly authoritarian context (neopopulist, in Rousseau's words) in which reforms have taken place. Maria Elena García takes a long-term view to examine the evolution of indigenous citizenship in Peru (2005), and in doing so, links up to the study of the dynamics of racial and class identities in a fragmented nation, as suggested by Marisol de la Cadena (2000). By examining intersecting inequalities, I intend to draw together the notions of race, class, and gender and show how these social divisions are intertwined in the exercise of citizenship. Although my case studies focus largely on the Fujimori period and a couple of years beyond, I trace the development of the policies directed at poor women to existing tensions between discourses and practices with regard to (economic) development on the one hand, and emancipation on the other. In doing so, I intend to highlight the deeper structures of inequality that highly influence not only the formulation of policy, but also the implementation, and thus the outcomes, of the discussed policies.

Peru: Persistent Inequalities

During the twentieth century the size and composition of the Peruvian population changed as a consequence of improvements in health care, migration and urbanization, industrialization, and the decline of agriculture. From being a mainly rural country with a large indigenous population, Peru became an urbanized and culturally, ethnically, and racially mixed society.[4] As elsewhere in Latin America, social and economic changes in Peru led to the emergence of populist political movements. In the early twentieth century, idealistic projects for a different, more inclusive nation were developed by intellectuals, who championed the indigenous population, the *indigenistas,* as well as by communists, socialists, and a small group of feminists.[5] At the same time, influential countercurrents were often highly negative about the Indian population, and favored a nation based on a European heritage. In the 1960s, socialist ideals—in a context of a highly unequal and exclusionary society in an era of Latin American revolutions—led to revolutionary guerrilla movements. These radical guerrilla initiatives were defeated by the Peruvian military, which, in 1968, took power through a coup d'état to rule through a "revolutionary" and leftist military dictatorship between 1968 and 1980, first under the leadership of General Juan Velasco

---

4. According the National Institute for Statistics (INEI), in 1940 64.6 percent of the population was rural, while in 2002 only 27.8 percent of the population lived in rural areas: http://www.inei.gob.pe. Besides indigenous, *mestizo* (mixed-race), and *criollo* (European-descended) populations, significant Afro-Peruvian and Asian groups live in the coastal areas. For an overview of Peruvian history, see Klarén (2000) and Contreras and Cueto (1999).

5. There is an extensive body of literature on *indigenismo* and *hispanismo* in Peru. A good overview of such literature and of early twentieth-century ideas and political projects generally is found in Hale (1996). More recent overviews can be found in the introduction to Cadena (2000) and García (2005, chap. 2).

Alvarado, and after 1975, when the rhetoric of "revolution" was abandoned, that of General Francisco Morales Bermúdez. This period was marked by well-intentioned but largely failed attempts to break with the old order, the oligarchy, and the extremes of inequality in order to establish a new national project that would incorporate the rural Indian population. In 1980, during the first democratic elections held in seventeen years, a group calling itself Shining Path declared war on the Peruvian state. During the next fifteen to twenty years, Peru was terrorized by Shining Path's violence and by the armed forces' counterinsurgency. In addition, incompetent governments, notably the Left-leaning populist government of Alan García (1985–90), brought the country to the edge of bankruptcy with an inflation of consumer prices of more than 7,000 percent in 1990 and with underemployment affecting 80 percent of the population (Figueroa 1998; Crabtree 1992). Only in 1992, after the capture of Shining Path's leader Abimael Guzmán and the implementation of shock structural economic adjustment policies, was pacification and economic stability achieved. This occurred in the context of the increasingly authoritarian and, as later would be revealed, corrupt, government of Alberto Fujimori (1990–2000). In 2001, after the spectacular fall of the third (and by many perceived as illegal) Fujimori administration the year before, a transition government installed a Truth and Reconciliation Commission (TRC) in order to investigate the violent events between 1980 and 2000.

Despite, or perhaps as a consequence of, the various intellectual, political, and violent projects that endeavored to transform Peruvian society into a more prosperous, equal, and just society, Peru continues to be highly unequal and fragmented. Cultural and political contradictions represented within Peru have generated a growing body of literature that focuses on the (failed) nation-state in order to explain Peru's persistent economic and political chaos, its profound inequality, and its inability to create a stable democracy for all Peruvians (e.g., Mallon 1983, 1995; Thurner 1997; Larson 2004; Mendez 2005; Drinot 2006). Arguably, the majority of Peruvians lived and still live with the daily experiences of "persistent violence (whether physical or not), poverty, and political and economic exclusion" (Drinot 2004). Several studies have claimed that in the 1960s and 1970s Peru had probably the most unequal distribution of wealth in Latin America (Webb 1977; Thorp and Bertram 1978). Only 5 percent of the population received 48 percent of the national income; 19 percent of this national income went to 1 percent of the population, whereas the bottom 20 percent of the population earned only 2.5 percent of national income (Klarèn 2000, 323). Since the 1970s, poverty has diminished slightly, but, according to the Living Standard Measurement Studies of the World Bank, in 1985, 42 percent of Peruvians still lived below the poverty line; the number increased only to 54 percent in 1991 (Figueroa 1998, 138), and was still 51 percent in 1997 (Ruggeri Laderchi 2001, 2).[6] Differences in income roughly coincide with where one lives and with ethnic background: the top incomes were mostly found among whites, referred to as *criollos*, of Spanish—or more broadly, European—descent, who live in the coastal urban centers, mainly in the capital Lima. In the 1970s, around 15 to 25 percent of the population was made up by the middle classes of urban *criollos* or *mestizos* (of mixed race).[7] The rest of the population consisted of the rural masses, indigenous, poor and largely landless people, urban migrants of indigenous descent, and a small group of Afro-Peruvians, descendents of slaves who worked on coastal plantations, as well as small immigrant communities that include Chinese, Japanese, and people from the Middle East (although many of these are part of the middle and upper classes). Although today parts of the urban internal migrant communities are doing increasingly well, the socioeconomic divide still runs along the same ethnic and geographical lines as before, and inequality is still high (World Bank 2007; UN 2005). Recently, national economic growth appears to have started to benefit the poor, reducing poverty from 54 percent in 2001 to 39.3 percent in 2007 (according to the national institute for statistics, INEI).

Women are particularly disadvantaged by the race- and class-based inequalities that characterize Peruvian society. According to the feminist organization Manuela Ramos, in 1991, men earned 47 percent more than women, a percentage that slowly decreased to 42 percent in 2000. Although since the 1960s women have increasingly had access to the education system, 16 percent of women are illiterate, compared to 5 percent of men (http://www.manuela.org.pe/empleo.asp). These numbers rise steeply when we look at the poorest rural areas: in the early 1990s in Huancavelica, in the south-central Andes, almost 50 percent of women were illiterate, compared to 10 percent of men (FLACSO 1993, 55). In 2004, the National Institute for Statistics calculated that 32 percent of women who did not live in Lima were illiterate (versus 11.3 percent of men), and 7.8 of women living in Lima (compared with 2 percent of men; http://www.inei.gob.pe).

---

6. I use the concept of poverty as it is used in the statistics produced to indicate Peru's poor population (Ruggeri Laderchi, Saith, and Stewart 2003). These are based on monetary calculations with a national poverty line. The "poor" are all those families living under a poverty line of U.S. $2 a day, while extreme poverty has a U.S. $1 poverty line, according to which 19 percent of Peruvians lived in extreme poverty in 1994. However, 35 percent of rural households lived on less than a dollar a day, against 5.5 percent of urban households (Ruggeri Laderchi 2001).

7. The urban middle classes were increasingly joined by migrants mainly from Europe and Asia, as Asians became another group that became racially stigmatized and discriminated against.

Additionally, there are particular issues that place women in a comparative disadvantage: four out of ten women suffer domestic violence, while 88 percent of reported cases of sexual violence are endured by girls under eighteen (ENDES 2005). Incest is a underdocumented phenomenon in Peru, but one study has suggested that of all pregnancies of girls aged twelve to sixteen in a maternity hospital in Lima in 1990, as many as 90 percent were the result of rape by the father, stepfather, or another close relative.[8] Social workers employed in centers and shelters for victims of domestic violence confirm that there is a high incidence of sexual abuse of girls in their own homes.[9] In relation to reproduction, it is estimated that of the total of yearly pregnancies, some 60 percent are unwanted, of which half end in abortions. Abortion is illegal and thus often performed in uncontrolled, inadequate circumstances. As a consequence, it is one of the most important causes of female mortality.[10] However, these numbers should be differentiated according to class, residence, and ethnicity, as access to reproductive health care, including abortion, is relatively good among the urban middle and upper classes compared to urban poor or rural areas. Access to services is impeded not only because of poverty and insufficient reach of medical services, but also because of discrimination, misunderstanding, and disrespect.[11] As we will see throughout this book, since the 1970s, national legislation concerning the situation of women has improved considerably. However, existing hierarchies based on gender, ethnicity, and class and the inadequate implementation of laws and programs have contributed to the persistence of inequality.

Peru remains a hierarchical society in which some are more "included" than others. Scholars repeatedly point to the racist basis of social inequality and to its devastating consequences for the majority of Peruvians and national development (Drinot 2006). The violent authoritarianism that keeps these hierarchies in place (Flores Galindo 1999) escalated during the war between Shining Path and the military that started in 1980. Nelson Manrique and Alberto Flores Galindo concluded already in 1986 that it was a paradox that Shining Path's so-called people's war—which was supposed to destroy existing power relations in favor of the poor—led to an escalation in violence against the already marginalized (Flores Galindo and Manrique 1986). Salomon Lerner (2003), the chair of the Truth and

8. According to a survey carried out by Manuela Ramos, as cited in Heise (1997, 415).
9. Interview with Emma Espinoza, Lima, December 2002; also Programa Integral de la Lucha Contra la Violencia Familiar y Sexual (2005).
10. According to a survey carried out by the U.S.-based Alan Guttmacher Institute, as cited in Centro de la Mujer Peruana Flora Tristán (2000).
11. See chapter 4 for further elaboration.

Reconciliation Commission, which investigated the atrocities committed by the insurgent groups as well as by the armed forces' counterinsurgency, today echoes their conclusions. Instead of the thirty-five thousand people initially thought to have been killed and disappeared because of the violence, the Commission now estimates the number to be seventy thousand. Eighty-five percent of these victims were Quechua-speaking and lived in rural areas. In his speech before then-president Alejandro Toledo, Salomón Lerner remarked that, "We live in a country in which exclusion is so absolute that it was possible for tens of thousands of citizens to disappear without anyone in the integrated society—in the society of the non-excluded—noticing . . . 35 thousand of our brothers disappeared without anyone [in the political community] missing them" (Lerner 2003).

Approach and Methodology: Researching Hierarchies

Studying the interaction between the state and poor women at the level of public discourse and practice, policy making, and daily experience can shed light on who confirms which hierarchical structure at which particular moment. I aim for an in-depth analysis of intersecting inequalities at different analytical levels in order to connect and juxtapose the everyday with the structural and institutional, the social with the political, and the discursive with the actual. Encounters in daily life with racism, sexism, and institutional and socioeconomic exclusion confirm ideas about "differences" that are disadvantageous for those on the negative end of such equations. In daily interactions, hierarchical positions are emphasized through sexualized and racialized images. At the same time, as Joan Scott reminds us, looking at the strategic use of specific representations also shows that differences along lines of gender, class, and race and/or ethnicity can be deployed as forms of resistance, negotiation, and change (1996, 12). By using the same markers of differentiation, however, these forms of resistance often confirm existing power relations as much as domination does. Women's emphasis on motherhood, for example, reifies the established gender hierarchy, but at the same time provides legitimacy to all-women's organizations and thus creates spaces for the development of multiple activities. This kind of resistance remains within the "permissible" margins of power and subordination, even if it can bring about unforeseen changes that in the end may undermine existing power relations.[12] For example, through talking with

---

12. According to James Scott, "the oppressed" have a "self-interest in conspiring to reinforce hegemonic appearances" in order to protect the little they have (1990, xii).

each other in mothers' clubs, women may develop a gendered consciousness, which may empower them to resist certain types of abuse or exclusion. In the long run, this empowerment may change their relations with their male partners, and possibly patriarchal relations in broader society. In the mean time, they do not challenge their assigned reproductive roles in the family or the community.[13]

I view Peru as a hierarchical society in which a complex system of sometimes small or imagined and often malleable and exaggerated differences attributed to whole groups results in the placing of one person in a dominant position in relation to another. As a consequence, minor differences often lead to large inequalities, which reinforce hierarchies and are deployed to serve the interests of some at the expense of others (J. W. Scott 1996, 12). As Marisol de la Cadena convincingly shows, the elements that are used to constitute differences need to be examined by looking at the function those differences appear to serve. That is, they must be grounded in the interests of the person or group that intends to make the difference instrumental (2000, 10–11). With such a perspective, fixed oppositions between dominant/subordinate become less plausible and thus less predictable and open to negotiation. Recent scholarship on the historical agency of peasants, women, workers, slaves, and servants in Peru and elsewhere indeed shows a less clear-cut hierarchy. Instead, power is constantly (re)produced through recurring interactions and negotiations between different social groups (e.g., J. C. Scott 1985, 1990; Bunster and Chaney 1985; Hünefeldt 2000; Christiansen 2004). The present study fits into this recent scholarship that aims to show the existence of subtleties in seemingly clear-cut power relations where "oppressors" seem to rule over the "oppressed." However, I do not want to underestimate the impact of subordination by exalting the creativity of so-called subalterns. Instead, I am interested in analyzing how major intersecting inequalities exist at the base of every social relationship in the daily lives of Peruvians, and consequently, within every negotiation over resources, services, and participation. In doing so, I am particularly interested in the agency of the less powerful, in this case, organized women from the lower socioeconomic strata.

In order to incorporate the different dynamics of Peruvian society in its cultural and geographical mix and diversity, I examine and link together three different localities: the coastal capital, Lima, and the south-central

---

13. See also the debates about other women's movements in the 1980s and 1980s, for example with regard to the Madres de Plaza de Mayo (e.g., Navarro 1989), but also other groups, e.g., Kaplan (1982), Radcliffe and Westwood (1993), Fisher (1993), Jaquette (1994), and Molyneux (2001).

Andean departments of Huancavelica and Ayacucho.[14] Ayacucho was the main area of activity of Shining Path and the army-led counterinsurgency between 1980 and more or less 1995, while neighboring Huancavelica was also severely affected. They are also among the poorest departments in Peru, relying mainly on agriculture. In both departments, many people, especially those who live in rural areas, speak Quechua and Spanish, or only Quechua. Although I do not speak Quechua, I was fortunate in always finding bilingual speakers who were willing to help me out when necessary. However, I could not conduct personal interviews with monolingual Quechua speakers. As a consequence, the focus of this study is more on Spanish-speaking urban migrants than on Quechua-speaking rural dwellers. It is often assumed that Lima is an entirely different cultural and sociopolitical space than the Andean highlands, but this is certainly not true for the millions of internal migrants living on the outskirts of the city. The ties and influences between women from rural Huancavelica and urban Lima, or from urban Ayacucho and urban Huancavelica or Lima, are strong. Urban migrants have extensive relations with rural communities. Some travel back and forth to maintain contacts with relatives; others trade between the urban and rural areas. Many of my urban interviewees were born in rural areas, whereas the younger generation had fewer memories of the communities their parents were born in. Still, many of the young went back with their fathers or mothers to visit relatives, or to contribute to rural development. With universities in the provincial capitals of Huancavelica and Ayacucho, some children of Quechua-speaking parents became anthropologists, studying the dynamics of the societies they partially grew up in, and still others became feminist activists or NGO workers. This indicates that the links between rural and urban are far stronger than they seem when seen from the perspective available to urban middle classes.

Considering the different themes I engage with in this book, the contemporary character of its history, the diversity of its actors, and, above all, my own interdisciplinary background, I approach my subject using a variety of sources and methodologies. I first explored written materials such as Peruvian feminist magazines from the 1980s and annual reports and fundraising reports of feminist NGOs, and I looked into various published testimonies of grassroots activists. To study policy, I used governmental promotion material, Internet-published speeches, and national newspapers from 1975 onwards. I was able to do this thanks to the Center for Women's

---

14. Peru is politically divided into regions, departments, provinces, and districts. Ayacucho is the name of a department, of a province, and of the capital city of both. The same is true of Huancavelica.

Documentation in Lima (CENDOC-Mujer), which did an excellent job of collecting press releases concerning women from 1975 through to 1996, made accessible via CD-ROM and a search engine. Last but not least, I was fortunate to find the woman in Ayacucho who kept a minute book of the Federation of Clubes de Madres of Huamanga, Ayacucho (1995–99). These minutes, which I use in chapter 3, contain a tremendous wealth of information about the locations, concerns, contacts, and problems of the women's organizations in Ayacucho.

Apart from these written materials, I interviewed people involved in grassroots organizations and in feminist NGOs and activist movements; I talked with civil servants in ministries, municipalities, and police stations; I interviewed lawyers and doctors; and I shared my experiences with Peruvian scholars. Besides attending meetings of grassroots organizations, I participated in many workshops organized by NGOs in urban settlements, rural towns, and villages. Both in Huancavelica and in several neighborhoods in Lima I was allowed to follow the *promotoras* (facilitators) of the NGO Manuela Ramos on their consciousness-raising missions and their provision of services in neighborhoods and communities that often lacked government-funded social services. Attending these meetings gave me a good insight into the "world of courses and workshops" in which grassroots women's organizations are often involved, and into the difficult relationship between women, the state, and NGOs. The *promotoras* in Huancavelica also shared valuable documents with me that they had produced with, among others, women in a community I had recently visited. These *autodiagnósticos* (literally "self-diagnoses") are documents in which rural women define concerns with regard to prevailing ideas about, and experiences with, reproductive health and contraceptives. As I further elaborate in chapter 4, these *autodiagnósticos* contain a wealth of information about reproductive health and sexuality.

Perhaps most valuable are the interviews with women involved in grassroots organizations. I have spoken with far more women, and visited far more organizations, than those that figure in this book. Nevertheless, all these voices are part of the narrative in having given perspective, affirmation, or strength to the stories of the women that do figure in the analysis. Although the majority of women were more than willing to tell their stories, I obviously do not claim that interviewees were completely open or sincere with me. They too had personal agendas in their encounter with me. Acknowledging this fact, however, does not invalidate their stories. In all interviews I conducted I needed to look at possible political agendas and cultural misunderstandings that could influence the conversation. I also needed to read between the lines and to think about possible interpretations (Sangster 2000, 87; see also

Leydesdorff, Passerini, and Thompson 1996, 6–7). For some women, talking to me may have been an expression of resistance or self-assurance. Luz, for example, a domestic worker in the house of friends and a participant in women's groups in her neighborhood, was interested in my work and wanted to tell me her side of the story. In the conversation I had with her, she criticized the women's organizations in her neighborhood and shared her experiences concerning the quality of women's cooking as well as the political manipulation on the part of the government and the municipality, thus warning me against writing too rosy a story. She also shared her hardships as a migrant, mother, and wife. By telling her story she highlighted her personal experiences, thus counterbalancing romanticized ideas about grassroots women's movements, and deliberately seeking an alliance with me when accusing her husband of abuse. Thus, even if Luz's story might not be her "factual" life story—I did not check if she really came from Loñagrande, or if she started to work at the age of six, and so forth—her experiences, as they were told to me, were invaluable. I interpret her, and others', decisions to offer me an interview before I even asked as an act of resistance against her own hardships, on the one hand, and an effort at influencing my opinions and actions, on the other. We might call Luz's agency a form of "subaltern resistance" as observed by James Scott in *Weapons of the Weak*.

In August 2003, the Truth and Reconciliation Commission published its report, a nine-volume work that investigated "what happened" in the years of political violence between 1980 and 2000. Apart from the detailed study of events, the report provides a sociopolitical history of contemporary Peru written by prominent sociologists, historians, and anthropologists. The researchers are writers and scholars, but, in the first place, they are Peruvians who are a part of the country's violent past. It is one of the most engaged and poignant documents I have read about contemporary Peruvian history. In its earnest efforts to uncover the truth about the events of the last decades of the twentieth century, the document confirms one's worst fears about sociopolitical hierarchies in Peru. Being the first Truth Commission internationally to deal with violence against women in a special committee, it includes a detailed analysis of gendered inequalities and its consequences for women during a period of political violence (TRC Final Report, vol. 8; see also Henriquez 2006; Boesten 2007, 2008). Although this book is not about political violence, the war is part of the context in which the study is placed. The report explicitly shows how inequalities based on ethnicity, gender, and class can be a basis for extreme violence and hatred, and for impunity and indifference. It shows how inequality and authoritarianism are untenable as a sociopolitical basis for a peaceful society. As such, the report confirms the relevance and necessity of researching intersecting inequalities in Peru in order to find ways in which to combat such inequalities.

In the next chapter, I will further elaborate on the historical and conceptual analysis of the relation between the state and women, broadening the context in which the case studies are placed. The chapter examines the state's approach towards the growing urban slums, and particularly looks at the rise of women's organizations in these migrant neighborhoods since the 1970s. This was also the time when feminist ideas took hold and a largely middle-class feminist movement emerged. The evolution of the relationship between the so-called popular women's movement, the feminist movement, and the state will be discussed, and the chapter will end with a discussion of the changes in state-society relations and gendered policy during the 1990s. I argue that although the 1990s were distinctive because of the implementation of neoliberal restructuring and the increasing international emphasis on women's rights, on the one hand, and the popular but authoritarian government of Fujimori, on the other, the underlying currents that shaped the discussed programs were rooted in deeper existing processes of persistent inequalities.

In chapter 3, I turn to my first case study, food distribution to women's organizations in Lima and Ayacucho. After tracing the politics of food aid and the relationship between the state and women as expressed in these policies, I examine how women's groups dealt with their assigned roles as food distributors in an era of political violence and poverty. In addition, using ethnographic material, I examine the power games played out in the relationship between state representatives and recipient women, and the strategies developed by women's organizations to negotiate their positions.

In chapter 4, I look at population policies and differentiated access to birth control methods. Because comprehensive population policies—and the expansion of reproductive health care—had long been opposed by the state, the overambitious and hands-on program designed and implemented in the 1990s was overwhelming for opponents and proponents alike. Whereas the program significantly expanded the formal rights of women to control their own fertility and improved their access to birth control methods, there was a clear racist and sexist undertone in how the program was set up and implemented. By looking closely at a parallel program that intended to empower women in reproductive health matters along side the medical program (both paid for by USAID), I examine the ideas and practices with regard to reproductive health among rural Andean women in the province of Huancavelica and the difficulties that they encounter in managing their fertility. The often-strained relationship between local medical personnel and rural women and men strongly contributed to the abuse that occurred during the implementation of the government's aggressive population program. In chapter 5, I examine the policies and programs designed to combat violence against women. I explore the extent to which gendered violence is related to political authoritarianism, and whether the government's efforts to counter violence against women contribute to democratization. I trace the development of policies against violence and how these relate to ideas about gender, race, and class. Using ethnographic material from Lima and Ayacucho, I explore women's use of legislation, special police stations, and emergency centers; in doing so, I also look at women's personal struggles with violence in their families, and how they use the women's groups to challenge patterns of violence and authoritarianism. Finally, in chapter 6, I follow up on the personal ambitions, gains, and losses of several women's leaders, bringing together the arguments made in the case studies by looking at what happened with the ambitions formulated in policy versus the practices that ensued from them.

2

THE PERUVIAN STATE AND (POOR) WOMEN

Any social, cultural or economic transformation can be sustained only if it involves women, who make up half of the world's population, and if it also eliminates the injustices endured by millions and millions of poor women around the planet.

I am convinced that in Latin America, and other parts of the world, the time has come to abandon, once and for all, the antiquated mental schemes which hinder the full development of women and, therefore, of humankind.

—*President Alberto Fujimori, Beijing, 1995*

In September 1995, President Fujimori was the only male head of state to address the official delegations at the Fourth World Conference on Women in Beijing. His speech not only celebrated women's achievements and their capacities and value for Peruvian society, but also recognized the long-term injustices suffered by women in general, and poor women in particular. In attending and addressing the Beijing conference and personally announcing a set of policies directed at gender equity and women's development, Fujimori made the "woman question" his personal concern. Surrounding himself with female legislators, ministers, and members of congress, and granting them ample space to develop proposals for policy and legal reform with regard to gender issues, the president further emphasized his personal concern for the well-being and emancipation of Peruvian women. Although Fujimori's presidency marked a decade of proequity legislation and policy, these changes did not appear out of nowhere. Both women's emancipation and the fight against poverty were long-standing, though not always successful, themes for debate, activism, and policy. These two aims, development and emancipation, came together in how the state addressed and targeted the poor women's organizations that arose in urban migrant neighborhoods in the 1960s and '70s and in rural areas in the 1970s and '80s. During the

1990s, the Fujimori government built on these developments, but largely failed to address the underlying inequalities.

Just as the proequity measures of the 1990s cannot entirely be accredited to the Fujimori government (Schmidt 2006), so are the ambiguous outcomes of policies and programs not only the result of bad policy design. Central to my argument throughout this book is the disjuncture between political discourse, underlying principles and interests, and the uses and effects policies have on the targeted population. Recognizing the complex nature of social policy forces us to look beyond the stated aims and objectives of policy documents, or even presidents' speeches (Shore and Wright 1997). The tensions between discourse and practice are easy to identify when analyzing Fujimori's speeches in retrospect, knowing what some of the damaging outcomes of policy practice were. But it demands more scrutiny to identify the connections between local, national, and global continuities and processes of change that influence how policies come about and how they are implemented. These processes are embedded in power relations and existing hierarchies that are simultaneously challenged and confirmed by policy: discursively, policy aims to generate change, while in practice, policies often confirm and reify inequalities embedded in state-society relations. In order to provide a long-term perspective as well as contemporary urgency to the three case studies examined in the upcoming chapters, we need to place the analysis of policy into a framework that includes the development of the relationship between the Peruvian state and women in general, and "poor" women in particular. On the one hand, we need to explore the historical-political background to policies directed at women in order to examine how gender, race, and class intersected at policy level. On the other hand, we need to discuss the relationships between women's organizations, the feminist movement, NGOs, and the state.

Central to such an exploration of the relation between the state and women is the tension between development on the one hand, and emancipation on the other.[1] Tensions between development and emancipation are not unique to Peru, but they surfaced with the introduction of a woman-inclusive approach in international development, associated with the publication of Ester Boserup's important book *Women's Role in Economic Development* in 1970. While Boserup's work made the necessity of including women in

---

1. Although emancipation is a somewhat outdated (or unfashionable) concept that has largely been replaced by terms such as "empowerment" and "gender equity," I believe that the emancipatory project, understood as a historical process that aims to free people, especially marginalized groups, from "legal, social or political restrictions" (Oxford Concise Dictionary) is appropriate in this context.

development processes credible and anticipated the Women in Development (WID) approach in international development discourse and practice, it also generated criticism. WID advocated equity in development, but, according to its critics, mainly promoted the inclusion of women as paid labor without questioning the underlining gender ideology that permeated society as well as development institutions (Vavrus and Richey 2003, 6). Critics argued that WID neglected the gender politics of policy and the "systemic nature of gender inequality and its connection with other forms of inequality" (Kabeer 2001, 38). These debates about women's inclusion, on the one hand, and the undermining of gender ideology, on the other, resulted in the formulation of a new approach, Gender and Development (GAD). Champions of GAD advocate women's empowerment and the restructuring of gendered power relations. The starting point of GAD is that gendered identities are social constructions—as opposed to biologically determined—which are influenced by differing processes of cultural and socioeconomic change. Thus, whereas WID approaches to development tend to promote the inclusion of women without addressing the underlining gender ideology that perpetuates inequality, GAD approaches explicitly seek to challenge gendered stereotypes and roles. Despite this structural approach to gender inequality, GAD has largely resulted in a technical idiom of "gender mainstreaming" that often overlooks more feminist critiques of underlying gendered power relations (Murdock 2003). In Latin America, as elsewhere, attempts at improving the positions of women often meet with existing inequalities based not only on gender but on ethnicity, race, and class (Molyneux 2000b).

First, I will look at the evolution of social policy in the form of tentative, scattered, and sometimes random, "politics of slums" since the mid-twentieth century, and how "women" became a separate category in Peruvian social policy. I will discuss the different approaches to the "woman question" and argue that with the rise of professional women and organized feminism, on the one hand, and the increasing growth and recognition of organized women in the slums as an important electorate, on the other, a class-based bifurcation of womanhood arose in political rhetoric and practice that did not reconcile developmental and emancipatory goals, but rather, perpetuated inequality based on gender and class. Opportunistic governments used social policy to mend dissatisfaction among both groups, and appeal for international approval at the same time. The lack of actual social citizenship (as opposed to citizenship in principle) for a majority of women, however, turned the relationship between state and citizen all too often into a relationship between patron and client.

A Politics of Slums: Clientelism and Paternalism

Politics in Peru during the second half of twentieth century shows some clear distinctions from regional trends: although Peru was ruled by military dictatorships in 1948–56, 1962–63, and 1968–80, these were not as repressive and violent as those in, for example, Brazil, Argentina, or Chile in the same period. The military government of General Juan Velasco Alvarado was particularly seen as an experiment in revolutionary politics, and was generally positively regarded by the Peruvian and Latin American Left until a politically more moderate dictator, Bermúdez Morales, replaced Velasco (see, e.g., Lowenthal 1975; Stepan 1978; McClintock and Lowenthal 1983; Kruijt 1994). The violence that paralyzed large parts of Peru between 1980 and 2000 was perpetrated by the uprising initiated by Shining Path and by the counterinsurgencies, which were sponsored by democratically elected governments. However, persistent inequality and poverty, made visible by rapid urbanization and population growth, facilitated modern electoral patron-client relations in all the post–World War II governments, albeit to different degrees. The growth of urban slums, built on waste land surrounding the cities by migrants from jungle, mountain, and coastal rural and provincial areas, went hand in hand with renewed interest in revolutionary politics and leftist ideals, feminism, and shifts in world politics and military power during the 1960s to 1980s.

Peru's demographic transition started around 1940; the population had doubled by 1970, and quadrupled by 2000, when it reached twenty-eight million. Economic change led to massive internal migration from rural areas to urban areas, bringing to the cities not only impoverished peasants but indigenous ones. This was the start of what came to be known as *cholificación*, a process of cultural change that went in hand in hand with mixing ethnic identities and increasing urban habits and expectations, including a steeply rising demand for education (Quijano 1967, 1980; Matos Mar 1984; Nugent 1992; Cadena 2000).[2] The political and economic elites concentrated in the capital, Lima, saw the migrant squatter settlements mainly as a breeding ground for social unrest. As David Collier points out (1976, 19), the settlements were frequently referred to as "socially deviant," a "social cancer," and "a belt of misery." Both *criollo* fear of, and disdain for, the "dirty masses" and an underestimation of the (political) power of

---

2. In 1940, 3,370 university students were counted; in 1970, 109,590; and in 1980, 257,220. According to FLACSO (1995), in 1970 30 percent of the university population was female. Primary and secondary education also went up.

these very same masses contributed to the indecisive and incoherent policies directed at the migrant settlements in urban areas.

But there were policies nevertheless. President Manuel Odría, the military dictator who ruled Peru from 1948 to 1956, recognized the potential of popular support among these newly literate (illiterate people had no suffrage until 1979) slum dwellers, and established clientelist networks by using charity as a favor to the poor.[3] Under the democratically elected Fernando Belaúnde (1963–68), such practices continued, although this president actively tried to stop the creation of new urban settlements around Lima. In the meanwhile, largely left to fend for themselves, male migrants organized in neighborhood committees, and women started to reformulate issues that had always belonged to the domestic sphere in terms of communal problems. As the vast literature on the subject shows, the resulting *comités de damas* (ladies' clubs) and *clubes de madres* (mothers' clubs) in the *Limeño* squatter settlements took part in the organization of necessary infrastructure; provided for a social network vital for migrants deprived of their old social structures such as kinship or community networks; organized courses to help people learn to read and write with the help of university volunteers; and created an alternative, informal social security system to take care of each others' children and of the sick, widows, orphans, or single mothers within their new communities (Barrig 1986, 1988; Blondet 1991; Blondet and Montero Checa 1995; Denegri 2000). In the 1970s, women's organizations were joined by—or transformed into—*comedores populares* (communal kitchens), while the female version of male neighborhood organizations, the *comités de damas*, largely disappeared. The *comedores populares* had a more specific task: they were set up for the immediate alleviation of poverty during the subsequent economic crises, many times with the financial and logistical support of NGOs, faith-based organizations, and governmental institutions (Anderson 1998).

A 1973 sociological study of the new phenomenon of massive shantytowns that were taking shape on the outskirts of the Peruvian capital argued that the "invaders," the migrants who occupied empty lands in order to build homes and neighborhoods, were being "invaded" (Rodrigues, Riofrío, and Welsh, 1973). The authors pointed at the growing caravan of priests, bureaucrats, students and professors, party leaders and political militants, and presidents' wives and other high-society charity ladies who entered the new urban districts for their own particular reasons. For governments,

---

3. Clientelism defined as client-patron relationships whereby favors are exchanged (e.g., food for votes). Odría was formally elected president of Peru in 1950.

the mushrooming women's groups became a welcome target for the distribution of benefits in return for votes. First ladies of the nation would distribute foodstuffs and kitchen utensils to women's organizations in poor neighborhoods during election time. These sporadic and paternalist campaigns were not devoid of attempts to do good by "civilizing" the poor. For example, Violeta Correa de Belaúnde, first lady of Peru from 1963 to 1968, personally visited the settlement of San Martín de Porres, Lima, and organized a contest among women's organizations. Those women who could show the cleanest houses, even the cleanest children, would receive sewing machines, cooking utilities, or food (Blondet 1986, 45). In such a way, and throughout the years, governments sought to bind organizations to the ruling party. Even General Velasco's strategy, which sought to regulate the development of the shantytowns and bring its inhabitants into the state, tied support to party politics.

The strategy of the Velasco regime in the early 1970s was directed at curtailing the creation of new settlements and illegal land occupations, as the "revolutionary" government was no supporter of the squatter populations around Lima either. However, the regime also intended to manage and control (or regulate and include) the existing urban migrants. The government issued property rights for the lands already taken, a very important and valuable measure for these people, who, through such licenses, not only felt they received a recognized place in Peruvian society, but also gained actual access to services they did not have as long as they lived illegally. With the slum population largely recognized, the government sought a way to control improvements in the infrastructure of the slums without taking too much responsibility on itself. To this end, Velasco called the progressive bishop Luís Bambarén of Lima, who had been active in the settlements since 1963, to his office to advise the government and to actively involve the Church in a new government program. Bambarén saw the squatter settlements not as a "social cancer" but as a positive alternative to the inner city's *callejones* (dark alleys). He renamed the settlements *pueblos jóvenes* (young villages), a term that was immediately made official by Velasco and is still current today. The philosophy of Bambarén—self-help action through organization, instead of reliance on "sporadic and paternalistic" government aid—was institutionalized and politicized (Stepan 1978, 161–62). Existing neighborhood organizations that managed and executed infrastructural demands and works were directly tied to government institutions. Although the organizations were well organized, the political interests in which most became involved did not further independent political participation. The idea of "self-help" became characteristic for the *pueblos jóvenes*, while it also indicates neglect on the part of the state.

Women were central to the idea of self-help, as they were the ones who organized in order to provide for the basic survival of their communities through their neighborhood-based grassroots women's organizations.

The Rise of the "Woman Question"

The increasing visibility of women in self-help organizations coincided with the rise of feminism in the middle classes. The first UN conference on women, held in Mexico in 1975, further highlighted the necessity for a politics directed at furthering the emancipation of women. However, throughout the late 1960s and 1970s, leftist perspectives dominated Peruvian politics and intellectual debate, and the woman question was initially read through a lens of class politics. In most scholarly analyses of the Velasco period, women play a marginal role. However, the Velasco regime was the first government in Peruvian history to address women specifically in a separate committee, the Comisión Nacional de la Mujer Peruana (National Commission for the Peruvian Woman, or CONAMUP), and the first to embrace specific policies that promoted the inclusion of women in public life (Anderson 1998). In first instance, CONAMUP was an attempt to bind women's organizations from all classes to the state in order to promote women's identification with the regime. According to a 1970 document (CONAMUP 1970), elements of CONAMUP were already active in that year; however, CONAMUP was officially activated only in late 1974, to prepare for the 1975 UN conference (Jara 1975). The government sent a Peruvian delegation to the conference, which was to promote the achievements of the revolutionary government in relation to the effective mobilization of women in "female grassroots organizations, located within the economically productive and political representative organizations of the workers and the people" (CONAMUP 1975, 11). The official standpoint of the government in relation to women's emancipation was based on the idea that equality would be achieved through a general revolution, not by means of a separate, feminist, struggle. "Patriarchy" was interpreted as a part of the legacy of colonialism and the Industrial Revolution and would thus be eliminated with the implementation and success of a Peruvian socialist revolution (CONAMUP 1975, 11). Feminism was even fiercely rejected: "We reject any form of feminist liberation as these only act in favor of women's rights . . . while these [rights] should be understood within the realm of general human liberation" (CONAMUP 1970). In its goals, CONAMUP showed strong parallels to Cuba's Federation of Cuban Women (FMC). For CONAMUP, as for the FMC, the creation of a large top-down women's organization controlled by the state "sought to achieve the political mobilization of women in order to consolidate political power and to implement a socialist program of economic and social transformation," whereby an "ethical commitment to women's emancipation [was] premised on women's entry into work, formal juridical equality, and social rights to health and education" (Molyneux 2000a, 295). In relation to the "woman question," the Peruvian military government seemed to support Friedrich Engels's analysis, reinterpreted by the Women in Development approach, of capitalism and the division of labor, in which women's oppression resulted from their exclusion from the labor market. In such an analysis, a feminist struggle was not necessary or would even be counterproductive for the general struggle against capitalist labor relations, as long as women were incorporated into the labor market (Kabeer 2001, 44–45).

As Maxine Molyneux observes (2001, 109), a rejection of feminism from a Marxist perspective did not prevent many communist states from being "the earliest to apply egalitarian principles in matters of law and policy." The first and most extensive policy to influence gender relations was the Velasco regime's educational reform of 1972, which called for a curriculum that would "dignify" women as persons and encourage the expansion of technical and vocational education for girls. Furthermore, it attempted to make the basic curriculum gender-neutral by assigning the same subjects to boys and girls, including knitting, sewing, and technical classes for all. Another goal was a gradual shift away from sex segregation in public and private schools (Anderson 1997, 80). While the Peruvian military government was no communist state, in some aspects—such as the woman question—it did follow Marxist principles.

The Velasco government did not only use an emancipatory, though not explicitly feminist, discourse while trying to tie organizations to the state, but also pointed specifically to the potential roles working-class women could fulfill in a national project of modernization. In a document from 1975, edited by CONAMUP, the final emphasis was put on women's reproductive responsibility. Women's functioning, like the activities of all citizens, should be in the service of the people, but women had "a unique and authentic basis in their decisive family function, and their reproductive participation in the process of transformation and perfection of Peruvian society" (CONAMUP 1975). Women's maternal and reproductive roles were emphasized and brought into the public sphere through an emphasis on the responsibility toward the future generation of Peru that they carried within them. Such a view should be seen in the light of women's growing activism in the urban migrant settlements. The Velasco regime used a combination of class and maternalist rhetoric to win the support of women's organizations and the emerging feminist organizations. Like other state institutions of the "Peruvian experiment" designed to encourage transformations at the grassroots level, CONAMUP never gained the broad-based support it aspired to, and after 1975, when Velasco was deposed by another, more moderate, military government, CONAMUP was gradually abolished.

From the Velasco period onwards, attention to the woman question dissipated as a result of the different approaches to the relation between development processes and women's emancipation, class positions, and feminist perspectives. This dissipation was mainly discussed as a separation of interests between *populares* (grassroots women's organizations), *políticas* (women politicians), and *feministas* (feminist activists) (Vargas 1991). The *populares* were seen as poor women fighting for basic needs; they lacked feminist consciousness, according to many feminists, or were in need of class struggle, according to others. The *políticas* fit the classical WID approach to women and development; they looked to the integration of women in development processes, without a primary interest in changing gender relations. *Feministas* saw themselves as the only autonomous group that questioned existing gender ideologies in pursuit of genuine equality. The *políticas*, in turn, considered feminists to be often unrealistic about class relations in Peru, while *populares* sometimes accused feminists of elitism (Grupo Autonomo de Mujeres 1983; Vargas 1991; Blondet 1995; Lievesley 1996).

The tensions between *feministas, populares,* and *políticas* were not unique to Peru. They were reflected as well in the discussions at the regional Latin American Feminist Meetings (Saporta Sternbach et al. 1992; Craske 1999, 2000; S. Alvarez et al. 2003). Whereas the tension between *feministas* and *políticas* mainly concerned the issue of autonomy versus double militancy— that is, whether one could be loyal to both feminism and a political party—the friction between *populares* and *feministas* was perhaps even more difficult. Did *populares* want feminism; did they not emphasize and further maternalism with their organizations for daily survival, such as the *comedores populares*? Were such activities not counterproductive to the feminist project? Were feminists not too elitist? Could middle-class women seek emancipation and empowerment for "all" women if they cheaply employed women from the slums to work in their houses and offices? Where did the project of seeking secure livelihoods meet the project of women's empowerment? These and other questions were endlessly discussed, and were also reflected in early attempts to seek rapprochement from both sides (Vargas 1991, 1992, 1995; Lievesley 1996).

On a theoretical level, two approaches gained ground throughout Latin America and in Peru. First, following ideas first developed by the U.S. black socialist movement—and an obvious predecessor of thinking in terms of intersecting inequalities—there was the idea that poor women were triply oppressed through the mechanisms of gender, class, and ethnicity (M. Francke 1990). According to the logic of triple oppression, poor women's struggles were separated from feminist struggles because of race and class. Rapprochement could be found in the common fight against the three pillars of oppression, but was constrained by the reality in which *criollo* middle-class feminists employed *mestiza* or indigenous working-class women as domestic servants. The second analysis of the schism between the feminist project and the large grassroots women's movement in Latin America, first developed by Maxine Molyneux (1985), was that both had particular women's interests, but that these interests differed in their practical and strategic priorities. Separating contemporary practical women's interests, such as feeding families, from strategic women's interests, such as legislation to improve political representation, helped to identify and clarify why debates between *populares* and *feministas* were so heated, but also offered a possibility for understanding between the two. María Elena Moyano, a grassroots activist and widely admired politician and feminist, understood this when she addressed a journalist on the issue of women's collective focus on domestic tasks in the *barrios*:

I think that if the feminist compañeras *say that we are [merely] transferring domestic tasks from the home to politics, they do not understand that we, popular women* [mujeres populares], *need to get out of the private space to be able to understand the public space; we need to understand that we are still oppressed, because first we will think about how to feed our children. The middle-class woman has her children well-fed, she has a husband who, if he does not help her in the domestic tasks, will have a* compañera *who will help her do so. (Moyano 1990)*

Moyano's critique pointed at what she thought to be several important aspects of the grassroots women's movement in relation to feminist politics: first, she noted that necessity comes first and should not be forgotten, that is, that practical interests are needs; second, she argued for the importance of organizing on behalf of these necessities; and third, she argued that in doing so, poor women gained a better understanding of forms of oppression. She thus pointed out that strategic and practical interests and needs were not exclusive. Furthermore, she indicated that the comfortable position of the middle classes, through their reliance on the labor of the poor, was in part dependent on the lower classes, even if she tried to neutralize class positions by calling both rich (*feministas*) and poor (*populares*) *compañera* (comrade).

The recognition of differing but not exclusive interests certainly helped in better understanding the tensions between *feministas* and *populares*.

However, the distinction between practical and strategic women's interests also provided a gender-friendly language for targeting women's groups in poor areas with poverty relief initiatives, without addressing underlying gendered inequalities (Wieringa 1994). The entanglement of a gender position that urges women to think about children first, with a class position that leaves little choice but to go public with demands for basic necessities, gave those organizations an image as collective carers in economic crisis, an image magnified, in turn, by political parties, the state, charities, the Church, and NGOs. During the 1980s and 1990s, grassroots women's organizations in Peru and elsewhere in Latin America were predominantly targeted as either carers for the community, or as part of communal self-help programs (see also Craske 1999, 2000; Lind 2005). As Wieringa argues (1994), this excessive attention to women's practical needs drew away attention from essential issues related to poor women's gendered oppression, including the premises on which they had become the carers for their families and communities.

During the Fujimori era, the different interests and positions within the women's movement once again shifted. The women in government or political parties and identified as *políticas* during the 1980s and early 1990s worked for state commissions and units designed and set up to address issues related to women. The issue of "double militancy" in both feminist organizations and leftist political parties became less relevant in the 1990s— mainly as a consequence of the breakdown of what used to be called the New Left, but also because of a gradual depolitization of the feminist movement as feminists increasingly cooperated with, and worked for, government institutions. Some of these feminist professionals became part of Fujimori's inner circle, while others were involved on the sidelines as advisers and consultants (Schmidt 2006). At the same time, what used to be the feminist movement—the autonomous *feministas*—are today working in NGOs that target what used to be the "popular" women's movement, or grassroots organizations (in Peru now referred to as *organizaciones sociales de base*). From the 1980s onwards, feminist NGOs started to play an important role in the further development of grassroots organizations and in the formulation of a feminist agenda as part of development discourses, a process referred to as the NGOization of social activism.

NGOization of the Feminist Movement

The NGOization of feminist organizations is the professionalization, institutionalization, and bureaucratization of feminist organizations earlier defined as relatively autonomous sociopolitical organizations (S. Alvarez, Dagnino, and Escobar 1998; Craske 1998, 2000; Schild 1998; Vargas 2004). Instead of being political activist/oppositionist organizations, NGOs often serve as intermediaries between the state and civil society. NGOs are often dependent on funding from outside sources, a dependence that has profound implications for the functioning of these organizations. In developing countries, structural adjustment imposed by the World Bank and the International Monetary Fund furthered the NGOization of civil organizations, which increasingly sought and found external funding and became specialists in certain areas of service delivery and advocacy, often working alongside transnational NGOs (Bondi and Laurie 2005). The Australian scholar Tessa Morris-Suzuki suggests that this trend was encouraged by the international community, and that it shifted state responsibility for social development onto civil organizations; she notes that the World Bank evaluated the presence of NGOs in developing countries as instruments of "good governance" (2000, 69).

Although the NGOization of feminism can be seen as a global trend, every region shows its own particularities in this development. In Peru, feminism became increasingly institutionalized during the 1980s under the influence of several factors. Besides political activism, feminist organizations linked up with grassroots organizations to organize projects. This was partly a result of feminists' interest in bridging the class divide, and was further encouraged by the growing international attention paid to gender in development—and the accompanying resources that were allocated for interventions in the realm of gender and poverty (Craske 1999, 128). Feminist organizations such as the Centro Flora Tristán, established in 1979, and the Movimiento Manuela Ramos (1980) took advantage of this trend and organized consciousness-raising workshops in the *pueblos jóvenes* with the financial support of international development organizations.[4] By 1985, increasing demand for support from feminist organizations came from the *pueblos jóvenes* themselves. Well-organized women in poorer neighborhoods apparently had the space, the network, and the desire for more collaboration with feminist groups. These collaborations were also financially beneficial to both parties: grassroots organizations saw an increase in the influx of small amounts of money for the realization of projects, while feminist organizations could increasingly professionalize and institutionalize. For example, by 1985 the leading actors in these feminist

4. See, e.g., the reports on meetings of Manuela Ramos in: "Las Manuelas se encuentran III," 567-5250-84 G ICCO, Utrecht Archives, 16; "La Situación de la Mujer, Collique 1983," 567-ICCO, Utrecht Archives, 13.

organizations were paid professionals financed by international funds. Development aspects—production workshops, financial management, nutrition, income generation—became main objectives of feminist NGOs' support to grassroots women's organizations. The rapid neoliberalization of the economy and the increasing authoritarianism under Fujimori further pushed feminist organizations to seek international funding and call themselves nongovernmental organizations. This trend had positive as well as negative aspects. Sonia Alvarez (1998) emphasizes the positive effects of the rise of transnational networks that were part and parcel of NGOization. In contrast, Arturo Escobar (1995) sees a "developmentalization" of women into clients of governmental and international nongovernmental projects that shift responsibility for national social welfare away from the state and onto the shoulders of women. Veronica Schild (1998) observes that while national and international development programs increasingly targeted women, there should be more attention to (poor) women's inclusion into a national welfare system through the granting and implementation of rights. The debate about the merits and disadvantages of NGOization as a process has died down with the consolidation of NGOs' roles in local, national, and global development projects. However, the nature of the contribution NGOs deliver to development in different contexts, and, especially, issues of accountability, representation and professionalization, are still widely discussed (e.g., Bondi and Laurie 2005; Bebbington, Hickey, and Mitlin 2007).

Of the various feminist organizations founded in Peru between 1978 and 1980, two grew steadily into NGOs during the 1980s: Movimiento Manuela Ramos and the Centro de la Mujer Flora Tristán. The NGOization of these two feminist groups created tensions between them and smaller feminist organizations, joined together under the umbrella feminist movement. The smaller organizations within the feminist movement criticized Manuela Ramos and Flora Tristán for becoming "centers" with office facilities, financed employees, and a specified program. In a controversy similar to that of the early 1980s over autonomy and double militancy in feminism and political parties, in the mid-1980s the centers were criticized for having a dubious double agenda. It was argued that because these centers had a stake in fulfilling the requirements of international funding agencies, they would not be able to develop feminist militancy and thus could not represent the feminist movement. Despite their criticism of the centers, however, the smaller organizations in the feminist movement did not distance themselves. After all, they also benefited from the facilities that only the centers could deliver; for example, the smaller organizations used the centers' office facilities, logistics, networks, and know-how when organizing activities.⁵ Thus, although tensions over political strategies and access to resources started at an early stage in the history of second-wave feminism in Peru, the different organizations also collaborated closely with one another (Vargas 2004).

Neoliberalism and Authoritarianism: 1980s–1990s

The NGOization of social movements and the neoliberalization of the political economy were not sudden events, but were intimately tied to the lasting economic and political crisis in the developing world in general, and Peru in particular. Beginning with the largely failed agrarian reforms of the 1970s, Peru had not achieved a stable economy. Poverty increased, and so did sociopolitical chaos. Basic needs such as food, health, and shelter were increasingly threatened and became issues for the locally organized networks of grassroots women's organizations and supportive NGOs.

The elections of 1980, the first in seventeen years, were important because of several events. First, they were the first elections in which illiterate citizens were allowed to vote after a constituent assembly extended suffrage in 1979. This measure expanded the electorate by 17 percent, of which the majority were women (Klarén 2000, 365). A quarter of the female population was illiterate, compared to 10 percent of men.⁶ Second, the normally fragmented political Left participated in these elections united under Izquierda Unida, but lost, a strong indication of the Left's inability to provide an alternative to more conservative, liberal, or populist and even violent opponents. Third, Shining Path chose these elections to announce its "people's war" by blowing up ballot boxes in the Ayacuchan village of Chuschi.

Fernando Belaúnde Terry, the president who had been overthrown by General Velasco and his soldiers in 1968, was the winner in the elections. To contain the violence of Shining Path, which the political classes thought to be far away in the *mancha India* (Indian stain) of the high Andes but in fact had started to terrorize the countryside, President Belaúnde increasingly militarized the affected areas and soon the whole country. For the majority of the population, the counterinsurgency war against Shining Path contributed to the insecurity in livelihood as well as the decline of physical safety of the majorities. The 1980s were, more than anything, marked by this devastating war and by the weakening of sociopolitical organizations at the grassroots,

---

5. *Mujer y Sociedad* (1984). By 1991, at least forty-two existing NGOs specialized in women's issues (Blondet et al. 1994, 122).

6. Ten percent of men were illiterate in 1981 (FLACSO 1993, 55).

which impoverished the already poor population and generated a new wave of internal migration (TRC 2003).

As we saw above, the 1980s were also a period of heightened feminist activism in the capital, Lima. Feminist organizations, and later NGOs, increased pressure on the state to take gender issues and women's rights into account. Several state institutions addressing women's issues followed the first governmental women's committee, the CONAMUP. Velasco's successor, General Francisco Morales Bermudez (1975–80), set up an institute for the family, the Instituto Nacional de Promoción del Menor y la Familia (National Institute for the Promotion of Minors and the Family).[7] In 1980, President Belaúnde created a new national women's commission, this time called the Oficina de la Mujer (Women's Office). Belaúnde's successor, President Alan García (1985–90), re-named this the Comisión de los Derechos de la Mujer and placed it under the Ministry of Justice. Such institutions worked mainly with women in the *pueblos jóvenes*. As the economic situation deteriorated, increasing attention was given to temporary poverty relief programs directed at women's organizations, which, as we will see in chapter 3, became responsible for the distribution of donated foodstuffs. Apart from these tasks in poverty relief, these state institutions kept a low profile and do not seem to have played important political roles.[8]

García was the promising young leader of Haya de la Torre's APRA, the Left-leaning populist party founded in the 1920s, which now, sixty years later, finally came to power. Its reformist program, directed at the masses, was widely supported. However, García's government was not able to establish solid and consistent policies, but instead kept changing policy with regard to the economy, international relations, and social integration. By the end of García's term in 1990, it was clear that the integration of the masses on economic, social and political levels had once again failed, as clientelist, authoritarian, and paternalist relations persisted. Again, as happened during the elections of 1980, the United Left was not able to present itself as a strong alternative, although it gained majorities in various municipalities in 1989. The problems the country struggled with were worsened by the political violence, while the battlefield shifted from the countryside to Lima. By the time of the presidential elections of 1990, Peru's social, economic, and political outlook was generally grim.

---

7. Today it is called INABIF and forms part of the Ministry of Women and Social Development (MIMDES).

8. These agencies are not even found in Jeanine Anderson's (1997) authoritative chapter on the subject. They were mentioned in 1987 in an article in a feminist magazine *La Tortuga* 1987).

The unforeseen and rapid rise of a previously unknown engineer, Alberto Fujimori, as a presidential candidate has been analyzed as a product of persistent low social integration and extreme insecurity having destroyed the electoral faith in established political actors (Jochamowitz 1993; Vega-Centeno B. 1994; Cotler 1994, 165–222; Crabtree and Thomas 1999).[9] Fujimori became president in 1990 because he was *not* a politician and especially because he was not a member of the traditional *criollo* upper classes. Many Peruvians seemed to have voted for him to block the election of the neoliberal coalition headed by the right-wing novelist Mario Vargas Llosa. Fujimori was no politician and did not pretend to be one: he did not even have a political party or a political program. He did promise "action" and "efficiency." Following these promises, formulated using concepts that seemed powerful after decades of increasing inefficiency, chaos, violence, and corruption, Fujimori created an authoritarian-populist regime. However, he also promised to give back democracy to the people: no white elite (the image of Vargas Llosa) would govern the people of Peru, but he, as a personal hero, would liberate the people.[10] Thus, from the start, Fujimori used the rhetoric of social integration and emancipation, albeit under the patriarchal direction of the president.

In his electoral campaign, Fujimori promised he would never give in to neoliberalism and the shock therapy, à la the IMF and World Bank, that had been his competitors' remedy to the economic abyss the country had fallen into. However, when elected, the new president started his government period in the second half of 1990 with economic measures that came to be known as "Fuji-shock." Fujimori implemented one of the most radical and rapid economic adjustments in Latin America. The national currency created in 1985, the inti, was replaced by the nuevo sol, which was worth one million intis. The government also began to pay off the external debt and stopped subsidizing and controlling prices and production. Initially, these measures hit the economy hard: inevitably prices and unemployment rose. The situation became so bad that increasing poverty, malnutrition, bad sanitation, and barely sufficient public health care brought back epidemics that were thought to have been extinct since the nineteenth century: malaria, yellow fever, dengue fever, tuberculosis, and cholera. In one July week in

---

9. Maybe the most enlightening account of the 1990 elections is the political memoir of Fujimori's opponent, Vargas Llosa (1994).

10. In 1992, an "independent" television station made a propagandistic miniseries that was broadcast by all national channels. In this program, which started a week before the elections for the Congreso Constituyente Democrático, Fujimori was presented as the savior of Peru. It pretended to cover the whole of Repúblican history, with the "big change" starting in 1990. See Vega-Centeno B. (1994).

1991, cholera spread from the northern coastal region to Lima, the highlands, and even the jungle provinces. In that year, 322,562 Peruvians were infected, while in early 1992, the World Health Organization reported cases in Ecuador, Brazil, and Bolivia (Poole and Renique 1992, 24; Cueto 1997). According to Marcos Cueto (Cueto 1997, 216–18), cholera became endemic in Peru because the recommendations to improve the public health system and the infrastructure for water supply and sanitation after the epidemic of 1991 were not implemented. Notwithstanding the high toll of the Fuji-shock, by 1994 the economy had stabilized, inflation had been contained, and international investment was on the rise (Kisic 1998).

As his unexpected economic changes already indicated, Fujimori was not troubled by democratic principles. On April 5, 1992, Fujimori staged a "self-coup" (*autogolpe*) with the support of the military. As discussed in the national newspaper *El Comercio,* the president appeared on television justifying his action as necessary for the continuity of his rule of "order, discipline, and national development, and to fight corruption" (cited in Contreras and Cueto 1999, 297). He replaced the two-chamber system with a one-chamber system; replaced administrators in ministries and the judicial and legislative branches as he saw fit; and rewrote the constitution, expanding the president's responsibilities and liberalizing the state's responsibilities in social policies. With the opposition weakened, grassroots organizations under continuous attack from Shining Path, the majority of the population impoverished, and many sick, protests against Fujimori's self-coup were limited, and many people even applauded the coup as a necessary measure. Fujimori's rule was consolidated when the army captured the leader of Shining Path, Abimael Guzmán, in September 1992. Despite pessimistic visions at the time (Poole and Renique 1992, 166), the capture of Guzmán weakened Shining Path rapidly, giving way to more arrests of leading Shining Path members and diminishing terrorist attacks considerably. In 1994, the economy recovered and began to grow again. However, this growth did not change income distribution: the segment of the population living in poverty had stayed more or less around 50 percent since 1970. It is also worth noting that in 1996 the GDP per capita had risen to reach what it had been in 1965 (Figueroa 1998). Despite these seemingly meager economic results, the increasingly authoritarian grip following Fujimori's self-coup, and consequently the president's increasing power over the judiciary and the expanding control of the secret service (SIN) over the population, Fujimori was reelected in 1995 with a majority of votes.

While the Fujimori regime steadily undermined democratic institutions, its rhetoric was framed in a discourse of social integration. The minimal, and often contradictory, effects that the corresponding policies had on the well-being of the people were offset by successes in other areas such as important and necessary infrastructure projects in the urban shantytowns and legislation that favored the poor and marginalized. In 1992, an existing emergency program for poverty relief was given new life. However, while basic necessities were provided, basic rights—for example, to education or health care—were not granted (Figueroa 1998, 146). These "social" measures, with which Fujimori gained support among poor voters and kept civil opposition low, were accompanied by more rhetoric and programs directed at women than ever before. Women offered several advantages to the interests of the Fujimori regime. First, grassroots women were well organized but politically debilitated as a consequence of internal disputes, increasing terrorist infiltration, and generalized poverty, a situation that made these groups particularly malleable. Second, well-organized poor women had a great caretaking capacity and had proven capable and willing to assume that responsibility, providing Fujimori the opportunity to expand maternalist practices in the service of state interests. And third, as various scholars and politicians have argued, women are often expected to "clean up" politics (Craske 1999, 200; Blondet 2002; Vargas 2002; 238–61; Schmidt 2006). The traditional image of women as morally superior and honest supported Fujimori in publicly presenting and justifying his own increasingly corrupt and authoritarian rule. He drafted many women from the available, highly educated middle-class sectors. He also mobilized female voters by using a maternalist and development discourse directed at the poor "mothers of the nation." In the pages that follow, I will discuss how Fujimori exploited the different existing perceptions of women.

Political Discourses and the Bifurcation of Womanhood

The increasing attention to the "woman question" in the 1990s was partly steeped in the modern language of women's empowerment, but this concealed an important factor: women were often addressed in stereotypes of femininity that have been called *marianismo,* a term coined by the scholar Evelyn Stevens in 1973 (e.g., Fuller 1993, 70–71). A debated concept, *marianismo* was thought to be the other face of *machismo,* terms that, according to Stevens, explained Latin American gender relations. *Marianismo* refers to a cult around femininity that "teaches women that they are morally superior and spiritually stronger than men" (Stevens, cited in Navarro 2002, 257).[11]

---

11. Navarro (2002) dismisses the concept, but gives an extensive overview of literature on *marianismo* since the 1970s.

Women's "holy" mothering role is emphasized through a comparison with the Virgin Mary, explaining her capacity to care and *abnegación*, self-sacrifice. In a similar vein, Elsa Chaney referred to women in Latin American politics as being treated like *supermadres* (supermothers) to foster the idea that women's participation was often interpreted as an extension of their domestic, mothering roles (Chaney 1979; Craske 1999, 13). When we look back at official standpoints on the "woman question" in Peru during the 1990s (and before), these images of woman as holy mother and carer are significantly present.

There was, however, a strong class bias in such images. Whereas middle-class professionals were approached as morally superior to (implicitly corrupt and undemocratic) male politicians and as modern women who encouraged women's emancipation, poor women were mainly approached as mothers who could help development through their resilience and caring capacities. Indeed, women who fought for improvements in their own and their families' positions through grassroots organizations were often portrayed as mothers fighting economic crisis, or, alternatively, fighting the government's politics of hunger (Vargas 1995). The rise of women's organizations that sought to improve their livelihoods collectively and the increased attention focused on these organizations brought practical women's needs into the public sphere. Yet grassroots women's activities were far more diverse than the caring activities emphasized in populist political discourse; their struggles for shelters, participation, and maintenance allowance after separation went largely unnoticed by the general public. For politicians, the grassroots women's organizations were useful in their efforts to cushion the effects of structural adjustment and for clientelist purposes. At the same time, feminist discourse was often appropriated in order to pacify the increasing number of female professionals and to comply with international agreements with regard to women's rights. Consequently, during the 1990s, a bifurcation of womanhood became apparent, in which maternalism and empowerment found their respective subjects.[12]

The emphasis on women's mothering roles in social policy was not new in itself. During the last thirty years of the twentieth century, maternalist discourses were used to consolidate power, to control potentially dangerous masses, and to divert responsibilities from the state to the people. It is striking how a whole body of social policies was embedded in maternalist discourses. Maternalist rhetoric was used to frame policies aimed at supporting poor women, even though these measures were not always in

---

12. On maternalism as a political strategy in the welfare state, see Skocpol (1992) and Koven and Michel (1993).

the interests of those women but rather in the interests of larger groups in society such as children, adolescents, families, or indeed whole communities. Women were mainly defined through their relationships with other people, not in their own right. During the early 1970s, General Velasco had proposed that women's reproductive responsibility be emphasized in the national struggle for the revolutionary "transformation" of society. The 1980s showed a moderate maternalist discourse directed at grassroots women's organizations in order to support and control community activities, and President Fujimori developed careful but far-reaching maternalist propaganda directed at the poor masses, coupled with a discourse of economic development and free-market policies.

For example, on Mother's Day in 1991, Fujimori gave a vigorous speech in which he called Peruvian mothers "heroines" and "self-sacrificing [*abnegadas*]," applauding the silence with which they performed their tasks "in the most perfect anonymity, the heroines of the great task called national reconstruction" (*Ojo* 1991). It was Fujimori's first year as president, which, after the Fuji-shock, brought hunger and despair to many people, and especially to those who were already poor. Communal kitchens, the *comedores populares*, appeared everywhere, but they were not able to feed the people either, as the *comedores* were too poor themselves. As leaders of the *comedores* started to protest against the "politics of hunger," Fujimori asked them for patience by exalting their *abnegación*. In succeeding years, Fujimori repeated his praise for the millions of mothers for their work in providing for the poor as well as their importance to the project of the "reconstruction" of the nation. On Mother's Day 1996, the president once again thanked mothers for their contribution to the "development of the fatherland" (*El Peruano* 1996). As mentioned above, both Belaúnde and García had deployed similar rhetoric directed at grassroots women and used food aid to appease mothers. However, Fujimori not only used these discourses but also, as I will further detail in chapter 3, institutionalized both food aid and the clientelism associated with it. Especially after 1993, Fujimori developed an increasingly sophisticated maternalism that was embedded in development discourses and actual policies that explicitly targeted grassroots women's organizations.

Fujimori's use of maternalist discourses has to be seen in light of the relationship between grassroots women's organizations and the government's intentions in relation to social development and gender equity. Following the World Conference on Women held in Beijing in 1995, Fujimori created the Ministry for the Advancement of Women and Human Development (Promoción de la Mujer y el Desarrollo Humano, or PROMUDEH). With the rhetoric of gender equality and the "advancement of women," on the one hand, and the important role of mothers in development, on the other, PROMUDEH was given the responsibility for all major and lesser social programs. These included the state programs for children, displaced persons, food distribution, social participation, indigenous peoples, literacy, child care, adolescents, and last and perhaps least, the advancement of women. Apparently, poverty relief and "soft sector" social policy were associated with the nation's female population. Women were first perceived as mothers and carers of other people, and only thereafter as citizens in their own right. In its promotion material, PROMUDEH is described as follows: "A ministry for women. To appreciate her, support her, promote her development and that of her family. To give her the primordial place in society and in the political and economic development of the country that she deserves." PROMUDEH was created "as recognition of her [the woman's] invaluable contribution." The promotion leaflet also states that the ministry would work for "a world of equity." This world of equity was mainly justified by a maternalist discourse of development and the role that women performed and should perform as "natural" mothers and caretakers of the family and the community. This coincided with the logic of PROMUDEH's task to work not only for gender equality but even more for basic development and poverty relief, in which women were viewed as a good source of voluntary labor. Effectively, the pictures in the leaflet resemble the images that international development agencies use to encourage the Western world to donate money: the front page shows a poor but enchanting indigenous girl with a dirty face and drippy nose. The whole leaflet radiates the government's commitment to reduce poverty with the support of Peruvian mothers, not its commitment to the advancement of women.

However, in his ten years of government, Fujimori simultaneously manipulated the feminist movement and international organizations with a discourse of empowerment. In doing so, he not only confused the Peruvian women's movement and the policy makers and bureaucrats who were genuinely trying to improve the position of women, but also further confused the relationship between development processes on the one hand, and women's emancipation on the other. Such an analysis raises several questions. For example, how are we to interpret a politics that is contradictory from its onset? How do development goals such as poverty relief and population control directed at poor women compare with measures to support and improve women's rights? Without discarding the possibility of actual ambiguity in Fujimori's rhetoric and programs, the following discussion will explore the purposeful exploitation of existing images and perceptions of womanhood in service of more instrumental causes.

Emancipation, "Honesty," and Female Loyalty

Fujimori's attitude towards women and the "woman question" was not a coherent exaltation of women as mothers of the poor; on the contrary, the president knew how to use educated middle-class women as political shields. Parallel to the motherhood and development discourse, Fujimori intelligently invoked women's involvement to foster trust and credibility in the more progressive national and international communities. He achieved this parallel goal by using two seemingly contradictory images: the traditional image of women as morally superior to and more honest and loyal than men, on the one hand, and as capable, efficient technocrats in a modern and emancipated country, on the other (Blondet 2002, 52–53). As poor mothers were lauded for their activities that could "save" the nation from poverty and hunger, educated women were conjured up as the emancipatory, professional faces of an increasingly corrupt regime. As Cecilia Blondet points out (1998, 1999, 2002), for many women, Fujimori's interest in their work was an opportunity to integrate into a world previously closed to them. Thus, although aware that they were working within a corrupt system, many women seized the opportunity. Fujimori's professional entourage, using the pool of educated female talent, which had expanded since the 1980s, assembled many more women than other governments or political parties. Although the collaboration of professional women had a sinister edge, which showed itself in personalized statements of loyalty to Fujimori on the part of some leading female *fujimoristas,* the opening of the policy arena to women from different political persuasions did feed into the most comprehensive set of women-friendly policies and legislative reforms that had been seen up to that time. Of course, women's increased political participation and representation was one of the most visible and high-impact effects.

Women's increased political participation was further encouraged by a 1997 law stipulating that all party lists for congress and municipal elections had to include at least 25 percent men and 25 percent women (Yáñez 2003; Schmidt 2004). This law, the result of the work of two female *fujimoristas,* was strongly supported by Fujimori himself (Schmidt 2006, 167). Overall, in the 1990s, female members of congress introduced laws concerning women's grassroots organizations, family planning, and domestic violence, all discussed in the following chapters. In addition, in 1997, the infamous provision in the criminal code that stipulated that a rapist was exempted from prosecution if he married the victim was abolished after a campaign headed by a congresswoman, Beatriz Merino (Schmidt 2006; Boesten 2007). The newly created ministry for women, PROMUDEH, was perhaps a repository for social programs that were intended more to buy votes than to alleviate poverty, but it also fitted into the increasing national and international quest for attention to gender issues and equality. In the 1990s, most Latin American countries established government institutions dedicated to women (S. Alvarez 1997; Chant and Craske 2003, 28–29; Lind 2005; Macaulay 2006). Apart from the immediate success of the gender quotas imposed on political parties, especially in the municipal elections of 1998 (Schmidt 2004), many of the reforms directed at women were insufficiently implemented and enforced, or, like the population policies, they were aggressively implemented and violated women's rights. As we will see in the following chapters, resources were often not allocated and personnel were often not trained. However, the increasing presence of gender-sensitive measures gave the regime a certain legitimacy vis-à-vis the international community and the national feminist NGOs working on the government's plans, proposals, and programs from the sideline. Among feminists, there was a continuing debate on whether they should support Fujimori's progressive emancipatory measures or oppose them out of democratic principle. Several women chose to resist based on "commitments to democracy, human rights, and civil liberty" (Schmidt 2006, 162), while in 1998 several previously cooperative feminists retreated from government institutions to join civic opposition movements (Blondet 2002, 45).

Fujimori, however, was not yet done with his personalized gender strategy. After his obviously fraudulent re-reelection of 2000 and the further undermining of his credibility by competing factions within his own political movement, an all-women steering committee was installed, which had to organize a coherent and credible government. These four women were ardent *fujimoristas,* not afraid to defend or deny violations of human rights. According to Gregory Schmidt, Fujimori had a habit of having his "geishas," loyal female journalists and politicians, defend his "dirty work." Among female *fujimoristas,* loyalty to the president seemed highly valued and far more important than any sense of gender solidarity, as the chair of the then congressional Committee on Women, Luz Salgado, proved in her 1998 defense of the sterilization program, even after it was proven to be extremely coercive (Schmidt 2006, 170). Whether the four women politicians were pushed forward in 2000 to show "innocent" female faces after fraud, or to represent unity in a political movement that was falling apart, or, indeed, to justify the unjustifiable remains unclear. It does seem clear that these women were supposed to radiate a more trustworthy, loyal, democratic, and honest political character than men. As the president of the four-woman steering committee, Martha Hildebrandt, said after the release of the first video that would lead to the fall and flight of Fujimori and his cronies: "We are four women defending the principle of loyalty, loyalty to Fujimori" (cited in Schmidt 2006, 166).

Gendered Citizenship and Social Policy

The relationship between the Peruvian state and women shows tensions in two main areas: (racialized) class and development and emancipation. In other words, the tension between development and emancipation in social policy directed at women is partly fed by the tensions between socioeconomic groups and their differentiated needs. Development policies are largely directed at the poor, who, in turn, are largely mestizo and indigenous. The needs of women in the so-called popular sectors, both urban and rural, are largely seen as practical and addressed as such; this class-based approach to women's needs is underpinned by a gender ideology that draws on Catholic images and duties of mothering and self-sacrifice. While in practice popular women's more emancipatory or strategic interests were often glossed over, strategic objectives such as increasing political participation, enacting legislation against violence, and expanding women's rights to control their fertility were finally addressed during the 1990s. But much of this increased inclusion through improved legislation was underpinned with maternalist rhetoric that reinforced the same stereotypes of mothering and self-sacrifice. To a great extent, then, the relation between the state and women since the Velasco regime to the end of the Fujimori era fits the Women in Development approach: an approach to women that pursues greater inclusion without questioning the premises on which inequality is based. Although legislation increasingly addressed inequality, implementation did not follow.

But the discussed dynamics are more complex; on the one hand, class divisions present a real conflict of interest between organizations of popular women and middle-class feminists and between development and emancipation. Whereas the division between practical and strategic needs is artificial and may play into the hands of politicians and policy makers who are not interested in changing the gendered status quo, the material starting point of different groups of women is real and unequal. Thus, development goals such as improving livelihoods and securing social security, let alone the need for improved social infrastructure such as health and education, particularly outside of Lima, are a reality. These development objectives *are* gendered, because of perceived roles and/or actual biological difference. As the social programs discussed in the next three chapters suggest, the pursuit of developmental goals directed at women and underpinned by gendered rhetoric (either confirming or challenging the stereotypes) does not allow much space to challenge the inequalities that underpin the positions of the targeted women in the first place. These inequalities are immersed in the complex and intersecting inequalities of race, class, and gender, and are difficult to tackle using rhetoric and discourses that (a) do not address this complexity of inequality, and (b) are not met by practice. By examining what happened with social policy at the grassroots, the following three chapters explore these tensions between theory and practice, rights and access, equality and marginalization, emancipation and development, and maternalism and empowerment.

3

FOOD AID, MOTHERHOOD, AND WOMEN'S WORK

In 2001, I met with Sra. Amalia, chair of a *vaso de leche* committee in one of the *pueblos jóvenes* in Lima. Amalia claimed that the local municipality, which was responsible for the distribution of milk to the *vaso de leche* committees in her district, used allocated funds to buy the cheapest and worst products, thus reaping profits. The municipality also caused disagreements between local committees—entirely made of volunteering mothers—by paying some leaders of *vaso de leche* committees as if they were employees, while demanding money for the "donated" products from others. But it was not only the municipal distribution coordinators whom Amalia accused of misconduct; she found that the system of selective distribution and clientelism had penetrated the women's organizations themselves. Some women, said Amalia, participated only to enrich themselves, not for need or even neighborhood solidarity. Although food support was institutionalized during the 1990s, Amalia's feeling of social security was completely undermined. Angrily, she insisted that it was "the law of the jungle, of the lion" (*la ley de la selva, del león*) reigning the social programs. She emphasized that the government "attacks the most vulnerable side: poverty."[1] Despite Amalia's complaints, she stuck to her job as chairperson of the neighborhood *vaso de leche* committee, and, as a meeting in her honor of various women's groups in her neighborhood showed, her peers appreciated her leadership and she was proud of her achievements.

The Vaso de Leche Program was set up in 1984 under the tutelage of the United Left municipal government of Lima. The program aimed to provide eight ounces of milk per day mixed with sugar, oatmeal, and quinoa, to be distributed to all needy preschool children (under the age of

---

1. Interview with Sra. Amalia, San Juan de Luringancho, Lima, 2001.

six). Mothers of the enrolled children were expected to contribute to the costs of fuel or bus fares and to take their turns in preparing and distributing the milk. The successful program was rolled out to rural areas in 1986. The *vaso de leche* committees added to the already existing myriad of women's groups in poor neighborhoods, albeit with different political ties, as the *vaso de leche* committees were tied to the municipal Left and the *comedores populares* received donations from various donors, including the state. The difficulties Amalia encountered in her work—corruption in and outside women's organizations, opportunism and improper use of funds and goods, internal and external manipulation and strife—as well as the gains, persistence and pride, were not unique to Amalia's municipality, or to *vaso de leche* committees. Rather, I argue in this chapter, both the corruption and clientelism in the national food distribution system and the resistance of women's organizations to internal and external constraints were increasingly institutionalized during the 1990s.

During the 1990s, policies of food aid were increasingly immersed in clientelist practices facilitated by the weak social and political position of marginalized women after the Fuji-shock of 1990, and the increasing violence of Shining Path in the capital. Women's organizations were left with little choice but to enter into clientelist relationships with the state, although, as we will see below, many organizations developed strategies to maintain a minimum of autonomy. Some sectors in government expected women to assume the basic caring responsibilities the population needed to survive periodic economic crises, while at the same time their efforts were used for political purposes such as electoral support (Palomino 2004). As Amy Lind (2005) observes with regard to similar processes in neighboring Ecuador, women's household and community labor was often central to neoliberal economic restructuring, and placed women's collective efforts in a paradoxical and maternalist alignment with state efforts to modernize at the expense of the poor. Peruvian women's active protests against the austerity measures of the early 1990s and their demands for an improvement in the politics of food were incorporated into the government's game of sometimes contradictory measures of emancipation and development. Women were increasingly pressured to dedicate themselves to the many social programs presumably designed to relieve poverty, even though these programs proved to contribute little to actual poverty reduction. As Nikki Craske observes, "women's preparedness to absorb the costs of adjustment allows states to withdraw services while minimizing social unrest" (2003).

Despite such ulterior motives and practices in state food programs, women such as Amalia were often keen to participate in women's groups and provided the state with an army of voluntary workers who contributed to poverty relief. So were these women the "heroic" and "self-sacrificing" mothers who worked to feed Peru's poor, as President Fujimori claimed? How did the emphasis put on women's mothering roles play out for the women involved? How do women perceive and negotiate their position in the implicit (and often explicit) hierarchies in the relationship between beneficiaries and donors? To answer these questions, I examine how women who participated in state-supported women's organizations dealt with manipulative practices and social marginalization and how they negotiated the limited sociopolitical space assigned to them. Besides extensive fieldwork among women's groups in Lima and Ayacucho, I use a minute book of the Federación Provincial de Clubes de Madres de Huamanga, Ayacucho (Provincial Federation of Clubes de Madres of Huamanga, Ayacucho, or FECMA). Strikingly, although the situation in Ayacucho was quite different from that in Lima and the *clubes de madres* in Ayacucho, as I discuss below, have a different background than the organizations in the capital, the problems that arose in the 1990s in relation to the practice of food aid were very similar. Neighborhood-based women's organizations in Lima had more experience with food distribution because they had been working since the late 1960s with a variety of institutions that provided food aid, while *clubes de madres* in Ayacucho organized around small-scale projects, and later in defense of human rights, during the 1980s and early 1990s. The first state-sponsored *comedores populares* in Ayacucho were set up during the government of Alan García (1985–90), which actively expanded its grip on the popular classes through the Programa de Asistencia Directa (Direct Assistance Program, or PAD). More independent *clubes de madres* operated parallel to state-sponsored *comedores*. The Vaso de Leche Program was set up in Ayacucho in 1986, two years after the first *vaso de leche* committee was set up in Lima. In both Ayacucho and Lima, women's groups soon established strong networks of women's organizations through umbrella organizations that tied together local groups. These networks increased their collective bargaining power with the diverse institutions from which they received aid.

The minute book of FECMA, founded in 1988, covers the years 1995–99 (FECMA 1995–99; in 2001 the minute book was in the hands of FECMA's president, Teodomira de la Cruz). In 1991, this provincial organization united with the federations of other Ayacucho provinces (Ayacucho is the name of a city, a province, and a department) under the umbrella Federación Departamental de Clubes de Madres de Ayacucho (Departmental Federation of Clubes de Madres of Ayacucho, or FEDECMA). By 1995, FEDECMA united 11 provincial federations, 1,400 clubes de madres, and 80,000 women (Coral 1998, 359). FECMA, in turn, united all women's organizations scattered throughout the province, from the smallest and most remote communities to the more visible organizations in the city of Ayacucho itself, representing 140 *clubes de madres* and 16,338 members (Asemblea extraordinaria, January 20, 1996, FECMA 1995–99, 41). The minute book is a record of meetings with local officials and program executives, such as mayors and program administrators, and with benevolent lawyers or NGO workers, as well as a record of meetings among members. The members consist of groups throughout the province, which, interestingly, include *comedores populares, vaso de leche* committees, and *clubes de madres* (i.e., women's groups without a specific feeding program). This was not always seen as acceptable; for example, according to the minutes of a meeting held in 1997, the municipal distribution centers that administered the Vaso de Leche Program tried to exclude the Federation from their activities. Apparently, the administrators claimed that the Federation managed *clubes de madres* and *comedores populares,* which benefited from government funds, while the municipality administered the *vaso de leche* committees. Whereas the Federation claimed that all those distinct women's organizations rightfully belonged to their umbrella organization, municipal officials accused women of taking advantage by combining the two programs (municipal and governmental) under the same organizing committee, suggesting that women were taking double portions of food. The Federation argued that neither individual women nor the organization was taking advantage of the donations: "The Vaso de Leche Program forms part of our organization while the participants in the *clubes de madres* are not all beneficiaries; only those who have children under the age of six, pregnant and breastfeeding mothers are." They argued that the beneficiaries, not the voluntary workers who prepared the food and milk, made up the difference between the two programs (Reunión extra-ordinaria, FECMA 1995–99, 287). In Lima these groups were not part of the same federation, as the Vaso de Leche Program was associated with the United Left municipal government and the federated women's groups tried to minimize political affiliations. A closer look, however, shows that in both Ayacucho and Lima there was as much collaboration and overlap as there was strife and competition between these differently sponsored groups. Therefore, I analyze these women's organizations and the aid programs directed at them as part of the same phenomenon: social programs that appealed to women's mothering roles and responsibilities, motivated by an often unclear set of government interests in poverty relief and clientelist networking, and with ambiguous results.

Food Aid and Clientelism

Food aid and women's organizations had become central to the politics of slums that took shape from 1960s onwards and became an institutionalized form of clientelism during the Fujimori period. Support for the construction and organization of new migrant neighborhoods in urban centers (in the form of food, money, technical support, and other material support) stretched far beyond the state and was pioneered by national charities, religious organizations, organizations such as USAID and the World Food Program and their local distributors, and international NGOs (Anderson 1998, 84). Such practices, in turn, encouraged women to organize, which suggests that women's organizations might have been less autonomous than they would like us to believe.[2] However, food aid was a particular favorite of the state and was (and largely still is) the cornerstone of internationally financed poverty relief. This centrality of food aid to international cooperation is historically linked to U.S. agricultural and foreign policy, under which the Food for Peace programs were started in 1954. Peru has received food aid since the 1950s, but more intensively since the second half of the 1970s after the leftist military government of Velasco (1968–75), which was skeptical of U.S. food donations, tried to reform existing food aid into programs for temporary interventions in times of crises (Grupo Impulsor Nacional/CESIP 2000).

Government food aid institutions were generally directly tied to the presidency in one way or another, whether through president's wife's charities (General Manuel Odría, 1948–56), presidential decree (Fernando Belaúnde Terry, 1963–68; 1980–85), or party politics (Alan García, APRA, 1985–90) (Collier 1978; Blondet and Montero 1995, 53; Lenten 1993). In the 1980s, with international food aid increasing and suffrage expanded to include illiterate people, the existing aid program was replaced by a long-term food-distribution system that specifically targeted women's organizations in the slums and later also in the rural highlands. Governments began to personalize women's organizations. For example, the second Belaúnde administration founded *cocinas familiares* (family kitchens) or *cocinas de Violeta*—named after

---

2. According to Cecilia Blondet, organizations exist because of the availability of donations: when there are donations, there is an organization; if not, there is not. Consequently, according to Blondet, all organizations are set up from above (in great part, according to Blondet, by religious organizations) and are not initiatives of women themselves. See Blondet (1986, 53) and Blondet and Montero Checa (1995, 56). Women who participated in setting up their organizations in the 1960s and 1970s tell a different story and like to emphasize autonomous organization. See Denegri (2000).

his wife—to work parallel to the existing *comedores populares*. Irene Jara, a leader of a women's organization in a Limeño *pueblo joven*, remembered the tensions that this generated: "Afterwards there were a lot [clubs], because [President] Belaúnde said: 'they should form *clubes de madres* to teach the women to help themselves—you agree, don't you?' And the majority rapidly organized, but just because of the government, because the government gave food, gave clothes, gave medicines. But we started and went on alone, independent. [Our club] is not political, it is united with everyone. We won't ask political people in, because they will want to dominate" (Denegri 2000, 216).

As Irene claims here, and as is verified by the boom in *clubes de madres*, many women did respond to the president's call to organize because the government provided basic necessities to those who organized under his party's surveillance. Such party-political use of food aid encouraged patron-client relations, which soon dominated the character and functioning of many women's organizations (see also Degregori, Blondet, and Lynch 1986; Blondet 1986). Between 1985 and 1990, during the government of Alan García, the Programa de Asistencia Directa (Direct Assistance Program, or PAD) was created, in which existing *clubes de madres* and *comedores populares* were merged. Although this program promised to cover more than food, the strong party links limited women's organizations once again in their autonomy.[3]

The Vaso de Leche Program, set up by leftist mayor of Lima, Alfonso Barrantes (1983, 1986), was meant to be different from these party political food programs in being established in the municipalities. Local municipalities received a budget to buy condensed milk or donated milk powder from Europe or the United States, which in turn would be handed over to local *vaso de leche* committees—consisting of organized mothers—who would prepare and distribute the milk to the population.[4] Despite the explicit avoidance of government manipulation or the threat of discontinuity of programs after a change in government (but tied to a political party), malpractice and corruption seemed to be as frequent in the Vaso de Leche Program as in government social programs, as Sra. Amalia claimed. Of course, local municipalities were subsidized by the Ministry of Finance, which made municipal employees dependent on the state, leading to

---

3. "Autonomous" does not mean completely independent; rather, organizations are perceived as autonomous if they maintain alliances with a variety of donors, without committing to a political and/or religious group.

4. On the actual reach of the program, see Ruggeri Laderchi (2001).

problems for the women's organizations that received, prepared, and distributed the milk similar to the problems for women of *comedores populares* and *clubes de madres*.[5]

A Politics of Motherhood and Resistance

As discussed in chapter 2, the 1980s and 1990s were periods not only of economic crisis, but of political violence. The politics of food aid, and the maternal identity that was emphasized through these politics, became an important factor in women's resistance against violence, while the associated link to the state also made them targets of Shining Path. In Ayacucho, the center of Shining Path activities during the 1980s, the violence played a central role in the identity of women's organizations. In 2001, Vilma Ortega, president of FEDECMA, stressed that the women's organizations mainly worked in secrecy during the years of political violence. She remembered that she and other women carried their minute books, hidden under their multiple skirts, all over the province to be able to organize as many women as possible.[6] Unfortunately, although Vilma assured me that they would be somewhere within reach, the minute books of both the provincial and the departmental federations in these years of war are not available because they are lost, or, more likely, are still in hiding. After I had searched for them for two days in the chaos of a recently moved archive, it became clear to me that they would not be recovered for study.

A minute book that the women did make available for study covers the years 1995–99, after Shining Path was severely weakened, pacification had set in, and external support from both the government and NGOs started to reach Ayacucho. The beginning of the book shows that the women felt as if a new era had began. Different *clubes de madres* reported on their situation to the Federation. One club noted that "there are signatures of commandos"; another explained that they "worked very well with the soldiers." However, no references are made to "soldiers" or "commandos" in the next four hundred pages. It seems likely that the Federation decided to omit such references on purpose after having confirmed a good working relationship. The famous *rondas campesinas*—armed peasant defense communities—and the national army were still present as late as 2001 to 2003, when I did the fieldwork for this book and tension between the military and human

---

5. The organization published a detailed history of the movement that lists all events, marches, laws, organizations and other relevant pieces of information (Garcia Naranjo Morales 2001).
6. Interview with Vilma Ortega, Ayacucho, August 2001.

rights groups, for example, was notable. It seems unlikely that between 1995 and 1999 the organizations had no issues whatsoever with either the army or the *rondas*. After all, the *rondas campesinas* consisted of members of women's own communities and families, and in many instances women themselves had actively participated in the *rondas* (Degregori et al. 1996; Starn 1999; Fumerton 2002).[7] Although in personal conversations individual women often voiced criticism of the military as well as of the *rondas campesinas,* both forces were also allies in women's quest for safety (see also Coral 1998, 360–62). It is likely that the omission of references to armed groups in the minute book was intentional in order to protect their political autonomy and personal security. Minute books also serve as written testimonies of political decisions: in this case, the wish to avoid an overt identification with or criticism of the different political factions.

As this shows, the *clubes de madres* were very aware of the political consequences of their actions, a lesson they had learned during their activism in the 1980s. When Shining Path declared its "people's war" in 1980, existing *clubes de madres* in Ayacucho rapidly transformed themselves into agents of protection and daily survival for a growing number of people. *Clubes de madres* in Ayacucho, but also in Huancavelica, coordinated hiding places for family members at risk, leaving the elderly in the communities and taking the youngest ones to travel around the region to keep kinship and refugee networks going. They organized searches for the disappeared, coordinated information on the dead, disappeared, and detained, and exchanged information on rights and legal procedures.[8] Women in Ayacucho performed these tasks by relying on their roles as "apolitical" mothers because this image of political "innocence" provided for a certain degree of protection against accusations of belonging to one or the other camp in the violent conflict. Of course, the use of maternal roles as a shield in political struggles, based on the idea that mothers cannot be killed, was widespread in Latin America and elsewhere (Kaplan 1982; Jelin, Zammit, and Thomson 1990; Radcliffe and Westwood 1993; Jaquette and Wolchik 1998; Eckstein and Garretón Merino 2001). As we will see in chapter 5, besides this use of motherhood as a form of protection against political violence, women also emphasized this role in their homes to cast off jealous and often violent husbands.

---

7. Meeting with the *club de madres* of Ccaturumi, La Mar, Ayacucho, January 2003. See also Final Report, vol. 8, 2.1, p. 54, http://www.cverdad.org.pe.

8. Interview with Francesca, Yauli, Huancavelica, February 2001; interview with Teodora Ayme, Ayacucho, January 2003; interview with Vilma Ortega, Ayacucho, August 2001; see also Coral (1998). The report of the Truth and Reconciliation Commission is a rich source concerning women's organizations and political violence: Final Report, vol. 8, 3.2.2, "Las Organizaciones de base de mujeres," http://www.cverdad.org.pe.

But motherhood and feeding families were not necessarily women's first concern in their activism. Many women participated because of anger and frustration after losing family members and friends. Maurita, for example, born in the 1950s and active in *clubes de madres* during the war, remembered that "when they killed my sister I retreated for various months, . . . then I went back, well, my brother, my cousins, made me swear I would never be leader again. . . . 'Yes,' I said, 'I won't go, I will not get involved.' . . . Seriously, I swore, but I don't know [where] this leadership came from; very silently I escaped, my brother asked me: 'Where are you going?' 'I am going to the market, just a moment,' but I did not go to the market, rather, I went to see señora Teodora."[9]

Maurita and her sisters' children had witnessed the violent killing of her sister and one of her brothers when four soldiers entered their home to look for suspected terrorists. Instead of being intimidated into submission, Maurita went to see the initiator of the resistance of *clubes de madres*, Sra. Teodora Ayme. Participating in the *clubes de madres* was her way of resisting the violence.

In contrast to the National Association of Family Members of Kidnapped, Imprisoned, and Missing Persons (ANFASEP), a mainly female organization set up in Ayacucho in 1983 (Tamayo 2003), the *clubes de madres* in Ayacucho were not openly dedicated to finding justice. Rather, they clandestinely supported struggles for human rights and expanded their networks of information around the department of Ayacucho. Because of the trust placed in the groups, based on their image as mothers working for the economic survival of their families, government poverty relief programs became increasingly available to them. When the Vaso de Leche Program reached Ayacucho in 1986, more women's committees were set up. During 1987 women started to talk about setting up an umbrella organization to unite the different *clubes de madres, comedores populares,* and *vaso de leche* committees in the province of Ayacucho. This was not an easy task, if only because a higher level of organization ran the risk of provoking serious opposition from both Shining Path and government officials. Teodora Ayme was not intimidated: "They [the priests] said, 'Don't get involved, don't do that,' [I said,] 'This is not about politics, this cannot be politics, we cannot fall into this political game, we are just defending our rights, everyone's rights. Look, now we are in the middle of this massacre, people are dying of hunger, they are dying and who claims for the already dead, who will?' Even the authorities lost their credibility, they lost their authority, they did not even come out of their offices anymore with so many massacres, that

---

9. Interview with Maurita, Ayacucho, December 2002.

is why we, women, organized."[10] Teodora, saying that women do not play the same political game that politicians do, denies that the women's organizations were political. The fact that people were dying of hunger was a reason for women to claim their rights to food. But Teodora not only refers to hunger, she explicitly refers to the violence as a reason for women to organize. She suggests that if women do not care for the dead, nobody will. Thus, if nobody else asserted the rights of the people, then the women would. Just like Maurita, who answered that she would not stop participating, as she was innocent and just wanted to defend her own rights and those of other innocent victims, Teodora claims female moral authority as her shield and her legitimacy.[11] Thus, while the activities of women's organizations were in fact political—claiming the rights of the people and resisting political violence—women's leaders used a discourse that appealed to nonpolitical domestic duties. Whatever women's personal interpretation of their activities in the *clubes de madres* during the war, the objectives that women such as Maurita and Teodora state—caring for the dead and the living—gave them the legitimacy to act as they did. Despite the claims to political innocence, the resulting umbrella organization, FECMA, set up in 1988, immediately became a target. According to Teodora, Carlota Morales, the elected president of the Federation, disappeared in the first month of its existence. Today, neither Teodora nor Maurita claims to know what happened and whether it was the army or Shining Path that was responsible for Morales's disappearance. According to the Ayacuchana activist and writer Isabel Coral (1998, 359), Carlota Morales was intimidated, assaulted, and received death threats from Shining Path, but Coral does not mention her disappearance. Despite the threats, the *clubes de madres* defied Shining Path at a public march for peace in 1988, at which at least twenty-five hundred women were present (FLACSO 1993, 115). Women physically threw from their midst Shining Path members who tried to get hold of the microphones. The women also experienced—and prevented—several attempts by Shining Path to infiltrate and command the Federation. Isabel Coral recollects that she had "never seen such strength, decision, and fury as when those women leaders went up to the dais and screamed and hit the intruders until they had to recede" (Coral 1998, 360).

Despite the strong opposition from her husband, Teodora took over the task of leading the Federation after Morales's disappearance. Maurita supported Teodora, and gave me an insight into their experiences during those frightful years:

10. Interview with Teodora Ayme, Ayacucho, January 2003.
11. Interview with Maurita, Ayacucho, December 2002.

Some women did not want to participate anymore: "because we could die, we put up with it but we are not even paid! What are we doing, risking our lives?" And there they went. I also wanted to leave, I was telling señora Teodora: "Better that I also withdraw, I am not going anymore, it is better if I go . . ." But she always made me come back . . . "We will have a meeting," is what she said; and I went. "If you promised how can you leave us. It is because of cowardliness," that's what Teodora said, "Because of cowardliness you all quit, ah," she said, "we will die defending our struggles," is what the señora said. Me too . . . only the two of us, with señora Teodora, that's all while others were afraid here and there, dead people until . . . well, [the women] did not want to participate anymore. But we were every morning in front of the Council, Teodora and me . . . we sat down, family members arrived crying, "This is what happened to my husband!" "They have killed me!" saying things like that they would come . . . "Now we have to go with this lady," is what I said, I was rather brave, "let's go, señora, let's go and see." "How are we going to be, we as leaders? At least we have to see what happens, we have to help," that is what we said. Señora Teodora was very daring.

To organize the Provincial Federation of Huamanga we had to visit communities. The people were afraid, señorita, they didn't want to go. Other leaders didn't want to go, "All kinds of things can happen to us," that is what they said. But me, as I was brave, I went, "I am going," that is what I told them. One time, just when I came back from Occros—over here, just a little farther up in Infernillo—they stopped a car; there were lots of terrorists, I almost jumped off the car as others did, "stand to attention, *carajo!*" that's what they said, and they were armed. "My God, now they will . . . yes, they will find me with this minute book" . . . I was afraid.[12]

Again, we see how Teodora and Maurita interpret their activities as revolving around helping others. They felt morally obliged to defend the defenseless, especially when everybody was afraid, but these two women—and others with them—found the courage to do so. Maurita recalls how they waited in front of the mayor's office to support women who would come during the day to ask for information about family members. Searching for family members was not without danger. Women would be shouted down, denied information, and dismissed. Sometimes soldiers demanded sexual favors in return for information; sometimes women were raped (TRC, Final Report, vol. 8, 2.1.3.1, 61). Knowing these difficulties made the necessity for organizing and supporting each other more urgent. As Maurita suggests, their women's organization stressed the importance of mobilizing women in

12. Ibid.

other provinces and persisted in organizing federations in all provinces of the department of Ayacucho. They succeeded in their efforts and, in 1991, organized a departmental federation that united the provincial federations. As a reading of the minute book of FECMA shows, the period 1995–99 was marked by the consolidation of the social support delivered by the state, as well as by the growing presence of NGOs. After the secrecy of the violent years 1980–95, the minute book functions as an official testimony of the work of the women, corroborated by the use of Spanish (the participants' language is predominantly Quechua) and the formalization of the book using participants' fingerprints and a notary's certification. This formalization meant that the federation was now recognized as an Organización Social de Base according to Law 25307 and had the right to make claims on the state.

In Lima, grassroots women's organizations also created coordinating committees at the level of districts and city zones to strengthen their negotiating position, defend themselves against government manipulation, and improve negotiations with the distinct donors. In the late 1980s, the organizations in Lima set up a national umbrella organization, the Comisión Nacional de Comedores Populares (National Commission of Community Kitchens, or CNC). As a result of fragmentation among women's groups, this network largely failed to create a strong negotiating position (Blondet and Montero 1995, 61). A new attempt was made when the economy collapsed between 1988 and 1991, this time focusing only on the vast organizations in the capital. The Federación de Centrales de Comedores Populares Autogestionarios de Lima y Callao (Federation of Self-Managed Communal Kitchen Centrals of Lima and Callao, or FECCPALC), was established in 1991 and was supported by international NGOs and national feminist organizations. The federation coordinated 1,600 *comedores populares,* 64 zone-based commissions or district committees, and 37,000 women.

By the 1990s, the core of Shining Path's violent campaign had shifted from Ayacucho to the shantytowns of Lima. Many expected that the well-organized *pueblos jóvenes* would easily resist infiltration by Shining Path, especially because progressive alternatives such as certain sectors of the Catholic Church, NGOs, and, in particular, Izquirda Unida (the United Left Party) were well-represented in the *pueblos jóvenes* and popular participation and association were high (Burt 1998, 268). However, by 1991 the battle for Lima was at its height, and it became crystal clear that the shantytowns were heavily infiltrated. However, Shining Path initially overlooked the importance of women's organizations, because of their seemingly apolitical emphasis on daily survival (Coral 1998, 367). But women turned their resistance against a politics of hunger, exemplified by "marches against hunger" during the late 1980s, to manifestations "against hunger and terror," "for life and peace," and with slogans such as "hunger nor terror will deter us from fighting for peace" (see, e.g., Aguirre 1991; *La República* 1991). Again, women discursively used their position as needy mothers to fight for peace at a time when political organizations seemed incapable of any form of resistance against the violence of Shining Path (*La República* 1991). Poverty, hunger, and violence were related in a complex rhetorical way that legitimized both women's resistance to political violence as well as their struggle for the survival of their families and their political activism as poor women. The grassroots women's movement was one of the very few openly resisting movements left, and perhaps the most visible resistance that Lima offered (Blondet 1996; Barrig 1998). In many ways exemplary to this activism was María Elena Moyano, a grassroots leader who became deputy mayor of the popular neighborhood Villa El Salvador. Interestingly, although Moyano had started her political career by setting up women's livelihood organizations, she did not focus only on them. She was active in municipal party politics for the Left and was a much-loved participant in middle-class feminist forums. Her resistance against Shining Path was open and loud, but short-lived.

By late 1991, Shining Path realized that dismissing the importance of the women's organizations was a mistake they had made in Ayacucho, and ferociously started to attack the women's groups in Lima (Coral 1998, 367). Increasingly, Shining Path infiltrated the women's organizations, which were forced to provide free food for combatants. When these refused, leaders were slandered and publicly denounced as being whores (*colchones*, mattresses) of the government. Receiving food aid became a hazard in itself (TRC, Final Report, vol. 3, 3.2.2; Burt 1998). Shining Path wanted the women's organizations to act as mothers and caretakers on behalf of the armed struggle; if not, they were accused of assisting imperialism. Grassroots women's leaders who resisted Shining Path—which many courageously did—were threatened or killed.[13] During 1991 and early 1992, at least forty neighborhood leaders in Lima were killed, among whom ten were leaders of local grassroots women's organizations (Barrig 1998, 118). In the rest of the country, an additional thirty-five women leaders were killed (TRC, Final Report, vol. 2, 3.2.2.1.6). The violent public killing of María Elena Moyano in 1992 became the symbol of popular women's courage and of all women's leaders who paid with their lives—or just escaped—for their resistance against Shining Path (Moyano and Miloslavich Túpac 1993; Barrig 1998). While Moyano's leadership had functioned as an inspiration

13. There were also, as suggested, many women active in Shining Path. See Kirk (1993) and the interesting though misguided book by Carol Andreas (1985).

for urban resistance, especially among women activists, her death broke popular resistance against the assault of Shining Path in the capital (Burt 1998, 292). Many women's organizations retreated from public spaces because of the extreme violence displayed and the resulting distrust and fear of each other as a consequence of Shining Path infiltrations. The remaining organizations dedicated themselves mainly to alleviating the growing severity of poverty but stayed away from any public manifestations. After 1995, when pacification had set in and the peak of the economic crisis had passed, the organizations slowly recovered.

Institutionalization of Food Aid

It was against the backdrop of violence and economic crisis that federations of women's organizations campaigned for the institutionalization of food aid to the poor. The Federation of Comedores Populares in Lima (FECCPALC) demanded an official recognition of all women's organizations as Organizaciones Sociales de Base (Grassroots Social Organizations). This would eliminate the stigma of being only community kitchens and give the organizations legal status, allowing them to engage in other activities such as workshops and speak on behalf of their communities. FECCPALC also hoped that as Grassroots Social Organizations they would have more powers to control distribution. The second demand the Federation made was for a commitment by the state to supplement the basic food baskets.[14] In 1991, the government issued Law 25307, mentioned above, which provided a legal framework for grassroots women's organizations. At the same time, the government needed to mobilize women's work—and appease the protesting women's movement—in order to relieve the worst effects of the Fuji-shock. As noted in chapter 2, Fujimori used a maternalist rhetoric to align the women's organizations, and he exploited Mother's Day festivities to praise women's work. He called women "heroines" and "self-sacrificing [*abnegadas*]," applauding the "silence" with which they performed their tasks (*Ojo* 1991). Crucially, women had not been silent, but had protested loud and visibly against both terror and hunger. However, the government realized that women's energy could be incorporated and mobilized for poverty relief efforts. An emergency program was set up (Programa de Emergencia Social) in which women's work, alongside that of NGOs and church groups, was central. In 1992, the government set up the Programa

---

14. Interview with Felicita Gallegos, president of the FEMOCCPAALC, Lima, March 2001, see also FEMOCCPAALC (n.d.).

Nacional de Asistencia Alimentaria (National Program for Food Aid, or PRONAA), which fused the various institutional leftovers from former governments since the 1970s. The aim of PRONAA was to raise nutrition levels among the most needy groups in society. The target groups of the program were children under the age of six, pregnant and breastfeeding mothers, old people, and victims of "temporary situations of emergency" (Portocarrero et al. 1998). Law 25307 supposedly supported PRONAA's activities on a legal level and protected women's organizations autonomy. In addition, *comedores populares* would receive kitchen utensils, support in the "integral development of women" (whatever that meant), technical assistance, literacy campaigns in rural areas, and, in Lima, financial support (Grupo Impulsor 2000). Autonomy, however, was not guaranteed at all, whereas technical or educational assistance was hardly supplied, and the "integral development of women" was little more than a slogan. Food was made available in a patchy fashion with conditions attached and not according to the agreements stipulated in the law. Whereas the law stated that the government should cover 65 percent of the budgets of all *comedores populares*, most *comedores* struggled to supplement the unpredictable contributions the government granted.

This lack of implementation, or the gap between discourse and practice, does not mean that such legislative tools were completely useless. Perhaps more than anything, Law 25307 served women's organizations as a means to put pressure on local authorities. For example, according to the minute book of the Federation of Clubes de Madres in Ayacucho, women used knowledge of their institutional rights to fight against deception and the politics of divide-and-rule. The Federation referred consistently to Law 25307, and the minutes are peppered with recurrent phrases such as "the *clubes de madres* have public records at their disposal and there is even a law that qualifies us as grassroots social organizations" (Reunión extra-ordinaria, July 15, 1997, FECMA 1995–99, 287). Despite the lack of implementation, legal recognition by the law was important for the organizations because it allowed them to defend themselves against the manipulative practices of public officials and demand the fair and adequate implementation of programs. On another occasion, in August 1997, the president of FECMA explicitly referred to the law in order to stress their rights: "[The president] states that the Vaso de Leche Program is a right. In *El Peruano* [the state newspaper in which legislation is published] it says how the administrative committee should be formed" (Asamblea general de los Clubes de Madres de Huamanga, August 2, 1997, FECMA 1995–99, 289). The women's organizations had, by law, the often-neglected right to form part of the administration of aid programs. In a similar vein, FECMA stressed the participative nature of food aid and insisted on seeing municipal accounts. They also demanded a voice in the administrative committees that supervised food distributions, as they were allowed to do according to the law (December 2, 1991, Law 25307, http://www.leyes.congreso.gob.pe).

However, familiarity with the law was not enough. The minute book shows that despite women's legal knowledge, they had little power to make sure that others would respect those laws. The Peruvian justice system displays a considerable gap between the law and law enforcement (Méndez, O'Donnell, and Pinheiro 1999; Poole 2004). Individual Peruvians, especially those placed in the lower echelons of social hierarchy, have little access to justice. Organizations such as the Federation of Clubes de Madres tend to be in a stronger position because they can inspire respect based on their representative role, activities, size, and alliances. Alliances are particularly important. For example, on June 28, 1996, Mario Cavalcanti Gamboa, a lawyer and during the 1980s dean of the Colegio de Abogados of Ayacucho (the most important lawyers' association), attended a meeting of the Federation. The women explained their problems to him in general terms: "the policies are bad," "we are mistreated," "there is a lack of unity," and "the Federation does not have enough experience and does not know about the laws" (a misleading claim, given the many references to the law in the minute book). Nonetheless, the supportive Cavalcanti was prepared to become "*consejero* [advisor] of the *clubes de madres* of Ayacucho" (Reunión extra-ordinaria de la FECMA-Hga, FECMA 1995–99, 134).[15] Like many grassroots civil organizations in Peru, the Federation searched for long-term alliances with professionals who might be able to defend the Federation's rights, or serve as *consejeros* when necessary.

The recurrent references to unfulfilled rights and fights with local authorities in the minute book indicate that it was not only food aid and women's organizations that was institutionalized but clientelism was as well. State spending on social programs was significantly increased prior to elections, especially directed at densely populated *pueblos jovenes* in Lima (Schady 1998; Portocarrero et al. 1998; Grupo Impulsor Nacional 2000). Foodstuffs came with aprons and cooking hats in orange, the color of Fujimori's movement, with the PRONAA logo on them. These items were accompanied by cans of orange paint so that the kitchen could be painted and PRONAA written on its front. A large picture of the "hero of

---

15. In his position as dean of the Colegio de Abogados (lawyers' association), Cavalcanti was one of those who defended and supported families of disappeared persons during the 1980s. He had to leave Ayacucho for Lima after receiving death threats but went back in the 1990s (see Tamayo 2003, 101–2).

the nation," Alberto Fujimori, had to be hung on the façade of the building as well. Loyalty to the government was enforced by the threat—made real when necessary—of the withdrawal of food aid (Grupo Impulsor Nacional 2000). Selected women leaders were paid to be in charge of local distribution centers, which created a top-down web of loyalty. Although it should be viewed as positive that at least some of the women were paid for their work, in this case the political loyalty of their district or neighborhood was demanded in return. These paid leaders became the pawns of Fujimori's system because they needed to protect their salaries, often at the expense of their political independence. The government would "encourage" the employees of the distribution centers to take as many people to political support rallies as they could, and the employees would, in turn, press the leaders of the local *comedores populares* or *clubes de madres* to take their members along under the threat of a stop in food supplies. Such threats went down to the individual household level. For example, one of my informants in Lima, Luz, told me that she left the organization she participated in after the leaders of those organizations threatened to cut off food supplies to her family if she did not attend a particular political meeting.[16] According to many other informants, such political demands had always existed. However, as the immense structure of PRONAA suggests and most participants in women's organizations have confirmed, during the Fujimori years clientelism became more visible than ever, and Law 25307 served as legal justification for that clientelism (Palomino 2004).[17]

Power and Prejudice

The hierarchical system created by the Fujimori regime, in which paid representatives of state institutions and social programs had the power of distribution under the watchful eye of the government, fed into the manipulative and often corrupt practices on the ground. The defense mechanisms pulled up by women's organizations—federations, alliances with NGOs, professionals, and feminists, and an "apolitical" image of caring—did not prevent the existing inequalities from being played out on a daily basis.

16. Interview with Luz, Lima, July 2001.
17. In 2000–2003, when I interviewed women about these practices, electoral clientelism was well known. During the elections of 2000, when mobilization was being carried out in support of one party or another, journalists would follow the buses that came out of poor neighborhoods ask participants which they had come to support. Many people did not know. Although the Fujimori government is gone, the system has not been entirely dismantled; subsequent responsible ministers have tried to transform PRONAA, but have apparently been obstructed by stronger forces. See, e.g., the work of Pedro Francke in *La República* (2003).

Many rural members of *clubes de madres* who took part in food aid programs were illiterate and spoke Quechua, not the language of power and bureaucracy, Spanish. Women's class position (poverty and lack of education), ethnicity (Quechua speakers), and gender roles (caring mothers) were exploited to the benefit of local bureaucrats. According to the president of FEDECMA, Vilma Ortega, in some rural communities co-coordinators of distribution centers would hand out fewer foodstuffs than formally allocated, while women were made to sign receipts for the promised amounts.[18] The Federation made a point of comparing the amounts of received goods of all *clubes de madres* in the department with the budget allocated to the different districts. This type of deceit was also a reason for the federation to campaign for literacy courses. For example, on December 16, 1998, the president of FECMA, Teodomira de la Cruz, reported on the literacy courses offered by a Limeño NGO. She had visited the projects in the countryside and concluded that it was very important for the women: "The illiterate mothers of the different districts benefit, so that they won't be deceived by the authorities because of their condition as illiterates" (Asamblea extra-ordinaria, December 16, 1998, FECMA 1995–99, 359). Thus, although officially it was the task of the state—as stipulated in Law 52307 and in the new social programs under the Ministry of Women and Social Development—to "promote [women's] development and that of her family" (PROMUDEH n.d.), in the end FECMA had to defend its members against blunt manipulation and corruption. In addition, it was not the state that provided literacy classes, but NGOs.[19]

The fear of deceit committed by a generic "authorities" emerges throughout the minute book, underscoring feelings of vulnerability and powerlessness among members of the Federation with regard to municipal or governmental officials. For example, in the minutes of August 7, 1997: "We also ask that the señor administrator stops dividing the *clubes de madres* and that he does not participate in internal organizational problems" (Asamblea general de Clubes de Madres de distrito de Huamanga, August 2, 1997, FECMA 1995–99, 287). On another occasion, the president of FECMA visited a member *club de madres* in a rural community (the actual name of the village is not mentioned in the minutes) and learned that "the mayor is corrupt and is not accountable. The Federation has the duty to support the grassroots and protect them in one way or the other" (Asamblea extra-ordinaria, February 16, 1996, FECMA 1995–99, 35). The minutes, in

---

18. Interview with Vilma Ortega, Ayacucho, August 2001.
19. Another NGO offered literacy courses in 1996. See Asamblea extra-ordinaria, January 20, 1996, FECMA 1995–99, 51.

other words, confirm the widely held interpretation that the government social programs often served interests other than feeding poor families. Local authorities seemed to use their power to enrich themselves or to secure the political loyalty of women's organizations in their regions. The minute book refers to various cases of games of divide-and-rule on the part of public officials who spread rumors, favored one organization over the other, or interfered in organizational structures. In one case, recorded in the minutes of September 17, 1996, "the club de madres of Los Angeles de Capillapata, claims that the señor mayor obliged them to change their executive committee," apparently because the mayor did not get on (*no se lleva bien*) with the present leaders (Reunión extra-ordinaria de San Juan Bautista, September 17, 1996, FECMA 1995–99, 163). As these cases indicate, the Federation of Clubes de Madres brought cases of doubtful public management out in the open and provided a platform to discuss particular cases of corruption or manipulation that *clubes de madres* encountered.

The Federation of Clubes de Madres was important because it helped to mediate in disputes with authorities and oversaw the politics of state institutions probably better than individual women's organizations. Nevertheless, the state institutions had the power of distribution, and therefore seemed to have the last word. For example, in January 1996 a "misunderstanding" occurred between an existing *club de madres* and a newly established *comedor popular* in a neighborhood called Neri García Zarate in Ayacucho. The president of the *club de madres,* Filomena, complained to FECMA that "the institutions do not show respect." These "institutions" had replaced the president of the *club de madres*—that is, they threw out Filomena and confiscated the *comedor* she managed. The institution in question appears to be the Instituto Nacional para el Bienestar Familiar (National Institute for the Well-Being of the Family, or INABIF), a program also under the supervision of the Ministry for Women. After the complaint of the leaders of the *club de madres* of Neri García Zarate, the Federation denounced INABIF for malpractice. The court, however, did not do anything. In response, the affected *club de madres* complained to the institution from which it used to receive food aid, PRONAA. In the end, according to the minute book, the *comedor* of the existing *club de madres* was given back to the women, while INABIF set up another *comedor popular* on the same street. Now the neighborhood had two *comedores populares* in one street, supported by two different government agencies, generating further competition among women's groups (Asamblea extra-ordinaria, January 16, 1996, FECMA 1995–99, 34). Whatever the underlying intentions of the coordinators responsible for the local offices of INABIF or PRONAA, their actions were challenged by the persistence of the women in finding solutions:

Teodora Ayme, the respected president of the Departmental Federation, FEDECMA, urged all women involved to defy the intrusive and manipulative state agencies (Asamblea extra-ordinaria de Neri García Zarate, 1996, FECMA 1995–99, 56). The minute book does not mention the two *comedores* further.

The state was not always the cause of conflicts among women, but they might be blamed for conflicts anyway. For example, on August 9, 1997, a meeting was held with a *club de madres* in one of the migrant settlements in the city of Ayacucho. The leaders of this club were accused of forcing every new member to pay a fee of three soles. When some new members (*socias*) refused to pay, other members joined in, claiming that "the old *socias* always marginalized them." Internal fights such as these can hardly be attributed to outsiders. However, on the next page of the minute book the secretary wrote that "the señor administrator is to blame for this division" (Asamblea general, August 9, 1997, FECMA 1995–99, 296). The shift from a relatively "normal" internal problem to the accusation that the (male) administrator was at fault may have been a way to deal with internal disputes and, at the same time, to strengthen solidarity.

As Sra. Amalia, presiding over a *vaso de leche* committee in a Limeño *pueblo joven,* already suggested, the management of the municipal program for the distribution of milk also generated many problems. In the minute book of FECMA we find a diatribe against a particular administrator of the program, who was "another one similar to the former." The women claimed that he "mistreats the mothers, lacks respect and is morally insulting; he doesn't let us speak; he asked for fingerprints and we don't know what for; he owes us two months of products; we had to pay; when we protest he insults us" (Asamblea extra-ordinaria, 1998, FECMA 1995–99, 353). These are serious allegations: once again, these administrators emphasize the inferior social position of poor women through insults when they come to claim their lawful rights to milk (powder). In addition, the milk often does not arrive, which must make the whole operation even more humiliating and, obviously, a waste of precious time. Of course, the women were no strangers to a bit of manipulation themselves: one way to solve the problem of insufficient portions was to register more beneficiaries than existed. The first few meetings covered in the minute book record an inventory of organizations, donations, possessions, and agreements for the upcoming period. These listings show that representatives of aid programs visited the *clubes de madres* to see how many actual beneficiaries lived in each district in order to determine the right portions "because there are ghost-*socias*, and no children but older people, and there are also women who say they are pregnant and [they check] if they are really pregnant or not" (Asamblea extra-ordinaria, 20-1-1996, FECMA 1995–99, 44). Women might have claimed more than that they rightfully deserved, but it was also possible that representatives of aid programs wrongfully accused them of lying. Probably both happened sometimes, reinforcing mutual mistrust, prejudice, and malpractice.

Asistencialismo

The minute book and the interviews show that the women's organizations made a point of defending themselves against manipulations and deceit; however, they do not show the political alliances that might have been submersed under façades of autonomy. We know that many *comedores populares*, *clubes de madres*, and *vaso de leche* committees were corrupt or pawns of the Fujimori regime. "Corruption" can mean various things; in this case it refers to the misuse of foodstuffs for other purposes than feeding the poor. Some women used foodstuffs to sell for profit, or used more for their own families than they were supposed to. After the fall of the Fujimori regime in 2000, the media highlighted the corruption and clientelism in state-sponsored *comedores populares*, radically revising the image of the grassroots women's organizations, from the brave militants of the early 1990s to self-serving manipulators. However, as often is the case, most organizations should be judged more mildly, as the binary corrupt/honest is not always clear-cut. In 2004, Rocío Palomino concluded that one of the problems was that women's groups were judged as if they were expected to reduce poverty, while in the end, women set up *comedores populares* to feed their own families collectively. Many women's groups had responded to the opportunity to receive food aid by organizing, not to help relieve the poverty of the country, but to help relieve their own poverty. They did not provide food aid for the poorest, and that had never been their aim, either. According to Palomino, the *comedores* and *vaso de leche* committees receiving food donations were judged on the wrong premises, suggesting that the objectives of the food aid benefactors and the women's groups differed significantly (Palomino 2004, 142). Despite Palomino's valid observation that there was a disjuncture between macro-level expectations and local-level practice, there were also many women's organizations that did actively seek to negotiate levels of financial and political autonomy to carry out other activities than feeding their own families. Not all organizations succeeded in doing so, and in both rural and urban areas there were major divisions between the more autonomous women's organizations and those that were seen as more dependent—and, as was assumed, therefore more clientelist.

The more autonomous organizations were the ones that set up federations and actively pursued their own political agendas, and those are the organizations studied here. However, these organizations did not escape internal divisions and accusations either. Central to such tensions were the often-heard critiques that food aid programs were "assistentialist," that is, giving assistance to people without transforming the structures that created the necessity for that assistance. Although there is some obvious truth in this, *assistencialismo* is also a negative label suggesting that women's organizations were dependent on food aid.

The idea of dependency weighed heavily on some women who expressed their concern that, in the end, receiving food provoked a social stigma of laziness. For example, Teodomira de la Cruz, at that time president of FECMA, defended herself before even being asked: "That we are lazy is silly. You can't live on two glasses of milk."[20] As she implied, women did not invent this accusatory discourse, but were repeatedly reminded of their supposed laziness by persons in positions of authority. Likewise, Shining Path had emphasized the assistentialist character of women's organizations, accusing participants of dependency on food aid and a lack of critical thinking, "unable to think beyond the next daily food ration they get as a 'gift'" (cited in Barrig 1998, 118, also Burt 1998). The former president of the Federation of Comedores Populares in Lima, Relinda Sosa Pérez, wrote in 1998 that it was often repeated that the *comedores* only asked for assistance without making any proposals to improve their own situations. Sosa Pérez noted that the organizations had many proposals, but that the state preferred emergency measures instead of collaborating with the women to expand their productive activities (cited in Arnillas 1998). However, the idea of women's organizations being dependent and lazy continued to be widely present.

Repeated references are made in the minute book to not wanting to be "assistentialist," especially when authorities are present at meetings. For example, on January 28, 1996, there was a meeting in the district of Chiara with representatives of the different organizational levels; the presidents of the departmental, provincial, and district federations, presidents of local *clubes de madres,* and some *socias.* The mayor, the deputy mayor, and the doctor of Chiara were also present. The reason for this meeting was to reestablish a district committee that could represent the thirteen *clubes de madres* operating in Chiara in the respective federations. The minutes contain various promises by both the authorities and women's organizations to

---

20. Asamblea general de Clubes de Madres de distrito de Huamanga, August 2, 1997, FECMA 1995–99, 287.

affirm their mutual commitment to feed the weakest among them. However, it is also emphasized "that they work together without egoism . . . and do not only wait for assistance, they also need to work harmoniously so that with our work we can earn together" (Asamblea ordinaria del distrito de Chiara, January 28, 1996, FECMA 1995–99, 64). Indeed, arguments against assistentialism were often used when authorities were present or when work needed to be done.

The core of such accusations is that women's activities are not valued as productive. Although women worked very hard to organize distributions, to transform food aid into actual nutrition, finding supplements and actually cooking and serving, and to take care of their households while performing additional jobs and community tasks, their activities were not viewed as "work." Within the gender division of labor, household tasks, including home workers' income-generating activities, were not appreciated as being sufficiently productive. Whereas the food aid women prepared and distributed was a welcome contribution to precarious livelihoods—and was meant to be just that—paternalist language urging women to behave a certain way often slipped in. The ambiguous status of long-term food-for-work programs exemplifies such attitudes.

Since the early 1960s, Peruvian men and women had been mobilized in "food-for-work" projects organized by governments as well as NGOs (Griffin 1979). Considering the indigenous custom of carrying out community works collectively, such projects were relatively easy to promote and organize. Food-for-work projects ranged from nonprofit food aid in exchange for help in building community infrastructure, to government food aid in exchange for labor in regional projects, to seasonal labor on *haciendas* (large farms), where wages were sometimes replaced by food. According to Maurita, she used to work on a *hacienda* during the 1970s, where she was paid only with basic foodstuffs.[21] According to Roelie Lenten (1993, 73), in the 1980s CARITAS and OFASA, in cooperation with the Peruvian government, offered food and other support in exchange for work programs while they also used these programs for evangelical purposes. In addition, since 1981 a system of improving agricultural skills through communal work in exchange for production materials and food has been institutionalized in a state institution, the Projecto Nacional de Manejo de Cuencas Hidrográficas y Conservación de Suelos (PRONAMACHCS). However, studies show the ambiguous benefits of food-for-work programs, as well as the multiple interests attached to such programs (Griffin 1979; Clay, Pillai, and Benson 1998). In the case of grassroots women's organizations and

---

21. Interview, Ayacucho, December 2002.

state-sponsored food aid, food-for-work programs exceeded the legal limits of the food allocations made to *comedores* and *clubes de madres*. Nevertheless, as the minute book suggests, the food aid women's organizations received was often offered in exchange for work, and was "legitimized" by using the language of women's laziness and dependency.

The minute book of FECMA sheds light on the mechanisms through which women were pulled into such projects. According to Law 25307, women's organizations in the rural areas would be supported in setting up vegetable gardens and small animal stocks, something women had been doing already for years without support. The government programs directed at women's organizations, as stipulated in the legislation, promised to support women in their own community-based work as well. Instead, however, women were often employed in, for example, state-led reforestation projects as a payment for the allocated foodstuffs (Reunión extra-ordinaria, February 27, 1996, FECMA 1995–99, 90). While most food aid consisted of foreign agricultural leftovers or processed products, food-for-work projects intended to "encourage local production."[22] Women were thus persuaded to participate because such projects would not only help them and their families to obtain food, but would also improve local markets.

Besides being persuaded to work with the argument of increasing and supporting local production, women were also talked into feelings of guilt about the support they received from the state. For example, at a meeting in 1996 in which an engineer from the agricultural state institution PRONAMACHCS talked with FECMA about several food-for-work projects that might increase women's monthly food supplies, the following sentence slipped in: "In order to receive, one has to change the work mentality" (Asamblea Ordinaria de San Juan Bautista, n.d., FECMA 1995–99, 97). This sounds as if it was thought that women did not work hard enough. At another meeting, the argument was "one has to work, and not wait for foodstuffs" (Reunión Extra-ordinario de Tambillos, April 19, 1996, FECMA 1995–99, 114). As such accusations were written down in the minute book by the secretary of the Federation without a critical note, they might be interpreted as "self-accusations." However, such remarks were often made in the presence of the responsible authorities. Perhaps women did not believe in their own dependency and laziness, but felt a need to justify the food aid they received in the presence of authorities in order not to lose the support.

Women would lose food aid if they did not comply with the demands imposed on them. After a meeting with the deputy mayor of the provincial council of Huamanga, Ayacucho, the minutes read: "We should not only

---

22. An intention that is mentioned in Law 25307; however, foreign food aid increased.

look at the support but we should work because if they take away [the food aid], where will we be then" (Reunión extra-ordinaria, January 27, 1996, FECMA 1995–99, 92). When I met several peasant women in Ccaturumi, Suca, and Quyupampa (agricultural communities in the province of La Mar, Ayacucho), we spoke extensively about the food-for-work program they were involved in. One of the things they said was that because they needed the extra nutrition for their children, they had no choice but to work according to the demands of PRONAA and PRONAMACHCS. Their farms had been largely destroyed during the war, and they were not yet back to a "normal" livelihood that could sustain their families without outside support. However, the plants PRONAMACHCS wanted them to develop meant that they had to reduce the number of goats they held in certain areas, even though goats delivered milk. For these women, cultivating plants that take years to grow in exchange for donated milk powder, rather than milking their own goats, seemed a bad deal (meeting in Ccaturumi, Suca, and Quyupampa, La Mar, Ayacucho, January 2003). These examples do not mean that all the work projects were ill-conceived or exploitative. It does mean, however, that power relations between authorities and women were complex and unequal, sometimes aggravated by insults. Instead of interpreting the voluntary efforts of organized women to take care of their communities as an economic activity that ensured the livelihood of many, those who sustained the clientelist politics of food in Peru imposed a discourse of dependency, laziness, and favoritism. As the minute book shows, the use of offensive language as a means of persuasion and manipulation was not uncommon and worked well since women themselves appropriated the idea that one should do "real" work in exchange for the donated food.

Criticism from former participants in women's organizations sometimes resembled the language used to discredit women's voluntary work. For example, in Lima women who had withdrawn from *comedores populares* or *vaso de leche* committees mimicked the same discourse of assistentialism, laziness, and dependency. Nelly, a woman who had been active in grass-roots women's organizations since the late 1970s and who works and lives in Chorrillos, Lima, claimed that the ideal of solidarity had vanished from the women's organizations. Instead, she argued, the population had become passive and lazy because of the constant food supply. The population was taught to be dependent. According to Nelly, women—and men—waited for PRONAA instead of developing their own productive activities. Nelly also thought that only the "real poor" should benefit from the programs, adding that this should not be the people in Limeño neighborhoods who could be working if only they put in a little more effort. She herself had started a relatively successful family business in sweets.[23] There is a certain logic to her argument—the studies discussed above show that overpopulated Limeño neighborhoods, although not the poorest, received much more food aid than did the poorest communities that were politically less relevant. But Nelly's accusations were not based on an economic assessment of government poverty relief programs. Rather, she explicitly referred to the corruption of her former colleagues by using the language of dependency and laziness often associated with receiving food aid. Even if some women's organizations were definitely corrupt, they were not necessarily "lazy" or "dependent."[24] However, women also accused each other of enriching themselves through the food supplies. Again, these allegations may be valid in some cases, but they were also a product of the same divide-and-rule politics deployed by public employees, since they used the same terminology to downplay the agency of the women involved. Moreover, an undertone of moral hierarchy is placed between those women who feed their families supported by food donations and those who are able to do without. In the end, all women I spoke to preferred earning their own subsistence; however, not all had the possibilities to do so.[25] Thus, accusations of laziness and dependence not only undermine solidarity, but produce and highlight new moral hierarchies between poor women themselves.

Food Aid, Poverty Relief, and Women's Empowerment

Women's—and others'—anxiety about assistentialism were not unfounded. The system of poverty relief through food aid, supposedly temporary and only directed at the poorest, had become an unaccountable industry. By 1995, at least 76,334 grassroots women's organizations provided food to 25 percent of the population, contributing almost five million U.S. dollars to the economy in voluntary work hours in the process of distributing goods and cash (Cueva Beteta and Falconi 2000). When it was clear that the Fujimori regime had created a monstrous bureaucracy allocating millions of

---

23. Interview with Nelly, Chorrillos, Lima, July 2001.
24. The corruption of women's organizations has been discussed extensively in the Peruvian press, especially because of some (nonautonomous) organizations' alliances with the Fujimori regime. See, e.g., Francke (2003).
25. After all, Law 25307 of 1991 promised technical support for women to set up production workshops in the urban areas, and vegetable gardens in rural areas. Most women said they would have preferred such support—adequately carried out—instead of food aid.

dollars worth in donated foodstuffs, economists started to do fundamental research concerning the economic impact of food aid on actual poverty levels. In 1996, just after the incorporation of social welfare programs into the then new Ministry for Women, the Peruvian parliament installed a commission of independent academics and professionals to modernize PRONAA into an efficient state agency. Although the president replaced the commission within half a year, the commission did manage to publish its findings. The study demonstrates that the majority of the assigned budget went to the most populated areas, which were not necessarily the neediest. Limeño districts, which were politically important but not all within the actual target group according to poverty measurements, received the bulk of the allocations. Rural areas with high rates of extreme poverty received far less material support (Portocarrero et al. 1998). As the minute book showed, providing access to assigned portions of foodstuffs in rural areas was often hampered by the corruption and brutality of the administrators of local distribution offices.

Nevertheless, the issuing of Law 25307 suggests that food aid was more than temporary poverty relief in times of crises, but instead promised to contribute to development of communities, poverty relief, and women's empowerment. The lingering question remains, of course, whether food aid actually contributed to poverty reduction. The literature on international food aid indicates that donor interests, other than humanitarian support, highly influence effectiveness and that persistent problems with targeting, monitoring, and evaluation of food transfers does not allow for a positive evaluation of food aid since the 1950s (Uvin 1992; Clay, Pillai, and Benson 1998; Barret 1998, 2001, 2002). The same can be said about national interests to deliver food aid. Statistics show that poverty has not been reduced since food aid was introduced. In 1970, 50 percent of the national population lived in poverty, a number that decreased slightly up until 1980. After 1985, poverty rose again to reach 54 percent in 1991. In 1997, poverty was still at 51 percent and malnutrition stood at 24 percent, despite the fact that food aid had consistently risen since the mid-1980s (FLACSO 1993, 18; Ruggeri Laderchi 2001). Data for 2000 show levels of 54 percent of Peruvians living in poverty, of which 27 percent lived in extreme poverty (Johannsen 2006). There is no demonstrable advantage to targeting women and "the poorest" (Clay, Pillai, and Benson 1998), which is perhaps not surprising considering the discussed levels of clientelism and corruption. The failure in targeting women and the poorest might be best exemplified in the persistent high prevalence of anemia among pregnant mothers and infants (50 percent and 78 percent, respectively; Sánchez-

Griñan 2002). Thus, although research suggests that food transfers have a positive effect on individual households (Ruggeri Lardechi 2001), these national poverty numbers confirm the long-term inefficiency of food aid as a poverty-reduction strategy.

The investigative committee looking into food transfers and the possible modernization of PRONAA came to the same conclusion (Portocarrero et al. 1998). According to the report, PRONAA was severely hampered by its political character. There was a lack of capacity and communication between PRONAA's executive and policy-making functionaries as a consequence of political interests. The report speaks of internal tensions between *tecnócratas* and *políticos* (technocrats and politicians) in the higher institutional echelons, respectively those who did want to transform PRONAA into an efficient and depoliticized institution and those who clung to and furthered political interests that government relief programs entailed (see also Velazco 1998). Considering the political interest the Fujimori government had in food aid, it is not surprising that by the year 2000 food distributions accounted for 40 percent of the budget allocated to poverty relief programs (Grupo Impulsor 2000).

However, Law 25307 promised more than food aid, which raises the question whether the food aid system has contributed to women's empowerment. In a roundabout, perverse way, it did. The positive side effect of the emphasis on food aid was that grassroots women's organizations became widespread in both urban and rural areas. As the above analysis shows, there is no doubt that poor women became more involved, empowered, vocal, and visible through their participation in grassroots organization (see also Barrig 1986, 1988, 1994, 1998; Blondet 1986, 1991; Blondet and Montero Checa 1995). During the late 1970s and through the 1980s, more women raised their voices in local politics, poor women got involved in feminist politics, and representatives of *comedores populares* and *vaso de leche* committees in Lima, and of *clubes de madres* in Ayacucho, gained a voice in policy making (Anderson 1998, 87). Although during the 1990s many women's organizations that received assistance from PRONAA became pawns of the Fujimori regime, many others resisted. Nonallied federations of women's groups in both Lima and Ayacucho engaged in a continuous struggle to claim social rights granted through the government programs and new legislation, even if this was a difficult and not always successful job. As it became increasingly clear that food aid was being used politically and that real political will to reduce poverty or promote women's empowerment was absent, women became more aware of and involved in politics. In chapter 6, I will discuss how this activism affected the careers of some of the women leaders here discussed.

Conclusion

The recent history of food aid in Peru shows that instead of reducing poverty, the state used food aid as a means to secure political support and to cushion economic crisis. The Fujimori government, in particular, expanded and institutionalized clientelist ties to a perverse degree: when the women's organizations were at their weakest because of political violence and severe economic crisis, Fujimori demanded an emblematic role from the women's organizations by compelling them to display loyalty to his regime in exchange for much-needed food aid. The food-distribution system represented a corrupt and clientelist system that started at the highest point, with the president, and was often reproduced by local bureaucrats and participants in the women's groups. Not only was food aid—and thus "temporary" poverty relief—institutionalized, but so were clientelist practices. Many local public officials or municipal administrators acceded to governmental demands in order to protect their jobs, and created a system of clientelism of their own that protected existing local power relations or reinforced new ones. Hierarchies based on gender, ethnicity, and class were efficiently deployed and enforced, as we saw, for example, in cases of deceit based on language.

Maternalist discourses directed at poor women were exploited to further emphasize women's responsibilities as unpaid caretakers of the community. Although presidents had used such discourses and practices since Odría (1948–56), the Fuji-shock of 1990 exacerbated the government's need for popular support, poverty relief, and women's work. With a deteriorating economy and increasing foreign food supplies, grassroots women's organizations became the distribution networks used by governments to distribute and prepare donated foodstuffs. The institutionalization of clientelism—made visible by the orange paint on the façades of many communal kitchens—did not help women's quest for recognition; the government's clientelism was translated into assistentialism on the ground and further eroded organized women's claims to be productive entities. The fact that women's work in the realm of poverty relief was associated with motherhood and self-sacrifice made it impossible for women's work to be recognized as productive. However, women's organizations also strategically used motherhood as a protective shield, on the one hand, and to legitimize protests against economic policies, on the other. Thus, the maternalist rhetoric was used and abused in ambiguous ways, from above as well as below.

The case of the women's organizations in Ayacucho, federated at departmental, provincial, and district levels, shows that women used a variety of strategies to protect their autonomy and to manage the food distributions.

First, by organizing on an increasingly larger scale, creating a layered system that reached remote communities, they managed to form a united front. Higher levels of organization gave women more possibilities to prevent deceit and corruption at the local level because together they had more knowledge and capacities at their disposal. Second, women knew the appropriate legislation and consistently referred to it when they felt their rights were violated. Although they had little power to enforce the law, knowing and defending it must have contributed to the respect they inspired in the local community, which helped them to protect their autonomy and the management of food distributions. Third, when the Federation had no other option, it could always fall back on the alliances it established with local NGOs, lawyers, and possibly other professionals. Mimicking discourses about the dependency and laziness of the beneficiaries that the assistentialist character of the food aid system generated might be called a fourth, though negative, strategy. Used in order to protect the continued allocation of food aid, this might have been a necessary option. However, when women deployed such negative arguments about the character of receiving aid against each other, it created a moral hierarchy in which those who received foodstuffs were seen as less valuable than those who did not.

The state limited the agency of women by characterizing them as poor mothers, not as full—and equal—citizens of the Peruvian nation (see also Craske 1998, 106–7). At the same time, the state appropriated the power of distribution of the organized women without implementing social reforms that would make the distribution of resources, knowledge, and power more equal. While subsequent governments treated them as clients of a benevolent state, the growing organizations (and federations) developed a discourse of rights in which "food" became the right of the women's organizations and the obligation of the state. The right to food aid, as established in Law 25307, issued in 1991, represented more than the right to a meal a day: for many grassroots women's organizations, it was a law that granted them a place in the national redistributive system of not only goods, but also social-political participation. Even if the stipulations in the law—e.g., participation in the administration of distributions, support in education, and productive activities—were often mostly neglected by the state, women could now make a legitimate claim on the state that was not guided by their mothering roles. As such, even though the system was clientelist or even assistentialist, and largely promoted using gendered stereotypes embedded in class difference, it expanded poor women's social citizenship.

4

POPULATION POLICIES, POVERTY, AND WOMEN'S BODIES

These women are ignorant. We just bribed them; they consented [to sterilization] if we gave them a bit of money for their basic needs.

—*Head physician in provincial hospital in La Mar, 2003*

In January 2003, I approached the physician on duty in the hospital of San Miguel, province of La Mar, department of Ayacucho, and asked him what had happened in his hospital during the much-denounced sterilization campaigns of the mid-1990s. He answered that he and his medical team did indeed sterilize many women, because "it was an authoritarian situation, we could not oppose. We went out to find women who we could sterilize."[1] Physical violence was not necessary, as women would easily consent in exchange for money or food. However, as the doctor indicates, they would not always know what they were consenting to, as these rural Quechua-speaking peasant women were "ignorant." The doctor and his team did not make any efforts to lift women and their families out of "ignorance" by supplying adequate information and care, but just "did their jobs" and sterilized them. As this anecdote suggests, an aggressive population policy imposed from above was relatively easily picked up at the local level, where many physicians and nurses acted upon their prejudices and accepted a neo-Malthusian policy directed at poor, mainly indigenous, women.[2]

This chapter looks at the ways in which aggressive population policies during the 1990s were embedded in prejudices concerning the reproductive character of Peruvians and, especially, of poor indigenous/mestiza women.

---

1. Interview, identity concealed, La Mar, January 2003
2. "Neo-Malthusian" refers to the nineteenth century ideas of Thomas Malthus applied to contemporary society. Central to neo-Malthusian thinking is the notion that population growth is unsustainable and hampers development.

I argue that population politics were overproportionally directed at poor women and grounded in the assumption that without a certain level of pressure, poor and indigenous women would not only produce "too many" children, but would reproduce the poverty in which they lived. Thus, poor women's bodies were used as a policy tool for poverty reduction in a neoliberal era. The Peruvian government set goals to reduce population growth substantially and promised to provide all Peruvian women with adequate reproductive health care and birth-control methods. By 1997, it was clear that a quota system had pushed medical personnel into sterilizing women (and some men) under inadequate and often coercive circumstances. Although the Peruvian government did not stipulate the use of force, the circumstances created did result in the use of deceit, excessive pressure, and sometimes physical force to meet the quotas set. Human rights organizations investigated what had happened, gathered evidence, and denounced the practices (CLADEM 1998, 1999; Defensoria del Pueblo n.d.; Comisión Especial sobre Actividades de Anticoncepción Quirúrgica Voluntaria 2002). Recently, scholars have placed the abuses committed in a broader perspective of global health sector reform and local politics (Ewig 2006a, 2006b; Rousseau 2007). In this chapter, I intend to widen the perspective by examining how far coercive population policies were related to long-term and widespread racism and sexism toward poor indigenous women; that is, I embed the coercive policies of the 1990s in a context that made them possible. As I will discuss below, Peru had been very conservative with regard to the use of contraceptive technology, and the opening offered by the policies of the Fujimori government seemed a progressive, even feminist, break with the past. However, looked at more closely, the president hijacked feminist discourse (Ewig 2006a) to implement racist and sexist policies, which would not have been out of place in early twentieth-century eugenic thinking (Boesten and Drinot 2004). Although the policies broke with a conservative past, the implementation of these policies, I argue, did not show a rupture with existing cultural norms, as the policies built upon the more generalized contempt for poor and indigenous women.

In order to examine how the relationship between local health care personnel and women could become so abusive, I examine self-assessment documents produced by grassroots women's organizations in the rural areas of the province of Huancavelica. These documents were produced in cooperation with a feminist NGO, Manuela Ramos, and assess issues of women's reproductive health. In doing so, I highlight not only how prejudice and disrespect is reproduced at a local level, but also how difficult it is for poor Peruvians to manage fertility when health care services are limited, hierarchical, and steeped in racist assumptions. Such a comprehensive and long-term analysis shows that although the sterilization campaigns were the result of a temporary and aggressive policy that was quickly reversed, they were possible because of poor women's continuous submission to humiliating reproductive health policies—a product of existing intersecting inequalities at both global and local levels.

Women's Bodies and Population Policies

If we discard eugenic discourses and practices of the first half of the twentieth century in the context of contemporary population policies, then international concern and fear about population growth, especially among poor and nonwhite groups, stem from the 1960s. In the United States, as scholars Jane Jaquette and Kathleen Staudt claim (1988), "near hysteria" emerged as a result of "scientific" studies regarding the possible economic and environmental consequences of uncontrolled population growth in poorer countries. One of the most influential books at that time was Paul Erhlich's *The Population Bomb*, published in 1968, in which population growth in the Third World was linked to economic "underdevelopment."[3] Influenced by such beliefs, USAID started to tie aid to restrictive population policies as part of development packages (Connelly 2008). Analyzing the contents of Erhlich's book and the attitudes of USAID and the U.S. Congress toward Third World population policies, Jaquette and Staudt conclude that these fears for population growth were steeped in racist and sexist fears regarding future changes in the world's power balance, or the lack thereof (1988).[4] The belief that poverty was caused by overpopulation (instead of overpopulation being a symptom of poverty, for example) and that reducing the population was a condition for development led to aggressive and often coercive practices in, for example, India, Indonesia, Bangladesh, and Kenya (Jaquette and Staudt 1988; Hartmann 1995; Kabeer 1992, 1994; Aripurnami 1997; Maternowska 2006; Connelly 2008). U.S. policymakers for population control were at the forefront of promoting family planning in the developing world, with USAID one of the main investors in the export of contraceptives, family planning clinics, and community projects. Although these policies were grounded in misguided fears and presumptions about the development of the world, U.S. policy makers never publicly endorsed coercive practices. However, as Helen

---

3. Ehrlich still supports his initial arguments; today he appears to be an environmentalist arguing that overpopulation within the United States will cause disaster. Consequently, he opposes migration, especially from poorer countries (Stein 1997, 593–99).

4. An early critique of such policies is Mamdani (1972).

Epstein reminds us, neither did they do much "to halt or at least distance themselves from the most abusive programs" (2008, 57).

The UN International Conference on Population and Development (ICPD), held in 1994 in Cairo, brought change: under pressure of feminist organizations, the debate shifted from demographic thinking to the incorporation of reproductive health and rights, in particular women's rights. Although this was potentially a major shift after almost thirty years of aggressive, top-down, and largely unsuccessful population politics, Betsy Hartmann (1995) concluded almost immediately that the new, post-Cairo consensus showed many gaps. According to critical observers and activists, the Cairo agreements left sufficient space for ambiguity for international cost-cutting and neoliberalism, religious opposition to women's rights and birth control, and the "Malthusian thinking ... ingrained in development institutions, donor agencies and government departments," to overshadow population programs throughout the world (Nair and Kirbat 2004, 30; see also Petchesky 2000; Hartmann 1995). Perhaps more importantly, the shift in discourse took place when the health sector underwent substantial changes in financing and delivery systems. This World Bank–guided neoliberal restructuring of the health sector often expected NGOs to participate by providing social safety nets and performing certain tasks that were shifted away from the state (Petchesky 2000). Especially in reproductive health, many nontechnical issues, including information and empowerment campaigns, became the responsibility of feminist NGOs and voluntary women's groups (Ewig 2006b). The reforms that were introduced in the Peruvian health sector have to be seen in this context.

Until the 1990s, however, Peru had gone against the global trends in population thinking and resisted international interference in population matters. This opposition came from two opposing camps: on the one hand, there was a powerful conservative Catholic movement that opposed any form of modern contraceptive technology; on the other hand, there was strong opposition against U.S. "imperialism," including the cheap importation of modern contraceptives, from the political Left. This does not mean that Peru was not experiencing similar problems to those in other developing countries: due to improved health care and high fertility rates, the Peruvian population tripled between 1950 and 1994, and urbanization accelerated (FLACSO 1993, 22). Poverty was not decreasing, and urban unemployment stayed high. The availability of modern contraceptives and increased female education, especially among the urban middle classes, did help reduce the fertility rate from 6.9 in 1950 to 6.0 in 1970, and 3.6 children per woman in 1990 (FLACSO 1993, 26). Interestingly, women's desired number of children was always lower than actual fertility rates suggest (FLACSO 1993, 84; Aramburú 2002). Urban fertility rates came close to the desired fertility rate, while national levels were long kept high because of high rural fertility rates. (In 1992, the urban birth rate was 2.7, while rural fertility stood at 5.9. By 2004, rural fertility rates had also decreased, to 3.6 children per woman.) These figures suggest that the unfulfilled wish to have fewer children was mainly a concern for rural women. At the same time, these processes suggest what many social scientists have known for some time: that women have fewer children if their position in society is improved as well as their living standards, and if both men and women get access to proper and respectful reproductive health care (Hartmann 1995, Aramburú 2002b). Continuous political and religious opposition against contraceptive technology exacerbated the geographical and class divide between those who had and those who did not have access to reproductive health care. As a result, it is estimated that in 1994 of the total of annual pregnancies, 40 percent were wanted, 30 percent were unwanted, and another 30 percent ended in abortions.[5] Illegal abortion was the second-most important cause of female mortality in Peru. According to ENDES, in 2000 infant mortality stood at 33 per 1,000 births and maternal mortality at 185 per 100,000 births, while abortion, still penalized today, had risen to 35 percent of all pregnancies since 1994 (as cited in Aramburú 2002a, 53; and also in Ferrando 2001). Thus, although it seems clear that a majority of women wanted to reduce the number of children they had, the conditions for doing so were inadequate, especially among the poorer and rural populations.

Before the state finally intervened in the 1990s, feminist organizations were actively promoting women's rights and reproductive health in Lima's *pueblos jovenes* (see, e.g., Movimiento Manuela Ramos 1984, 16). However, institutional preconditions were absent: there was no equal access to education, health care, and contraceptives or to the economic resources needed to obtain such services. Feminist campaigns for improved contraceptive rights, including abortion, were continuously undermined, not only by the conservative sectors, but also by the feminist movement's supposed allies among the political Left (Portugal 1987; see also *Marka* 1979). As a consequence of the illegality of abortion and of the concentration of medical care in urban middle-class centers, many abortions are carried out by nonprofessionals or self-induced, which leads to complications and high maternal mortality rates, especially among the poor (*Marka* 1979; see also Centro de la Mujer Peruana Flora Tristán 2000). It is clear that women

---

5. With an average fertility rate of 3.5, as cited in Centro de la Mujer Peruana Flora Tristán (2000, 35).

with low incomes and without proper health care services to turn to have the most problems with unwanted pregnancies.

In 1985, the government of Alan García issued a National Law on Population, which "guaranteed" the rights of individuals to decide freely how many children they wanted to have (Bonfiglio 1999). However, again opposition from the Church proved strong. In this period, the first rumors of forced sterilizations emerged: the Church accused the government and some international agencies of sterilizing poor people (¡Viva! 1985). At this point, sterilization was not government policy, and it has never been proven whether sterilizations were illegally carried out. Nevertheless, it is clear that during the period from the late 1960s into the 1990s, the United States actively supported aggressive sterilization programs throughout the Americas and Asia; there is just not sufficient evidence to prove if this actually happened in Peru as well. Although the feminist periodical ¡Viva! reported the Church's denunciation, no follow-up action was taken (1985). Unfortunately, accusations of forced sterilizations have become a powerful argument among conservative sectors to oppose and obstruct making contraceptive methods available on a larger scale. As a result, this first population program did not substantially improve the situation for the majority of poor people, especially those in rural areas (Aramburú 2002b; Bonfiglio 1999; Arroyo 2002).

President Fujimori took the issue of population politics more seriously and deliberately and openly challenged the Church's hegemony in reproductive matters. When he came to power in 1990, his government designed a National Population Program and expanded the existing law of 1985. The goals of this new program were to reduce population growth to a maximum of an annual 2 percent by 1995, to decrease fertility from 3.6 to 2.5 children per woman in 2000, and to improve maternal and child health. The program emphasized the freedom to choose, the reproductive rights of persons, and gender equity (CLADEM 1998). Thus, the Fujimori government not only promoted family planning for developmental reasons, but explicitly—and repeatedly—emphasized the need for equal access to birth control methods for women of all classes. That was the message the president brought to the Fourth UN World Conference on Women in Beijing in 1995, at which he combined rhetoric regarding women's emancipation and the "right to choose" with developmental goals for the benefit of the poor. Newspaper articles from 1995 show Fujimori's double standard in relation to the conference on women: his emancipatory discourse covered an aggressive politics directed at poor and indigenous women. Fujimori stated in a national newspaper, El Comercio, that he went to the conference to support the "important work of the women's movement" and to emphasize his "dedication to the improvement of the position of 50 percent of the population which has been excluded for a long time" (*El Comercio* 1995). In Beijing, Fujimori could not stress enough that women had the right to control their fertility and that he would be the one to guarantee this right for women "of all classes" (Fujimori 1995). This rhetoric was in sharp contrast to his politics; as Christine Ewig observes (2006a), Fujimori skillfully hijacked a progressive feminist discourse, furthered in the Cairo and Beijing agreements, to implement aggressive population policies directed at poor and indigenous women.

In 1995, voluntary sterilization was incorporated into the law as an approved contraceptive method. This provoked a heated debate between the government and the Church, while the media supported the measure (Bonfiglio 1998). The Church again attempted to impose its conditions, preventing the state from implementing liberal sex education in schools by opposing the spread of educational material that the Ministry of Health had issued in 1996. Initially the sex education guides the Ministry published included homosexuality as a sexual preference, and provided information about abortion and about voluntary sterilization as a birth control method. However, under pressure from conservative sectors, the government revised the guides and eliminated some of the more progressive references in order to promote "family values." But the "war of the guides" went on; the bishop of Ayacucho and one of the most conservative and influential Church authorities in Peru (and member of Opus Dei), Monsignor Cipriani, developed his own educational material, stressing responsible parenthood and family planning based on abstinence. According to feminist writer Mariella Sala (1996), this conservative material was distributed as school material to students, while the Ministry's material—revised but still more informative—became available to teachers only. The Church knew too well how to influence public opinion against the government; Fujimori, for his part, had to take these disagreements into account and did so using a progressive global feminist discourse. In a national newspaper, *La República*, the minister of health declared there were no disagreements with the Church, because the government was just "giving in to the demands of the population to control their fertility according to their rights" (*La República* 1995). In the meanwhile, Fujimori accused the Church of impeding women from exercising their rights by saying in his speech to the World Conference on Women in Beijing: "I am convinced that in Latin America, and other parts of the world, the time has come to abandon, once and for all, the antiquated mental schemes which hinder the full development of women and, therefore, of humankind. This does not mean that we create alliances to attack any particular institution, but instead we must promote a debate of the highest ethical and humane standards" (Fujimori 1995). In this way, Fujimori deployed international discourses of women's rights and appealed to demands for equality to justify a fertility reduction program directed at poor, rural and urban, women.

Fujimori's proposals to actively pursue a decrease in population growth while reforming the health sector into a system that would explicitly benefit women and the poor was welcomed by the World Bank, which agreed to finance educational campaigns on family planning (Bonfiglio 1998, 134). USAID also supported the new population program and vouched to donate a yearly sum of approximately U.S. $14 million plus several tons of foodstuffs. A feminist NGO, Manuela Ramos, was mobilized to carry out an innovative and participatory program aimed at empowering and informing poor women. The government swiftly set up information campaigns, and family planning services were provided without a fee, including sterilization. However, no improvements in the quality of rural health care services, such as hygiene and the availability of medical supplies, or even beds, were provided. Thus, while the proposals with regard to reproductive health found broad support in progressive sectors and in the world of international cooperation, necessary reforms in the health sector were not carried out.

Instead, the government improvised mobile medical services for the rural areas; local rural doctors received orders to sterilize women in their regions according to a quota system and to "ensure that all women accepted a contraceptive method after giving birth" (Aramburú 2002b). As the fact-finding research of the feminist human rights lawyer Guilia Tamayo uncovered (CLADEM 1998, 1999), local health care personnel had to determine the number of "women of fertile age" in their region and sterilize a certain number of these women according to established quotas. The medical officers who met quotas received goods or money. Donated food was used as a bribe for women to agree to sterilization. Highlighting the interests of U.S. international policy, according to one newspaper, the offer of "free sterilizations for the poor" was made public at the very moment when the minister of health received almost twenty thousand tons of foodstuffs from USAID in the harbor of Lima (*Expreso* 1995). Such U.S.-backed practices of food-for-sterilization would not have been out of place in 1960s and 1970s international development policy. Although several investigating committees differ about the extent to which the Peruvian government forced sterilization upon women during the Fujimori period, all agree that it occurred (CLADEM 1998, 1999; Defensoria del Pueblo n.d.; Comisión Especial sobre Actividades de Anticoncepción Quirúrgica Voluntaria 2002). Fujimori's motives for these extreme measures were economic; they had little to do with providing equal access to services for all, or with ensuring the well-being of women. Carlos Aramburú, who was briefly president of the National Population Council in 1996, observed that Fujimori's personal interest in decreasing population growth through the most cost-effective method was clear-cut. Aramburú recalls that in 1996, the prime minister declared to the press that "the government cannot reduce poverty efficiently if poor families continue to have seven children on average" (Aramburú 2002b). The minister's formulation shows the Malthusian notion that unchecked fertility contributes to poverty and underdevelopment, a notion that has dominated thinking about population throughout the world.

In mid-1996, responding to reports from rural parishes, the Church accused Fujimori of using force in his sterilization program, but of course accusations were dismissed with the already prepared argument that the Church was a conservative force that did not support the freedom of women to use modern contraceptives. Indeed, human rights and feminist movements had initially supported Fujimori's plans. However, from late 1996 onward, it became clear to feminist organizations, human rights movements, and the national ombudsman that there was something seriously wrong with Fujimori's population program. In late 1997, the Peruvian press released the first testimony from female victims of forced sterilization, and human rights advocates started to investigate the issue. Because the program was largely financed by USAID, activists accused USAID of involvement. In January 1998, the U.S. Congress sent a human rights researcher to study the practices in the population program in Peru. After reaching the conclusion that USAID was not directly involved, because its personnel did not know anything about quotas, USAID pressed the Peruvian government to cancel the quota system and to stop the "voluntary" sterilization program; international funding disappeared and the government was forced to reform its program drastically (Bonfiglio 1998; Aramburú 2002b). In March 1998, the Peruvian government announced reforms in the population program, an investigation into malpractice, and proper punishment for the "guilty."

In sum, the population policies implemented by the Fujimori regime used poor women's bodies as a policy tool to reduce poverty. Biological reproduction was thought to be predominantly a female concern, while the reproduction of poverty was strongly linked to the bearing of children among the poorest and those perceived as racially of a lower status. Adding to the racist undertone of earlier national and international debates about populations in developing countries, such bias suggests a deterministic view upon who and what poor women are, and, in particular, about how poverty is maintained and reproduced. Such views largely legitimized the use of quotas and coercion in achieving the goals of the population program. As we will see in the next section, prejudice about racial difference and disrespect for poor women further helped the Peruvian government in implementing a highly questionable population program.

Perceptions and Practices of Reproductive Health: ReproSalud in Huancavelica

ReproSalud was (and still is) a community reproductive health program designed and commissioned by USAID staff to accompany USAID-funded population programs, and was carried out by Manuela Ramos. The contradictions and ambiguities of such an approach—neoliberal health sector reforms relying on NGOs and women's voluntary labor and the collaboration of a feminist NGO in a dubious population program—and the position of Manuela Ramos will be discussed below, after the actual project has been examined. The core of the ReproSalud program is the collaboration between professional facilitators, trained and financed by Manuela Ramos, and women's groups such as the *comedores populares, clubes de madres,* and *vaso de leche* committees. Using innovative techniques, facilitators and participants make an *autodiagnóstico*, a self-diagnosis of reproductive health issues in the community. The assumption of such a participatory action research approach is that information about women's situations was reciprocally constituted and thus closer to local realities, while simultaneously providing a learning opportunity for all involved. This potentially transformative strategy aims to empower women to make claims on the health care system.

Apart from providing a learning experience for participants and a potential wealth of information for health care providers, the a*utodiagnósticos* are a great source for studying the perceptions and practices of reproductive health in Andean communities. The *autodiagnósticos* show the sometimes contradictory experiences of "traditional" or local versus "modern" biomedical beliefs concerning health care and reproduction. These contradictory experiences feed into the complex relationships between men and women and between health care personnel and their patients. The relationship between women and medical personnel, in turn, is grounded in sociocultural misunderstandings that are entrenched in racism and sexism toward rural indigenous women and periurban migrants. Unpacking these relationships, drawing on *autodiagnósticos* drawn up in the Andean province of Huancavelica, helps explain how it was possible for medical personnel to use aggressive methods in family planning programs.

Huancavelica is a province and a department with a capital of the same name, situated in the cold and arid heights of the Andes at approximately twelve thousand feet. It is in one of the poorest and least served regions of Peru. People mainly live from cattle, wool, and some agricultural products such as potatoes, corn, and quinoa, a cereal product used as a staple food. The communities and the provincial capital are linked mainly by unpaved roads. Public transportation and private cars are available only to a group of traders, authorities, and NGO workers, and the roads between the provincial capital and the other departments are poor and often inaccessible due to flooding. Peasants walk to local markets in order to sell their goods. The history of Huancavelica is, in addition, a violent one: it used to be an area of mercury extraction, at high cost for the local population in terms of labor exploitation (see, e.g., Contreras 1982). Bordering the department of Ayacucho, it was also one of the main areas of warfare between Shining Path and counterinsurgency forces from 1980 to 2000. Despite its geographical, political, economic, and social isolation, in 1990 a university was established in the capital of Huancavelica, opening up new perspectives.

A group of young women born and raised in the region run the Huancavelica branch of Manuela Ramos's ReproSalud. They studied at the local university and followed courses offered by the Manuela Ramos office in Lima. However, these *promotoras* (facilitators) are neither doctors nor nurses and do not have the power to instruct local medical personnel. They provide *capacitaciones* (workshops) to women in the hope that the women will become "empowered" through sharing information regarding leadership, civil participation, women's rights, and reproductive health problems. In January 2001, these *promotoras* took me with them on their trips into the field. The following analysis is based on that experience.

The *promotoras* of Huancavelica visit rural communities equipped with pens, paper, and, necessarily, warm clothes and sleeping bags. On request, they had one four-wheel-drive car and a driver at their disposal; regular transport was not available. The roads were poor, when there were roads at all. The *promotoras* left early in the morning, at three, four, or five A.M., to be able to start a workshop at eight or nine, depending on the community they would visit. Many times the *promotoras* stayed over for the weekend, sleeping on the floor of one of the participant's houses or, when available and empty, in the beds of a *posta de salud* (local health care center). The participants in the courses came from surrounding communities. The geography of the area implies that the majority walked three to four hours over the hills, carrying their smallest children on their backs, to reach the place where courses take place. Various women indicated that getting their husband's permission to leave the family for a day or two was a bigger obstacle than the long walk itself. The participants were members of women's organizations such as *clubes de madres* or *comedores populares*, which had been approached by the *promotoras* of Manuela Ramos.

The *autodiagnósticos* contain a special form of making "life stories': together, the participants made up a "typical" life of a woman born in their village. Through discussion, everyone made her personal contribution to the collective story. In this way, different possibilities in the course of a life in a small village were chronicled. Questions were asked and speculations made: "The husband was sad because it was a girl, or maybe he was not so sad"; "After she menstruates, what will become of this girl?"; "This man might hit her." Together they speculated on their own lives and experiences. Women talked about existing beliefs and traditions in their culture, and how they experienced social relations. The life stories were meant to contribute to a discussion about reproductive health. As such, they tend to be more about sexuality than, for example, work.

After drawing up the life stories, women discussed the distinct visions and problems that emerged during the life story session. The *promotoras* discussed particular themes by asking questions and making lists of answers on large sheets of paper pinned up on the wall. Questions immediately related to women's own interpretations of reproductive health were asked, such as: Why does giving birth hurt? Who helps you give birth? What do you do when you feel pain? Why does one get sick? Is getting older a problem? How can one avoid having many children? Questions directed at development issues, such as the functioning of the health care center and the role of nutrition in relation to their health, were also discussed. Furthermore, questions related to women's positions were reviewed, most directly in the deceptively simple question: What is a happy woman?

The *autodiagnósticos* that are analyzed here were performed by women organized in *clubes de madres* in four different communities in Huancavelica.[6] The communities are hours walking away from each other, but although villages, dates, and personal experiences can differ, the experiences concerning reproductive health among women in rural Huancavelica have much in common. Therefore, I present the four *autodiagnósticos* within a

---

6. The *autodiagnósticos* have also been studied by Carmen Yon Leau (2000) as part of Manuela Ramos's intent to learn from women's reproductive preferences. Various of my observations based on the *autodiagnósticos* of Huancavelica are obviously also made by Yon Leau. The four *autodiagnósticos* from Huancavelica that I use here are photocopies of the originals drawn up by the local office of Manuela Ramos: Autodiagnóstico Club de Madres "Maria Parado de Bellido," Matipaccana, Yauli, Huancavelica November 1996; Club de Madres "Virgen del Rosario" Pallallas, Acoria, Huancavelica 1998; Club de Madres "Sor Ana de los Angeles," Churcampa, Huancavelica, April 27–May 1 1999; Club de Madre "Virgen de Fatima," Centro poblado menor de San Juan de Ccarhuacc, zona Chopcca, Yauli, Huancavelica, July 6–10, 1999.

single narrative in order to show a general image of how women in the region interpret their realities.[7] Although I obviously do not pretend to transmit women's own "reality" here, I think it is possible and also useful to extrapolate certain beliefs and practices that influence rural women's reproductive lives. Since Peruvian women in general indicate the desire to control their fertility but do not seem able to do so, considering the high fertility rates in rural and poor areas, it is useful to ask what they regard as obstacles in managing their fertility. While governments have acted as if poor women do not want to or cannot manage and reduce the number of children they have, the analysis here suggests that there are other problems that serve as impediments in the exercise of women's right to control their own bodies.

Autodiagnósticos: Growing Up, Marriage, and Childbirth

The women start their life stories at birth. Born as women, they discuss the distinct parental appraisal of having a girl or a boy and conclude that, generally, men want sons and women want daughters. Growing up helping their mothers from an early age, girls will not have many opportunities for schooling. According to the women—and confirmed by statistics—girls get less education than boys, since female education is perceived as less important. However, the mothers of today would like their daughters to go to school. Unfortunately, girls often do not want to go to school. Some of the young mothers present at the meetings say that they were treated so badly at school that it was no use going: "It's just that they do not teach us well here, they punish us, the teachers throw sticks at our heads, and with that fear, we'd rather drop out." This may sound like an extreme observation. However, the work of anthropologist Patricia Oliart confirms the ambiguity between the respect for schools and teachers and the humiliation experienced by students. Oliart studied teaching methods

---

7. This operation generates a number of problems arising from the transposition of women's ideas about themselves and the world they live in as contained in the *autodiagnósticos*. First, these ideas were originally transmitted in Quechua, which has its own characteristics and linguistic rhythm. Second, in translating the reports into Spanish, the *promotoras* who wrote down these ideas might impose their own worldview or opinions on the text through their selection of Spanish words. And finally, in translating quotes from the *autodiagnósticos* into English, I have further modified the original sense of the *autodiagnósticos*. Because of the multiple transpositions, the Spanish in the texts is not always grammatically "correct." Some "mistakes" in language are also interesting, such as when the perspective is changed from "they" into "we" or from "she" into "I" in one sentence, which reveals something about the intimacy of the "invented" life stories.

and the reproduction of inequalities in rural primary schools in Peru, and concludes that teachers mirror those elements of society that reflect authoritarianism through humiliation, in which they, the teachers, project the inequalities and *sufrimientos* (suffering/ordeals) they themselves endured onto their pupils. Although for some pupils the experience of education creates "the illusion of being someone," at the same time, pupils in this situation develop a "strong feeling of *fracaso* (failure)" (Oliart 1999, 218–19). Indeed, in the life stories of these Huancavelican women, the idea of education as a way of advancement for their daughters is as much present as the knowledge that most girls will encounter humiliating treatment at school.

For many girls who do attend primary school, the start of their menstruation cycle often causes them to drop out. This is related to the perception that girls become women and not in need of education when their reproductive life starts, but also to their desire to avoid the shame and discomfort of being in public spaces when menstruating and no hygienic facilities are available (Red Nacional de la Promoción de la Mujer 2002). The start of menstruation is a life-changing and frightening event. All the *autodiagnósticos* indicate that prior to puberty there is hardly any communication between mothers and daughters about the changes the female body undergoes. Thus, when girls reach thirteen or fourteen, most of them will experience their first menstruation without warning; some will think "they are dying." Others will think it is "bad," that they have done something wrong and that blood is their punishment. After talking with friends or older sisters about their fears, they will realize it is normal. Some women say that they did not trust their mothers enough to tell them about their menstruation; for example: "I told my sister about it [first bleeding] and she said that I would definitely die now; she asked 'how are we going to tell this to our mama, we should not tell her, maybe she will hit you.' That's what she told me, and I did not say anything." However, other mothers do reassure their daughters: "Our mother never told us, so it frightened us the first time, but afterwards my mother saw me with blood and she told me that this will happen every month and it is normal."

Urban migrants confirmed the lack of communication and the presence of confusing stories about their bodies. In conversations I had with first-generation Andean migrants who are now in their thirties and live in Lima, women recalled not knowing anything about their own bodies and sexuality until they had their own children. Rather, they said, they grew up with *mitos negativos*, negative myths that engendered fear and shame about being female, such as the story of Maria Marimacha, the girl who would be cut into pieces if and when she behaved "like a boy" (Rivera 1993). Several migrants said they did not want their daughters to grow up like that—or like the daughters of "others" (never their own) who became pregnant too young. In order to avoid such experiences, women in Lima actively sought out information about sex education to share with their children.[8] However, access to information in Lima is significantly greater than in rural Huancavelica. The adult women who speak in the *autodiagnósticos* could not agree about the nature of menstruation. According to some, it is ugly and dirty blood. Others believe that it is good that the blood comes out, because it will cleanse the body of "sickness." Many women explain that the blood serves to conceive children, because some women maintained that babies are created when the blood of men and women is united.

In the *autodiagnósticos*, limited or absent communication is a recurring theme in the relationships between mothers and daughters. When girls start having sexual relationships at the age of thirteen, fourteen, or fifteen, it is blamed to a great extent on the family: "Their mothers do not tell them anything, they do not talk with them, that is why they get pregnant, girls are behaving like crazy." Other women give a more social explanation for the young age at which girls become sexually active; they say that girls think they can have a better life living with a young man than with their own families, where they face many "problems," that is, violence. In the next chapter, the story of Nelly, a twenty-year old Ayacuchana, confirms this argument when she explains that she preferred to go and live with an abusive boyfriend and have children with him than to stay at home with her parents, where she felt even less safe. Besides the suggestion of violence at home, these "problems" also point to the few alternatives that rural women have in managing their own lives.

The idea that it is bad that girls get pregnant at a young age is interesting in itself.[9] In cities, the rejection of early pregnancy is linked to the pursuit of education and professionalism (Olthoff 2006). In rural areas, as we just saw, the idea of education exists but is less of an option than in the cities. Rather, children are expected to help out in the family household and production unit. However, Manuela Ramos teaches women that giving birth before eighteen years is bad for their bodies. At the same time, the *autodiagnósticos* indicate that women recognize that postponing sexual relations is a way of limiting the number of children they will give birth to in their life cycle. Thus, while educational and professional opportunities are not necessarily expanding in rural areas, girls are encouraged to postpone sexual relations

---

8. Conversations with organized women in San Juan de Luringancho and Pamplona Alta, Lima, 2001.

9. Ward (1995) provides an interesting parallel in her analysis of the moral undertone in the condemnation of "teenage pregnancy," as early motherhood is referred to in the developed world.

through a discourse that emphasizes the incorrectness of getting pregnant at a young age. The phrase "girls are behaving like crazy" is a direct moral condemnation of adolescents who get involved in sexual relations, while those girls' mothers—who now complain about their daughters' behavior—also had their first children before the age of eighteen.

In the constructed life stories, most women say that the first years of *convivir*, living together with a man, will be nice. However, after the first children are born, couples start to quarrel. Women indicate that husbands start blaming their wives for the behavior of the children: "[We fight] when the children cry or get dirty" or if children behave badly. Gossip and mothers-in-law are perceived to do much harm as well: "Other mothers-in-law hate their daughters-in-law, they put stories in the heads of their sons so that they will quarrel with their wives." According to anthropologist Penelope Harvey (1994, 73–78), it is common in many Andean communities for the woman to leave her own family behind to move in with, or at least close to, her husband's family. This means that the woman needs to find a new position as a wife and a daughter-in-law: a recently married woman does not simply gain freedom from her own family and its authoritative structures, but she also has to gain the friendship and respect of elder women in her new family. According to Harvey, this task is complicated by the absence of a mutually acceptable hierarchy and the usually strong ties between mother and son. Thus, after the initial period of marriage, where a woman feels safe because she is now responsible for her own family, the marriage becomes more conflictive and, in some cases, violent.

As a consequence of the low level of communication between mothers and daughters about sexuality and the body, most women know little about procreation and motherhood. For most women the first baby was a surprise: "My mother didn't know, she didn't tell me anything either. I asked myself, where will it be born, shall it come out of the vagina?" As a consequence, young girls are afraid during their first pregnancy. In some cases, there is even little solidarity among family members during pregnancy and delivery, and some women recall that they had to deliver their babies on their own: "I am not supported by anyone, I endure the birth on my own, I feel constantly like urinating, then my mother-in-law or the neighbors come in, they come when I am already done with the delivery, so they can cut the umbilical cord." According to the now classic work of Susan Bourque and Kay Warren in the community of Mayobamba, Ayacucho, women who give birth without assistance do so out of personal choice and both men and women see them as particularly valiant (Bourque and Warren 1981, 93). However, in the *autodiagnósticos* most women say that they are helped during birth by female relatives, mothers-in law, or even neighbors (midwives are rarely mentioned). Although not always possible, the presence of their husbands at the time of birth is crucial, according to some women, an observation also made by Bourque and Warren in the community of Chiuchin in the department of Lima. Few women go to the health care center to give birth, and only in cases of emergency do they consider doing so.

Three to nine days after giving birth, women go back to work—not because they feel well, but because "the husband is bored with taking care of us," or because "I feel ashamed in front of my mother-in-law," suggesting that mothers-in-law expect a certain endurance and bravery and, especially, wives for their sons. Working, during and after pregnancy, can also be seen as healthy exercise for the mother (Bourque and Warren 1981, 90). After the first child is born, children start arriving one after the other. Because of the quick succession of pregnancies, the mother's health deteriorates and she becomes weak. As the *autodiagnósticos* show, pregnancy and delivery can be difficult for mother and child, as mothers usually continue to do their daily chores until the last hour before delivery, and some give birth on their own. Women might use herbs but no medication in case of an emergency, and they are vulnerable to complications during pregnancies, which are rarely attended to.

If we look at the available statistics on abortion and maternal mortality in Peru, then we might expect the worst for the women in this poor district of Huancavelica. However, abortion is not mentioned as a major problem in the *autodiagnósticos*. It may be that women do not talk about abortion, but it is more likely that *promotoras* are not allowed to report on abortions. Given that the project was funded by USAID and the Peruvian state, Manuela Ramos has to follow official policies on such themes. The backlash on reproductive freedom since George W. Bush took office in the United States in 2001 made talking about abortion even harder. However, despite the possible omission of conversations about abortion, the one *autodiagnóstico* that does mention abortion suggests that it is not as common as the statistics indicate; the Huancavelica *autodiagnósticos* suggest a high percentage of unwanted pregnancies, but few self-induced abortions.[10] The stories do indicate a fear of spontaneous abortions—or miscarriages—

---

10. Bourque and Warren came to similar conclusions: in their study they did not find evidence of abortion as a way to control family size, although most of their interviewees did know about the possibilities and dangers (89). However, there are widespread rumors about Andean women leaving unwanted children behind to die as soon as they are born. Such an occasion is, for example, narrated in the testimony of Irene Jara in Denegri (2000). The anthropologist Kimberley Theidon indicates that the practice of letting babies die when they are born with physical problems or after rape is long established among many Andean communities (2004, 126–27).

just as much as the fear of other diseases and treatments related to pregnancy and childbirth. Some women believe that they can get cancer from abortion, or that the dead child has to be taken out of the belly in little pieces, or that the mothers will become seriously ill. In sum, these rural Huancavelican women may not have practiced induced abortions, they may not call them such, or Manuela Ramos may have felt obliged to omit the references.

Gender, Sexuality, and Violence

The disadvantaged socioeconomic position of women in relation to men, their vulnerable physical position, and the cultural meanings attached to decency, honor, and sexuality often produce violent relationships that shape their reproductive lives and their sexuality. The *autodiagnósticos* are peppered with stories of violent husbands and unwanted children conceived against women's will. The image that arises from the *autodiagnósticos* in communities in Huancavelica is a certain resignation on the part of the women: "Being married, we always have to tolerate this life." According to one woman, it is not so bad as "they only hit us when they drink." The main cause of male anger and violence, however, is jealousy, although "they are the ones that look for another woman, and in their conscience they start to compare, the devil makes them see things that are not there and they hit the child and everything. When the children have problems the mother is guilty, they pay with us." Men also humiliate women when they are ill: they accuse their wives of *hacer arte,* faking illness so they will not have to work. After all, a good wife is never "lazy." One of the women answered a discussion with the *promotoras* of Manuela Ramos about violence with the remark that "you don't have to worry [about the workshop], but we will be beaten because we talked." In fact, according to the *promotoras,* one of the groups refused to allow the use of a tape recorder when they discussed violence in the family. The mere fact of talking could provoke the anger of men, or at least some women feared.

Having many children seems to confirm the husband's virility and the wife's loyalty, but that does not necessarily make women proud—or safe. In a discussion about abusive husbands, one woman, Juana, observed: "Men get ideas from their friends, they look for affairs, they give us abuse and we women criticize each other, saying that we have children like guinea pigs. Therefore, as I feel ashamed when I am pregnant, I wrap myself up; my husband, when he sees that I am covering myself, he calls me, he says to me: 'why do you cover yourself, or is it because you are carrying the child of another man?'" Juana juxtaposes the points of view of men and women; men encourage and incite each other to have sexual relations, while women find their consecutive pregnancies shameful. Whether this shame is a consequence of sexual shame is difficult to tell, but it might well be, because many women acknowledge the violence with which pregnancies are forced upon them. Women perceive sexual violence as an important health problem for themselves and their future children: "Against her will, señorita, when her husband forces her, that's why she gets pregnant. . . . She will not be correctly pregnant, she will be bored with her belly and her husband already wants her to have the child. She does not want to have children anymore." Unwanted children who are conceived by force appear as a recurring problem in the *autodiagnósticos* and a serious health problem for mother and child. The *autodiagnósticos* also indicate that women find that having many children, with little time in between, causes their bodies to deteriorate, makes every delivery more difficult, and is a burden on the household economy. Considering the sexual violence of husbands and the shame and fear of wives, the means to control their own fertility are limited indeed. Juana feels ashamed among other women when she is pregnant again, which is why she tries to hide it. However, her pregnancy is the proof of her husband's sexual potency—unless someone else has made her pregnant. Violence, sexuality, and reproductive health collide and intersect: Juana's husband uses her sexuality to show his (masculine) power over women.[11]

Mixing Myths: Local and Biomedical Beliefs About Reproduction

Overall, these *autodiagnósticos* offered by women in communities of Huancavelica confirm national statistics indicating that the majority of women do not want to have large numbers of children.[12] The idea that people in peasant societies want many children in order to support the old and to work the land is refuted by these women, who said that their families cannot support so many children and that their bodies suffer as a result of every

---

11. The intersection of violence, sexuality, gender, and public health in relation to family planning policies has also been studied by Heise (1997).
12. According to the Encuesta Demográfica y de Salud 1991–1992 (Demographic and Health Survey), the majority of Peruvian women believed two children was the ideal number, while the rural fertility rate was 6.2 children per woman (FLACSO 1993, 84). In 1981, Bourque and Warren concluded that the ideal number of children according to men and women in the rural Andes was maybe two or three children, but not more (88). Today, rural women still express the wish to have two children, and the official fertility rate has gone down to 3.6 children per woman. For fertility statistics, see http://www.inei.gob.pe.

new birth (see, e.g., Guzmán 1996, 193). The question is thus twofold: first, why did women not find ways to reduce their fertility; and second, why could the state health care personnel not hand out information and contraceptives instead of using coercion? The *autodiagnósticos* show that disparities between, and sometimes outright incompatibility of, biomedical and local beliefs about the body, reproduction, and gender relations have obstructed a fruitful and positive experience between rural women, men, and health care providers.[13] To further explore the problems women have with regard to birth control, I will analyze the possible fears conveyed in the *autodiagnósticos* in relation to reproduction and modern contraceptives. First, some women are afraid of their husbands' responses to their reproductive wishes. Second, many women are apprehensive about the methods themselves. Most importantly, because it reinforces the first two anxieties, women distrust the health care workers, who fail to respect rural women and men, the supposed beneficiaries of the family planning program.

The "traditional" obstacle for women in using contraceptives, that is, the one that is often emphasized and based on stereotypes of men as machos, is the resistance of their husbands.[14] Women sometimes fear their husbands' response because they might associate the use of contraceptives with the risk of their wives' infidelity. In the *autodiagnósticos*, women said that if they wanted to use modern contraceptives, husbands prevented them from doing so: "One time I talked about [birth control] with my husband and he called me *ccacha warmi* [unfaithful woman], and said, 'Why do you not want to have my children, or do you want to go with another man?'" The connection between motherhood, decency, and the reproduction of the community is strong. Women are viewed as the "guardians" of moral codes. Interference of an unknown "modernity" by way of contraceptives is not easily accepted by everyone. Yet, according to the *autodiagnósticos*, men do accept women's use of traditional herbs or natural methods to prevent or postpone pregnancy. Male resistance to modern contraceptives may partly be grounded in a fear of female sexual autonomy and the subversion of tangible male virility. In such an analysis, pregnancy is proof of masculinity and female loyalty.[15]

---

13. Similar conclusions on the incompatibility of biomedical and local beliefs concerning the body and reproductive health were drawn in a study conducted in Jamaica (Sobo 1993).

14. Fort (1989, 88–94) had already observed that the fear of violence from, desertion by, or accusations of infidelity from their partners if women brought up the issue of birth control was a major obstacle for women who legally needed their partners' consent before they were allowed the use of contraceptives. Cited in Heise (1997, 420). Guzmán et al. draw similar conclusions (1996, 430–31).

15. See also Maternowska on similar patterns in Haiti (2006).

On the other hand, men's opposition to modern contraceptives might also derive from feelings of exclusion because of the emphasis on women in the politics of reproductive health. In the *autodiagnósticos* of Huancavelica, some women said that their husbands would be prepared to consider modern birth control if it was explained to both of them: "My husband says, 'if they explain to me, then we can use them. But they do not explain well, they only explain to the women." The emphasis on women and women's own desire to understand and use birth control methods made men suspicious about their wives' sexual behavior, even though men might be happy to be involved in the process. The health care providers instead excluded men from the birth control process. Strikingly, since 1996, women have been able to ask for modern methods at a health care center without the permission of their husbands, which they could not do before. Although this change in the law increased the freedom and autonomy of women with respect to their husbands, and has therefore received ample approval from progressive forces such as feminists, it has also made it easier for health care providers to deceive women, as rural women are less likely to be literate. Just as in the case of food distributions, representatives of the state might persuade women to sign papers they cannot read, with potentially devastating consequences.[16] The suggestion made by the women in the *autodiagnósticos* to involve rather than exclude men from reproductive issues is today an accepted view among international reproductive health advocates, as it is thought that focusing on men's involvement "is designed to increase the likelihood that women's male partners are educated about, supportive of, and positively involved in the range of reproductive health concerns that both women and men face" (Makhlouf Obermeyer 1999). Following this new approach, recent programs set up by NGOs in Limeño *pueblos jóvenes* confirm the positive effect of informing men and women alike.[17] Men are more than willing to attend workshops on family planning as long as they are considered as part of the process. However, during the Fujimori years the national health care services treated family planning primarily as a female concern.

---

16. In early 1996, after Fujimori's sterilization quota system had been implemented for some months, the law was altered to allow women to ask for contraception, including sterilization, without the signature of their male partners. The coincidence of time should be viewed with suspicion; did the government strategically remove this rule to be able to reach women more easily? Also observed in Zauzig (2000, 88).

17. According to *promotoras* of Manuela Ramos in Pamplona Alta, Lima, personal conversation, 2001. A similar project in Nicaragua also shows positive outcomes and was largely a response to the demands of women in poor communities (Sternberg 2000, 89–99).

The many myths and misunderstandings concerning modern contraceptives that circulate in Andean communities are indications of the lack of information that people have access to. This has created a fear of the methods themselves. In the *autodiagnósticos* of Huancavelica, people indicate that sterilization would change the woman's character, make her quarrel with her husband, and "burn" (*quemar*) the body: "they become thin and dry out." Pills and injections would also burn the body. Women strongly believe that modern birth control makes women sick, cancer, heavy bleedings, extreme loss of weight, and a bad temper being mentioned most often. But not only women will suffer. Stories about deformed children because of the use of birth control methods circulate as well. These reservations also indicate that the women do not really believe that contraceptives work. The stories are generated by a general concern about the unknown because incomplete information (although not necessarily wrong information, as many contraceptives have side effects and are not 100 percent safe) is mixed with traditional fears that are projected onto that which is new. For example, other reasons given for a woman giving birth to a deformed child are the mother standing in a rainbow while menstruating, or looking at or carrying a cat while pregnant. Modern contraceptives became a part of these beliefs, a new reason for having deformed children. The integration of "modernity" and "tradition" in blaming the woman for giving birth to a deformed child might make the woman a "traitor" to the community. Blaming mothers emphasizes women's responsibility for both biological reproduction and maintaining the cultural identity of the collective.[18]

Some women say that they know about the menstruation cycle and try to use it for birth control. It is a method that needs the participation of the husband, which can reduce feelings of exclusion among men, although some women say that men also "abuse" this control: if men feel like it, they demand intercourse whenever they want it. Other problems occur in relation to using the period as a birth control method; for example, women say that "we cannot control our cycle as we do not get our blood," suggesting that mothers might get pregnant again before they have the chance to control their menstruation. Another obstacle in relying on the menstrual cycle is the belief among some people that conception occurs when the paternal and maternal blood unite. According to health care promoters in both Lima and Huancavelica, women might remember explanations of the rhythm the other way around and have intercourse in the middle of the cycle and not during menstruation. In such a construction of

---

18. On women as representatives of indigeneity, see, e.g., Cadena (1991).

conception, the "body is open" to fertilization during menstruation. Following such views, the openness of the female body will cause pregnancy and the child will then live the first months on maternal blood, which is why menstruation stops. According to the *promotoras* of Manuela Ramos in Huancavelica, health care personnel explain this method to women without taking into account possible contradictory ideas about conception. These instructions are given only once and are not written down or discussed with the husband. According to the *promotoras*, women might get confused or simply forget what they have learned, since the biomedical knowledge refutes what they have learned since childhood about their bodies. Thus, not only do different ideas about the body and conception cause difficulties in controlling fertility, but the communication between health care provider and the couple asking for birth control methods lacks continuity and trust.

From Miscommunication to Sterilization

The lack of information and the resulting misgivings about contraceptives had everything to do with inadequate communication between health care provider and user. If we look at the stories, testimonies, and investigations, health care personnel often mistreated women on the assumption that poor and indigenous women were too ignorant to care, too stupid to understand, and too powerless to protest. In the zeal to comply with quotas set by the government, local health care personnel did not inform the partners equally on birth control, but imposed methods on women without much explanation. For example, in the *autodiagnósticos* women said that the *posta de salud* gave them contraceptive pills for the treatment of, for example, a headache. One woman said that the health care center had placed an IUD (intrauterine device) while doing a checkup. She only found out when she went to another hospital because she felt pain. The lack of constructive communication about certain beliefs held both by women and health care personnel generated, on the one hand, suspicion among women and men and disrespect, and on the other, discrimination on the part of health care workers. This situation contributed to what became the scandal of forced sterilizations based on the government's quota system.

A study carried out by the Latin American and Caribbean Committee for the Defense of Women's Rights (CLADEM) gives a full account of the results of Fujimori's quota system. According to this report, health care personnel deployed many tricks to win the consent of women for sterilization in order to comply with the set quotas. Birth control campaigns (Ferias de Salud; see Vasquez del Aguila 2006) promised medical consultations by "specialists from Lima" and free health treatments for the whole population. They also promised free food and clothing. Another tactic, hardly to convince women but rather to round them up, was to organize food distributions to women's organizations and then take them to the health center or mobile facilities. When women protested, threats of imprisonment, fines, and the deprivation of medical services for the whole family in the future were made. Pure physical force and confinement were a last resort used by health care personnel. The government even ordered health care centers in marginalized areas (rural or urban) to "make sure that women who enter for delivery or abortion, walk out with a sufficient method to prevent future pregnancies" (CLADEM 1999, 66). In practice, this led to some women walking out sterilized without even knowing it.

The consequences were severe. Although the full impact of the damage is difficult to assess, at least seventeen women died and many were left permanently injured as a result of badly executed sterilizations (Defensoría del Pueblo n.d.). Besides the coercive methods used, the quality of health care was also poor. The *postas de salud* in rural areas frequently lacked the necessary equipment and medical knowledge to carry out the operations, the clinics were not cleaned properly, and women received no care before or after operations, which could lead to serious medical complications and physical harm.

Accordingly, the pressing question is, what compelled local health care personnel to meet the government's demands? First of all, just like the targeted women, health care personnel were tempted through a system of reward and punishment. The *posta de salud* or hospital that met the established quotas received, as a reward, computers and other useful equipment. Individual professionals received bonuses when they met personal quotas of four to six sterilizations a month. Not participating could mean losing one's job or receiving a lower monthly salary (CLADEM 1999, 56–57). The situation was summarized by a physician in San Miguel, who claimed that "it was an authoritarian situation, we could not oppose."[19]

However, although health care personnel acted under pressure, it seems that many did not try to improve the situation either. Women in Huancavelica as well as in Lima said that doctors and nurses humiliated them constantly. They kept ordering women to use contraceptives, underlining this "need" with accusations that they, as indigenous women, produced children like guinea pigs. In 2001, women in the district of Pamplona Alta in Lima drew up an extensive list of the humiliating treatment they were

---

19. Interview, identity concealed, La Mar, January 2003.

used to receiving from health care personnel. According to these women, every time they used state hospitals they were treated as irresponsible and stupid. Supported by *promotoras* of Manuela Ramos, they demanded that doctors not criticize them about the number of children they had and that they be allowed to give birth in their preferred position and under hygienic circumstances. They also insisted that doctors and nurses refrain from shouting at them or "pushing and pulling" them during treatment. They requested that contraceptives be explained before being prescribed or applied.[20] Just as Manuela Ramos supported these Limeño women in their demands to the health care providers, they asked women in Huancavelica about their concerns. Accordingly, at a workshop in Pallallas, a rural community in Huancavelica, women made a similar list, in which they mentioned, for example, that they wanted doctors to believe them and that they did not want to be threatened.[21] The above-cited CLADEM report also includes charges regarding denigrating remarks about women's sexual behavior, their stupidity, their marginal position, and their weak legal status (the last as a threat to prevent them from openly complaining). Poor urban and rural women claimed to feel discriminated against, or rather, *maltratado* (abused), by the health care personnel.

Inequality thus operates at several often-intersecting levels, serving distinct purposes. For example, the physician in San Miguel quoted at the opening of this chapter was distinguished from his patients by his education. He himself was from the southeastern highlands of Puno and proudly introduced himself as being of Aymara-speaking indigenous descent. He also claimed to be happy to serve in a Quechua-speaking region, saying he loved the culture of the area. However, after four years in the La Mar area, he did not yet speak the language. Although he lamented his inability to communicate with the population, he did not seem to find it essential. This doctor presented himself as dedicated to the indigenous population, but saw himself as an educated, state-appointed doctor among a poor and "ignorant" population. In the end, he, as the educated doctor who possessed the "truth" of biomedical science, did not believe in the rationality of his patients and believed that indigenous women and men were not capable of understanding birth control methods and the use of family planning. Powerful vis-à-vis the population but powerless vis-à-vis the higher authorities, this doctor and his personnel complied with the demands that the central

---

20. Meetings at the Casa de Bienestar, Pamplona Alta, Lima, supervised by local representatives of Manuela Ramos, February 2001.

21. Workshop Manuela Ramos, Pallallas, Huancavelica, June 2001.

government made on them.[22] His testimony shows the paternalistic and hierarchical application of medical practices in a culture where biomedical knowledge often contradicts local knowledge about the body and reproductive health.

Ethnicity and gender are palpable pillars of inequality that have influenced the prejudice and miscommunication between health care providers and users. To justify their stress on the need for birth control, health care workers tend to view Andean women as ignorant and promiscuous. Strikingly, among many couples in Andean communities, the idea of promiscuity is the exact opposite; a woman is viewed as promiscuous when she shows interest in using modern contraceptives. These contradictory attitudes emphasize the need for mutual understanding and a constant questioning of assumptions about reproductive health among both users and health care workers.[23] As Bonnie Shepard, program officer for the Ford Foundation, who was in charge of the organization's sexual and reproductive health program in the region from 1995 to 1999, concluded: "In the traditionally vertical context of the biomedical setting both providers and users are prisoners of unspoken assumptions and corresponding roles in a paternalistic system" (Shepard 2002).

The Ambiguity of Collaboration: The Role of the NGO

Much of the information above was retrieved from the work of the feminist NGO Manuela Ramos, which suggests that this organization was well aware of the issue of coercive practices in the provision of health care to poor and rural women. The ReproSalud project was designed and commissioned by USAID and formally represented an integral part of the population program as developed in 1995. The information gathered in the *autodiagnósticos* was meant to contribute to the improvement of national health care services and communication between provider and client, which, in the long run, would lead to a "natural" reduction in fertility rates according to women's own wishes (Manuela Ramos 2001; USAID n.d.). Unfortunately, the Peruvian government found faster ways to reduce fertility rates and did not have the patience or interest to take such information seriously (Guzmán

---

22. A parallel should be made to the teachers in Oliart's study (1999): both Oliart's teachers and these doctors are authoritarian and even dominant in relation to lesser educated, while they reproduce the humiliating circumstances and treatment they themselves received when they (or their parents) were in the position of their now students/patients.

23. Catherine Maternowska draws similar conclusions with regard to a USAID-financed community reproductive health project in Cité Soleil, Haiti (2006).

Chaganaquí 2002, 197). A similar experience involved UNICEF, which had a project in Cusco and Cajamarca concerning reproductive health, strengthening the capacity of health care personnel, participation of the community, and cultural adjustment of services. According to Alfredo Guzmán Chaganaquí (2002), the state did not make use of the important experience this project entailed. Guzmán Chaganaquí also observes that the project of Manuela Ramos discussed here was not made any better use of because of the "fragmentation of projects and programs during the 1990s" (198). Although this fragmentation was and is indeed an obstacle to adapting policies nationally, the actual practices of the state as examined here do not indicate that there was any political will to do so. On the other hand, for reasons explained below, Manuela Ramos contributed little to a public denunciation of coercive practices in the health care system at the time, nor did the NGO provide legal support to women with complaints against health care providers. Manuela Ramos's close collaboration in the national population program could easily lead to accusations of complicity to the events. A closer look at its role is therefore justified.

First of all, all feminist organizations in Peru, and indeed the international community, supported Fujimori's initial plans for improving access to reproductive health care and birth control methods. The legalization of voluntary sterilization was received positively and opened the possibility of a debate about decriminalization, or even legalization, of abortion. It was not in feminist interests to protest against the perhaps overambitious aims of the program. This ambiguity—improved legislation and opening up of debates concerning reproductive rights, accompanied by an overambitious and eventually aggressive targeting of certain populations—was at the heart of the slow and fragmented response of the feminist movement to the revelations of forced sterilizations in 1996 (Barrig 2002). Of course, as we have seen, Fujimori also deliberately played upon this ambiguity to mobilize support for the population program.

Within the feminist movement the position of Manuela Ramos was, of course, even more constrained. In implementing the ReproSalud program, the organization was part of the population program and received millions from USAID. Although interviews and annual reports show that Manuela Ramos strongly opposed any coercive sterilization project, it did not publicly denounce the program either.[24] The *autodiagnósticos* discussed

---

24. Strong criticism of the Fujimori government is found in an internal document (Movimiento Manuela Ramos 1997). In an interview held in April 2000, the then head of ReproSalud Manuela Ramos, Ella Carrasco, stressed the importance of working with the government if one wants to influence policies.

imply that the organization could have been aware of what was happening, as women mention coercion and deceit used by the health care personnel. On the other hand, as I have suggested above, the abuse women received from the health care personnel was not unique to the years of Fujimori's aggressive population policies, but was far more institutionalized. In that context, Manuela Ramos chose to aim for long-term "change from within," a position that perhaps compromises the critical role a feminist nongovernmental organization should have; however, they did not want to jeopardize the ReproSalud program either. As Manuela Ramos itself recognized, their "dual role of collaborating and critiquing" (Galdos and Feringa 1998, cited in Petchesky 2000, 38) put them in a very difficult position.

As Petchesky observes (2000, 38), the tension between collaboration and critiquing that the NGO encountered in the issue of forced sterilizations also highlighted the fact that while Manuela Ramos provides important public health services, it "has neither the *authority* nor the *accountability* of a government agency" (emphasis in original). Despite the millions from USAID, ReproSalud was one of several community-based projects that could not surpass the existing fragmentation of programs. This lack of authority and accountability, added to the organization's loss of its activist role through its collaboration with an authoritarian government, made the ReproSalud program institutionally weak.

On the ground, this weakness is particularly evident in the gap between what the project teaches and what it can offer materially. As long as NGOs provide only information but not the resources that can solve everyday problems discussed in the workshops and courses, many participants will reject the usefulness of such efforts. As one woman at a workshop about reproductive rights in Pallallas, a rural community in Huancavelica, said: "The workers at the health care centers have all these rights [to give to us], but here, the personnel never stay."[25] Indeed, the health care workers at the *posta de salud* should confirm and respect the rights women learn they have, and they should also have the means, such as medicines, treatment, and diagnostic skills, to make women's rights a reality. The *posta de salud* of Pallallas, however, which is supposed to have at least one nurse, is often not staffed. According to the *promotoras* of Manuela Ramos, nurses tend to flee from these remote areas. Ernestina, the nurse who was there when I visited this particular community in 2001, had nothing to do because she had no equipment or medicines. Although the *posta* was the sole building in the community with electricity, she only used it for her radio. There was no running water. Very few people in the community said they

---

25. Workshop ReproSalud, Pallallas, Huancavelica, June 2001.

relied on her advice, as they believed that she would soon go anyway. Ernestina had been there only a couple of weeks and had made no attempt to establish a long-term relationship of trust with community members. And now the *promotoras* of Manuela Ramos came to tell the women of Pallallas to use the *posta de salud* more efficiently, an activity in which Ernestina hardly participated. ReproSalud was thus constrained by the lack of communication between the *promotoras* of Manuela Ramos and the state health care personnel, pointing at existing tensions between the two. In addition, the program was constrained by the failure of the state health care personnel, represented by Ernestina, to engage with the population. But the situation in Pallallas also confirmed a lack of institutional support from the state in the form of genuine health sector reform, giving Ernestina little means to carry out her job. ReproSalud, a USAID-financed program carried out by a national NGO and intended to provide support to reform within the health sector, was severely constrained by unchanging structures and was thus not able to provide the services it promoted.

The observation that NGOs have been unable to replace state responsibilities does not necessarily lead to the conclusion that ReproSalud has failed in its objectives. A crucial question is whether the program helped rural women in managing their reproductive health better. Based on the *autodiagnósticos* and the number of women reached (2,528 grassroots women's organizations around the country), Manuela Ramos has concluded that the first five years of ReproSalud were very successful. The organization claims that the project resulted in increased contraceptive use by participants, improved knowledge about reproductive health, changing ideas about family planning, improved communication among sexual partners, and improved knowledge about health care services (http://www.manuela.org.pe/Repro_ext.pdf). In Pallallas I observed some evidence of this success; for example, the women I met handed over surveys they had carried out in their communities. Together, the ten participants, leaders of *clubes de madres* and *comedores populares*, had interviewed 493 women and 161 men about reproductive health. They had gathered information about birth control methods used, the prevalence of diseases related to sexuality, violence in the family, and how and where women give birth. According to one participant, Augustina, she had found gathering this information difficult at the beginning as she had felt ashamed to talk about such themes. However, she claimed that she had become used to it and that her neighbors, both women and men, would now visit her, since she was now *capacitada* (trained) because of the workshops, to ask questions related to their reproductive health. Despite the fact it did not improve the functioning of *postas de salud,* according to many women in Pallallas the work of Manuela Ramos generated knowledge that empowered both women and men to manage their reproductive health and fertility in a better way.

Arguably, Manuela Ramos achieved even more than the ReproSalud program aimed for. In contrast to the more limited objectives of ReproSalud, Manuela Ramos wanted to improve the conditions in which rural women lived by empowering them in all aspects of their lives. This meant that the organization and their participants actively confronted reluctant local authorities, family members (including husbands), and institutions. For example, when we arrived in Pallallas to meet women for the workshops, the mayor of the community wanted to know why we had come. The *promotoras* explained that improving women's knowledge about health (they did not say *reproductive* health) would contribute to the well-being of the whole community. The mayor responded that the community would rather have projects directed at improving the infrastructure of the community. However, considering the repeated turnout of women from different localities, women seemed to think differently. They obviously did value the workshops—even if that sometimes included more instrumental interests such as a free meal or the opportunity to talk with neighbors. Thus, Manuela Ramos aimed to help change power relations and improve the position of women in the community as a development strategy of that community, sometimes going against the ideas of male authorities in those communities. In challenging material and linear notions of development at local levels and providing a space for women to develop their own ideas, Manuela Ramos certainly has made a contribution to the empowerment of women in the area.

Conclusion

We can draw several conclusions from the analysis above of the implementation of aggressive population policies directed at poor and mostly indigenous women during the Fujimori governments: (1) women's bodies were used as tools for demographic purposes in a post-Cairo world; (2) the Fujimori government cleverly used a progressive discourse to manipulate public opinion; (3) internationally encouraged neoliberal health sector reform further obstructed the improvements necessary to provide for comprehensive health care in neglected areas; and (4) existing inequalities based on gender, race, and class facilitated the complicity of local health care personnel in carrying out those policies.

Because women give birth, they are perceived as responsible for the number and "quality" of children they have. Often men are overlooked in reproductive health matters, and are not always held responsible for the excessive number of children being conceived.[26] As we saw in this chapter, governments and concerned international organizations aim policies to control national birth rates at women. Despite bearing this responsibility, women are paradoxically not always perceived as capable of managing their own sexuality and are therefore often excluded from controlling their own fertility. As the analysis in this chapter confirms, the relationship between health care providers and low-income, indigenous women is by definition unequal, and abuses of power are at the core of such relations. Moreover, men sometimes attempt to control women's sexual behavior in order to maintain a certain power inequity within marriage and the family. Male anxieties about women's use of modern contraceptives are reinforced by their exclusion from the "modern" family planning process. In the end, both men and health care providers approach women as solely responsible for reproduction, while at the same time, those same actors frustrate the possibilities for women to manage their own fertility.

By the time a Peruvian government defied religious and political opposition to population policies in the 1990s, the international discourse concerning population had shifted its emphasis from a demographic to a women's rights approach. However, these shifts left sufficient space for neoliberal restructuring and aggressive demographic goals. President Fujimori used this space by invoking a feminist discourse of women's rights, while the government's first priority was reducing the growth of the poor population. There was a clear emphasis on the rapid reduction of fertility rates among poor, rural indigenous and urban poor women. The weakness of the targeted groups' position vis-à-vis agents of the state also facilitated coercive practices on the ground. Women, perceived as the reproducers of poverty, suffered great humiliation, physical harm, and even death because the government thought that one "cannot reduce poverty efficiently if poor families continue having on average seven children" (Aramburú 2002b, 9). Although an openly racist position toward the designated "problem" population was never expressed, the areas, methods, and goals of the population program leave little doubt about the hidden prejudices that sustained the policies. The racism entrenched in Peruvian society and in its institutions largely secured effective collaboration from health care personnel without the need to explicate or justify the policies too extensively. Accordingly, parallels could be drawn between late twentieth-century population policies and

---

26. A sinister fact has to be added: According to the CLADEM report (1999), apart from women in the fertile age group, a number of male homosexuals were targeted to be sterilized. While this is a important accusation that needs further analysis, it is not in the reach of this chapter. As an exception to the rule, in aggressive population policies in India, men were targeted rather than women.

early twentieth-century anxieties about the evolution of Peru's population as mainly indigenous, "backward," and poor (Boesten and Drinot 2004).

Paradoxically, it is also clear that the majority of targeted women were very interested in reducing their number of pregnancies. Other obstacles in their lives, however, prevented them from successfully using birth control methods. Biomedical ideas about the body often clashed with local ideas about and practices of reproduction. The role and function of women's sexuality and the female reproductive body in local culture as well as the cultural prejudices of health care providers prevented an adequate exercise of reproductive rights. The absence of a solid notion of reproductive rights among both health care providers and users encouraged vertical and paternalist relationships. In addition, the low esteem of women in their own localities and the power imbalance between men and women further prevented successful birth control. The program set up to empower women and provide them with the adequate information about reproductive health and rights, the USAID-funded ReproSalud, carried out by the feminist NGO Manuela Ramos, was severely obstructed by the lack of actual health sector reform. The program's attempt to change poor urban and rural women's situation in relation to reproductive health and fertility control was insufficiently supported by necessary reforms in the health sector. Nevertheless, the work of Manuela Ramos with grassroots women's organizations contributed to participants' knowledge and to communication about reproductive health, and seems to have contributed to an overall improved position for the women involved.

Lastly, to avoid misinterpretations, I wish to close this chapter by highlighting the political attention the episode of forced sterilization in Peruvian population programs received after the fall of the Fujimori regime. The campaign against the Fujimori government's population program was headed by a peculiar alliance: for once, the Church and feminists formed part of the same (uncomfortable) political camp. Unfortunately, the abuses committed opened "the door to a strong political backlash against family planning" (Rousseau 2007). This backlash was supported by USAID, for the United States returned to a prolife religious-conservative position in population matters as well. Because of the political viability of using previous abuses in population programs for the purpose of opposing the liberalization of reproductive health care, feminists were reluctant to emphasize such abuses. Pro-birth control advocates prefer to highlight the positive sides of the Fujimori program, including legalization of voluntary sterilization, wider access to birth control methods, and the legal independence for women to decide about the use of contraceptives, rather than the negative consequences. In this chapter, I have emphasized the negative rather than the positive in order to show how legal improvements can be used against the women for whom those improvements were meant, and how such abuses are underpinned by institutionalized inequality. Politically, this does not mean that these legal improvements or further liberalization of birth control are not crucial, but rather, that access to birth control needs to be accompanied by substantial improvement in health care services and respect for human rights.

5

VIOLENCE, DEMOCRACY, AND RESISTANCE

I started this book by narrating the misfortunes of Dori, a young Quechua-speaking woman, as witnessed at the special police station for women in Ayacucho.[1] Dori had been severely beaten by her partner, who, as the police officer's version of Dori's story implied, also abused her sexually and never contributed to her or her children's costs of living. Although Dori probably understood very well what was going on, her Spanish was not good enough to respond, and the officer used this fact to give his own version of her misfortune. Unsolicited, he told her story to us in Spanish, even though I had come with a Quechua-speaking student who could have translated for me; the one-room police office was filled with other women and officers, and with the doors wide open, waiting partners and family members, including Dori's abusive boyfriend, could listen in as well. Dori's fragile and humiliating position was of no importance to the officer. As the foreigner, I was probably of more interest to him than she was.

Related to the issue of language is Dori's status as an illiterate indigenous woman in an urban setting. As we saw in the previous chapters, being an indigenous woman invites little respect from more urban and literate people. Her status explains not only the power the officer had over her, but also why she could not simply walk away. Not only did the officer found Dori less important than others, but she herself probably did as well. She had been severely beaten, had nothing to feed herself and her children with, and had no place to go to. And her abusive lover—Dori could not claim marital status—was waiting outside, which cannot have been a comforting idea

---

1. At the police station for women in Ayacucho, I held several interviews, some with the help of a Spanish-Quechua–speaking anthropology student, Kelly Alanya. All names of women whose personal stories are told in this chapter have been changed. Interviews were held between 2001 and 2003, transcribed by a Peruvian, and the translations to English are my own.

for her either. The abuse she received at home was thus continued at the police station. This brings us to another factor in the hierarchies displayed at the station: the status of the police officer. The officer was male, spoke Spanish, was literate, and was in a position of authority. As Marisol de la Cadena would say, these factors "mestizised" him; despite his indigenous background, his education and position placed him in "another social class" than Dori (2000). Feeling no obligation to show respect to her, the officer put extra emphasis on Dori having *allowed* herself to be not only beaten, but raped and deceived; after all, he emphasized, she was stupid enough to have stayed with this abusive man who made her pregnant all the time without ever helping out financially. That she was not a legal wife made her claims to protection even more feeble.

Besides the ethnic and class bias in the relation between Dori and the police officer, there was obviously a gender bias. "Male solidarity" made him see Dori not as a victim of male violence, but as an accessory to her own miserable situation. As members of the community, police officers are local men who take part in the construction of masculinity and, more often than not, identify with fellow male community members, as the officer in this case identified more with the aggressor than the victim. Police routinely receive accusations against neighbors or even friends. According to Delia Zamudio, who manages a *casa de refugio,* a shelter for women, in a Limeño neighborhood, the wives of local police officers would sometimes denounce them to her for violence in their homes. However, reports against officers or their friends or family never resulted in prosecutions, as the paperwork always miraculously got "lost."[2]

The police station in Ayacucho is part of the state-funded program against domestic violence, or "family violence," in Peruvian terminology.[3] As Dori's story suggests, and I will further elaborate in this chapter, well-intentioned state policies against domestic violence were often constrained by the existing racism and sexism, both in society and in the state institutions designed to combat violence. Despite the important leap forward the state made during the 1990s in improving legislation and designing programs to deal with violence against women, several major problems remain. Some

---

2. Personal conversation with Delia, San Juan de Luringancho, Lima, November 2001.
3. The first law against domestic violence, in 1993, did not include a clear enough definition of what "domestic" was and what kind of relationships would fit into such a definition. Today, the term "intrafamily violence" is used to include extended family members, including ex-partners who do not live in the same household as the victim. I use the terms "domestic" and "family" violence interchangeably without making a statement about the marital status of partners. This chapter mainly looks at intimate violence by men against women, however, and includes less discussion of violence against children, elderly, or men—which all fall under the definition of "intrafamily violence."

of these problems are embedded in the structures of Peruvian society, and indeed in most others, and are as difficult to change as the violence itself as they are rooted in the same gender ideology. Other problems were specific to how the program was set up and implemented. In the following, through a discussion of the evolution of legal reform and the design and implementation of policies, on the one hand, and women's response to and interpretation of the violence they experience, on the other, I examine the constraints to changing deeply rooted discriminative and violent social structures through an interaction between state and society.

Feminist Activism, Democracy, and Legal Reform

As in the previous two case studies, the social policies discussed here served broader interests than merely complying with women's rights or responding to demands from society; in this case, they were directed toward the right to a life free of violence. Food aid and the support for popular women's organizations were embedded in clientelism and poverty relief, emphasizing women's caring roles. As stated earlier, the population policies, aimed at expanding access to birth control methods and reproductive health services, were underpinned by a neo-Malthusian notion that linked population to economic development and poverty. Poor and indigenous women's reproductive roles were emphasized in a negative light. The policies to combat violence against women had a different ideological background and were unrelated to poverty-reduction strategies or clientelism. They did serve political goals, helping further the idea that despite the clear signs of increasing authoritarianism and continuing state violence, Peru was democratizing. Nevertheless, the legal reforms and the policies that followed were long due and signaled a definite start toward a system that would not only protect women from violence, but provide the basis for a society-wide debate about the role of violence and authoritarianism at home and beyond.

In Latin America, the struggle against domestic violence has always been strongly linked to the struggle for democracy, perhaps best represented in the activist phrase "democracy in the country and at home" (Matear 1999; Jaquette 1994; Jaquette and Wolchik 1998). Often, as Laura Weldon observes, legal reform in this area does indeed go hand in hand with improved collaboration between democratic governments, women's movements, and government institutions, that is, with more general democratizing developments (2002, 5). In Peru, however, policies against family violence were implemented at a time when Peru was perhaps not undergoing a process of democratization, but was in a process of pacification. Starting in the 1980s, male violence against women became more visible; women grew less tolerant and feminist activism more fierce. Several studies suggest that male violence toward women also increased in the 1990s, especially in areas that had been particularly affected by political violence (CEPRODEP 1997; TRC 2002, 2003).[4] The war had made a bad situation worse. According to a conservative estimate of the Encuesta Demográfica y de Salud Familiar (ENDES; Survey of Demography and Family Health), held in 2000, 41 percent of Peruvian women were beaten at least once in their life by their partners (Guzmán Chaganaquí 2002, 217). An influential study by Ana Güezmes, Nancy Palomino, and Miguel Ramos shows higher prevalence rates, from 51 percent of women in Lima to 69 percent in Cusco (2002).[5] In a 2005 study in the department of Ayacucho, where the majority of the interviews for this chapter were held, 54.5 percent of surveyed women had suffered domestic violence, 30.7 percent systematically (ranging from every three months to every day; Programa Integral de la Lucha Contra la Violencia Familiar y Sexual 2005). Considering the lack of reliable data for prewar years, we have to rely on local anecdotal evidence suggesting that these figures are higher than "normal" due to war-related aggression and trauma. Nevertheless, high as the Peruvian figures seem, these numbers are not completely removed from prevalence estimates elsewhere: according to different studies carried out in the 1990s, about 25 to 30 percent of women in Canada, the United States, Belgium, and the Netherlands are regular victims of domestic violence (Weldon 2002, 211–17; Netherlands Ministry of Justice 2002). Surveys carried out in Nicaragua, Colombia, and Costa Rica reported, respectively, 29, 60, and 51 percent of women as suffering from domestic violence (Heise 1997, 416; Sternberg 2000, 91). Despite the difficulty of accurately estimating domestic violence levels and the use of different sampling techniques and statistical calculations across surveys, one can conclude that Peru ranks high on the score when compared with other countries, but that the degree of domestic violence is not unique to Peru.[6]

The link between political violence and violence against women was made explicit at the first Latin American Feminist Meeting of 1981, held in Bogotá. This meeting nominated November 25, the date in 1960 on which

---

4. This is consistent with studies that suggest that domestic violence increases in post-conflict situations: Pankhurst (2003, 2007), Kelly (2000).

5. Movimiento Manuela Ramos (n.d.) claims that seven out of ten women suffer from domestic violence, based on a study carried out by PROMUDEH.

6. Both Heise and Weldon list percentages of wife abuse reported in different country studies side by side, but the different measurements and sample sizes and characteristics make these comparisons difficult. A recently published study by the World Health Organization uses country studies for comparison, but reportedly streamlines methodological issues. Peru also ranks high in this comparison (World Health Organization 2005).

the Trujillo regime in the Dominican Republic killed the Mirabal sisters, *El Día No Más Violencia contra la Mujer* (the Day of No More Violence Against Women).[7] Since then, November 25 has served each year as a worldwide opportunity to protest against ongoing violence against women in both the political and domestic, the public and private, spheres. Whereas in policy the link between family violence and political violence is often separated, feminist scholars, following activists, have long recognized that political and domestic violence are linked in more than one way (see, e.g., Herman 1992; Enloe 2000; Jacobs, Jacobson, and Marchbank 2000; Meintjes, Pillay, and Turshen 2001; Pankhurst 2003, 2007; Boesten 2007, 2008). Peru experienced military regimes between 1968 and 1980, but, although authoritarian and repressive, they did not generate the same widespread political violence, disappearances, unlawful imprisonment, and deaths as occurred in, for example, the Dominican Republic, Chile, or Argentina. However, during the early 1980s, the brutality of Shining Path and the counterinsurgency established and confirmed the gendered nature of political violence in Peru as well. Denunciations against military and police were often made, but never led to any official charges or prosecution (Cisneros 1984; *Marka* 1984; *El Observador* 1984). In the *zonas de emergencia*—highland zones that President Belaúnde declared in "emergency" in December 1982 to enable the start of the counterinsurgency campaign by the army—the situation for women regarding sexual violence was becoming particularly alarming. According to an article published in 1990 in a feminist periodical, *Mujer y Sociedad*, rape, forced pregnancies and abortions, and forced prostitution were such problems in these areas that female representatives of the zones pleaded for the state of emergency to be lifted because it only "legitimized atrocities against their integrity" (Barrantes 1990). The racist views that coastal, mainly urban mestizo soldiers fighting terrorism in the Andes had of the local population also aided and abetted sexual violence against indigenous women (Manrique 2002).[8] In 2003, the Truth and Reconciliation

---

7. Julia Alvarez wrote an influential account of this episode, also made into a film (1994).
8. Although the use of rape as a weapon of war in ethnic conflicts has been extensively studied in relation to the Yugoslavian wars, the Peruvian situation is considerably different. Sexual violence was grounded in both sexism and racism; however, it was not an ethnic strategy. This war, after all, was no ethnic war. It was a racist war, which generated far more victims in the poor and indigenous regions than among other social groups. Although the idea of racial difference facilitated the rape of indigenous women perpetrated by soldiers, one can also argue that for some soldiers, descendants of indigenous families themselves, participating in the violence against the Andean population (including raping women) might have provided entrance into an otherwise closed-off mestizo identity and created deliberate distance from an indigenous heritage. In the Andes, armies tend to provide a possibility for integration, whitening, mestizing for the poor and disenfranchised (Nelson 1999; Canessa 2005; Boesten 2008).

Commission confirmed that the cultivation of a violent and sexualized masculinity in the military fed into a culture of abuse against Andean women. Although the TRC concluded that the majority of systematic rape was perpetrated by the army and police forces, Shining Path and even the *rondas campesinas* were also found guilty of rape and sexual abuse (TRC 2003, VII, 2, 2.1).

Cases of sexual violence—publicly perceived as "collateral" to war—certainly helped activists in placing violence against women on the political agenda. In 1983, the first shelter for battered women was set up in Lima by community activist and feminist Rosa Deuñas.[9] In 1984, middle-class feminists initiated an intense campaign for legislative change. Feminist lawyers studied the existing legislation on women's rights and campaigned against the maintenance of legislation drawn up in 1924 (Sala 1984; *Mujer y Sociedad* 1987). In the penal code of 1924, rape was defined as a crime *contra las buenas costumbres* (against good custom) and *contra la libertad y el honor sexual* (against freedom and sexual honor). The complicity of women in cases of sexual harassment and rape was embedded in such honor codes. In 1989, the Peruvian feminist movement together with the Latin American Committee in Defense of Women's Rights (CLADEM-Peru) drafted a detailed proposal for reform of the penal code with regard to violence against women and sexual harassment (*Mujer y Sociedad* 1989). In 1991, Fujimori introduced a new penal code, adopting recommendations of the feminist lobby, that made sexual violence a criminal offence.

Following these changes in the existing legislation, Law 26260 "against family violence" was passed in 1993. This law decreed that family violence should be approached from a holistic perspective that involved education, special police stations, and temporary shelters for women and their children. These developments were a great victory for the feminist movement, and gave Fujimori—after his *autogolpe* of 1992—a positive, progressive, and to a certain extent even democratic image. The governing party also used the successful adoption of Law 26260 in its rhetoric to emphasize the "modernity" of its policies and its governance. Because the law had been the result of cooperation between feminists and congresswomen of all parties, the women in the ruling party, the *fujimoristas*, exhaustively pointed to the unanimity with which the law was designed and adopted, while stressing that this was the result of "women working together." In doing so, they emphasized once again an essentialist image of women as morally superior to, and more democratic than, men (Blondet 2002, 48). The president needed this

---

9. Personal communication with Rosa Deuñas, Lima, October 2001.

display of unity, democracy, and woman-friendly policy making desperately, as, simultaneously with the process of law reform, Fujimori was separating from his wife and "used all the means at his disposal to isolate and publicly humiliate" her (Vargas 2002, 211; Schmidt 2006, 156). According to Virginia Vargas, the president, while pretending to be dedicated to advancing democratic relations "in the country and at home," opened the undemocratic relations in his own family to public inspection.

Of course, the law against family violence was part of the Fujimori government's package of women-friendly legislation to win the hearts and minds of Peruvians on the political Left, the women's movement, and the international community. In the same year, the United Nations World Conference on Human Rights in Vienna confirmed women's rights as an integral part of, and not subordinate to, human rights. In addition, the UN Declaration on Violence Against Women, issued in 1993, argues that "violence against women is a manifestation of historically unequal power relations between men and women" and that it is "one of the crucial mechanisms by which women are forced into a subordinate position compared to men." The UN defines violence against women as "any act of gender-based violence that results in, or is likely to result in, physical, sexual or psychological harm or suffering to women, including threats of such acts, coercion or arbitrary deprivations of liberty, whether occurring in public or in private life" (UN Declaration on Violence Against Women, quoted in Weldon 2002, 9–13). The coercive family planning program, wartime rapes, sexual harassment at work or on the streets, and all other forms of psychological, physical, and sexual violence fall under this definition. Nevertheless, in policy making, violence in the private spaces of the home figured most prominently because the family was often perceived as the "cornerstone" or even the "breeding place" of society.

The emphasis on the domestic in legislation and policy generated several problems. For example, the concepts used in the 1993 law were too vague and undefined. Consequently, several adjustments to the law have since been made to define what constitutes "family violence"; what types of social relationships should be included under the category "family"; how one defines, detects, and proves psychological violence; what sort of acts should be considered "sexual violence"; and what constitutes "severe" or "minor" physical harm and to what extent it should determine the character of further legal proceedings. To the dismay of feminist lawyers, men could only be prosecuted if the injuries of the victim kept her "incapacitated" for more than ten days. If not, a perpetrator could only be held for twenty-four hours, according to the police in Ayacucho a "sobering-up" period.[10] The law failed to provide sufficient judicial guidelines or intervention mechanisms for judges and the police to be able to protect women or prosecute men. The law was even less specific on how to prevent violence. In addition, the roles and responsibilities of the different legal institutions and social services needed to be negotiated, and penalties established. According to feminist lawyer Silvia Loli (2001), this space for creativity in the law worked against victims, as judges and prosecutors were not sufficiently familiar with, nor interested in, cases of family violence to encourage creativity. To add to the confusion, the judicial system is often slow and victims have to be very patient in seeing their cases go to court. The protection of victims is also a major problem as plans for shelters have been poorly implemented and the imprisonment of perpetrators is rare. If perpetrators are found guilty at all, they receive fines or community service (ibid.).

To problems of definition and protection, we can add problems of interpretation, as not only did the law leave significant space for creativity, but the workforce dealing with cases of violence is predominantly male-biased. For example, the *médicos legistas* (doctors) are responsible for confirming the veracity of denunciations of rape and whether physical harm done falls under the category of "severe" or "minor" injury. This categorization determines whether an aggressor is charged and, thus, whether the victim will receive any protection, albeit minimal. The categorization of injury and punishment is dependent on the responsible doctor's, or sometimes police officer's, interpretation of the injury inflicted on a woman in her home, that is, in private. Cases rarely get to court, but if they do, convictions of perpetrators are rare because most male judges are of the opinion that "for the sake of the family, marriage and the children, women need to tolerate a certain amount of violence" (Egan 2000). In 2000, a Human Rights Watch report claimed that the examinations by doctors are often inadequate and minimize the physical harm done, and that attorneys and judges tend to see domestic violence as not important enough to warrant a claim. Similarly, in a recent evaluation of the possibilities for justice for victims of sexual violence, Flor de María Valdez Arroyo (2006) confirmed the persistence of sexism in the justice system and the persistent interrogation of victims in rape cases about their behavior and dress during the attack.

---

10. The idea that perpetrators use violence only when they drink, or only in otherwise particular circumstances, still dominates much popular debate about the causes of domestic violence. Such beliefs—extensively rebutted by evidence—suggest that violence is incidental and only happens "when provoked." According to evidence gathered by the Peruvian Ministry of Justice for the first half year of 2007, the state's facilities received 57,472 denunciations of violence; in 66 percent of the cases the perpetrator had been *ecuánime* (level-headed). See http://www.manuela.org.pe/violencia.asp.

Even Janet Tello, judge of the High Court in Lima, claimed that judges' male bias often resulted in a negative outcome for women in cases of sexual violence (TRC 2002). In rural areas, justices of the peace deal with domestic violence cases according to customary law. Justices of the peace are respected representatives of the community, not trained lawyers or judges, and predominantly male. "Minor" injury will most likely escape the attention of justices of the peace. In 2003, I had a conversation with two justices of the peace, a father and daughter, in the province of La Mar, department of Ayacucho. The father claimed that in his district domestic violence was not a problem and that it had never been. This came as a surprise, especially as I had spent the day interviewing victims of violence in his community. Two days later, in a private interview, the daughter told me that her father had always beaten and abused her mother and that in her family the word of her father was the law, enforced with violence if necessary. If a justice of the peace thinks that violence is a good means to solve family conflicts, how can this same man implement national laws against domestic violence? The daughter, who had replaced her father as justice of the peace in 2002 and actively engaged with cases of domestic violence in their community, was voted out of office in 2005.

Despite these problems, both in rural and urban spaces, denunciations of domestic violence rapidly soared after the law was issued in 1993. The existing system did not seem prepared for the increase in cases. At the same time, a new initiative aimed to increase efficiency and access to justice for the traditionally excluded—the urban poor and rural indigenous people—was designed. Judicial reforms, funded and supported by USAID, the Inter-American Development Bank, and the World Bank, stipulated a network of arbitration that "would be overseen by the national judiciary, but would not be directly part of it" (Poole 2004, 53). A law on conciliation was issued in 1997, and simultaneously, amendments were made to Law 26260 on family violence. The linking of the two laws made conciliation compulsory in all cases of family violence (Espinoza Matos 2000, 13). The laws provide an "alternative mechanism for the solution of conflicts" (Ley de Conciliación, no. 26872, http://www.leyes.congreso.gob.pe), as conflicts including cases of maintenance allowances, divorce, and domestic violence were subjected to compulsory, extrajudicial mediation by a third party, which might be a special conciliation office or a public prosecutor in urban areas, or a justice of the peace in rural areas. According to Silvia Loli, the new provisions of the law were the result not only of the neoliberal restructuring of the judicial system under the guidance of the international financial institutions, but in great part of a conservative commission of female politicians and lawyers who intended to create protection for women against violence in the family while also preventing divorce. Loli implies that the principle behind conciliation in family matters, including violence, was preservation—maybe even "improvement"—of the family structure as the cornerstone of Peruvian society.[11] Such a focus prioritizes family unity over women's and, arguably, children's health and safety. Moreover, because acts of male domestic violence lead to conciliation rather than prosecution under the criminal law, the result might be the legitimization of male dominance over women and to a certain extent even the use of violence.

Deborah Poole observes that the compulsory law on conciliation created a shadow legal system that was neither within nor outside of the state (2004, 53). Instead of reforming the system so that it becomes a more inclusive system of justice, "the new generation of reforms suggest that people should be asked to avoid the judicial system as a court of first instance, and to turn instead to a network of "informal" dispute resolution centers with hazily defined ties to the national judicial and legal system" (54). The result is that women are again excluded; they are told to forget about justice, about the legal system, and about civil/women's rights. The state, for its part, can avoid the "escalating load of domestic violence hearings, while the women who are the most frequently victims of this form of criminal violence are shuttled into a system where no legal sanctions can be brought against her attacker" (55). Similar criticism emerged from feminist organizations, which argued that conciliation could only succeed between equal partners. Domestic violence is grounded inherently in unequal power relations, which means that conciliation should not be an option. The law was modified in 2001 to prohibit conciliation procedures in cases of domestic violence, although this change in legislation does not mean that it is not used anymore (Estremadoyro 2001).

Conciliation in violent domestic conflicts not only suggests a political preference for the preservation of the family but, according to some scholars, serves a cultural logic. For example, the lawyer Julieta Estremadoyro, in her study of domestic violence and the law in the Peruvian Andes, focused her attention on the relevance of conciliatory practices as part of Andean culture. According to Estremadoyro, community-based Andean women were not helped by "Western feminist solutions" such as separation and punishment, but preferred conciliation by family members higher in the hierarchy, such as parents, godparents, or community leaders like the justices of the peace who traditionally performed extrajudicial mediation in local disputes (Estremadoyro 2001). In this vision, the Andean family unit is analyzed as an ideal type of male-female reciprocity and complementarity (Harris 1978; Isbell 1979; Silverblatt 1987; Reynaga Farfán 1996). Arguably, such

11. Personal communication, October 2003.

views obscure the inequality within households and between indigenous households and the wider society (Barrig 2001; Theidon 2003). Estremadoyro does not reject the idea of gender inequality in Andean culture, but she considers inequality in large part to be a product of "modernization" and the region's increasing incorporation into the market economy. Domestic violence, in this vision, is something that can be repaired and should benefit from conciliation according to local customary law. After interviewing men and women in Andean communities in the Cusco area, Estremadoyro also asserts that rural women *expect* conciliation with their partners through the intervention of third parties. Although we shall see below that, to a certain extent, this is valid, she does not sufficiently consider the economic aspect of female dependency on men, which makes women's resistance against violence a more difficult task. In the end, the emphasis on conciliation in the formal legal process implies that after failed efforts at conciliation by kinship networks, women have no alternative option but to tolerate the violence they might experience.

In practice, the law on conciliation meant that women wishing to denounce aggressive partners to higher authorities, often after years of coping with everyday violence in their homes, were obliged to conciliate their differences in a paralegal space where volunteers or low-paid trained personnel such as justices of the peace, special mediators, or public prosecutors would mediate between husband and wife until an agreement was made and signed. This normally means a woman forgives in exchange for a promise. As Estremadoyro emphasizes, many indigenous Andean couples do go through processes of conciliation with the help of kinship networks and, in the last instance, community authorities. In many communities, godparents have the responsibility to watch over domestic conflicts among their godchildren, and are expected to mediate between spouses when necessary. In Ayacucho, conciliation procedures involving parents, godparents, and local authorities seemed a common first step. The justice system was brought in only when violence exceeded their control. For example, Gloria, a young woman of eighteen years of age, lived in Antolinayocc, a village in the province of Ayacucho. She, her father, and her one-year-old baby traveled to the city of Ayacucho, where I met them at the police station, to report Gloria's partner, who had beaten her since they started living together two years earlier. Gloria's father had tried everything to stop the violence against his daughter. Not only he, but, as he told us, also the parents of the young man, the godfather, and finally the local deputy governor (*teniente gobernador*) talked to the man. However, the man also became violent with the mediators, even with his own parents. The family saw no other solution but to go to the police in order to report the aggressor officially, in the hope that the police could do something about it. Secondly, they hoped for an alimony agreement so that Gloria could leave her partner without burdening her family too much.[12] It is important to note that neither Gloria nor her father asked the judicial system for additional conciliation, but instead sought more severe intervention. Thus, Gloria's story appears to suggest that in the first instance people are prepared to use local social structures to try to solve conflicts. However, once these mediations fail to reach an acceptable, nonviolent reconciliation, they do not appeal to the judicial system for further attempts at conciliation. Rather, they ask the legal system for protection, separation, and/or alimony at a moment when there is nothing left to reconcile. Gloria's story confirms that people might rely on mediation using local networks, but expect the judiciary to offer alternative solutions. Hence, the compulsory stipulation of conciliation through an extrajudicial mediator on top of community-level mediation structures was a misconceived attempt at discouraging women to denounce husbands who were out of the control of traditional mediators.

In Ayacucho, however, local social structures are increasingly subject to radical changes. Displacement, disappearances, and deaths caused by the war have torn families apart. Young couples often leave their parents' communities in search of a better life elsewhere. This means the loss of family ties that could otherwise provide women with social resources providing protection and negotiation. As a result, migrants in urban centers report their husbands without having gone through a process of family conciliation because, due to changed social surroundings, there is no supportive family network. Hence, it is difficult to know whether high indices of domestic violence in urban migrant centers mean that domestic violence is more frequent in migrant communities than in nonmigrant communities. It could be that in migrant communities people visit state services more often than elsewhere simply because they have access to services not available to them before. It is also possible that women approach the state services because they provide the mediatory role of the kinship networks they could previously rely on. Such an analysis might explain the high visibility of domestic violence in urban settlements—and the concentration of both state and nongovernmental services offered in poor migrant neighborhoods as opposed to richer or rural settlements—and the popularity of mediation services offered by Manuela Ramos in the *pueblo joven* Pamplona Alta in Lima.

An important argument in the proconciliation camp is that "Western" concepts of justice—as upheld in the national justice system—simply do

---

12. Personal conversation with Gloria and her father in front of the police station for women, Ayacucho, December 2002.

not apply to Andean people, as Andean women do not seek punishment or separation (Estremadoyro 2001). While the idea of punishment might not be central to women's expectations, this does not necessarily mean that they wish for conciliation either. For example, Julia, whom I met at the same police station where I met Gloria and her family, said that she had married at the age of seventeen. After enduring eighteen years of physical abuse, she was still married. She claimed to have been too shy and afraid to denounce her husband to the authorities. She also said that she did not dare to report him because she originally came from the village of Vinchos and had no family in the city of Ayacucho, where she had married. Although her husband had left her seven years ago with three children, he occasionally came back *para pegarla* (to hit her). Recently, one of Julia's sisters had taken her to the police to accuse the husband of violence. Julia hoped that the police could force her husband to pay for the hospital where she had to go after his last visit when he beat her and that he would be obliged to support her children financially.[13] As a result of her migration (and possibly the consequences of political violence, which was particularly intense in her area of origin, although Julia did not comment on that), Julia lacked the option of mediation that kinship networks could offer. However, through another family connection, her sister, she became aware of her rights as a citizen and the services the formal justice system offered: she could go to the police, and she could even demand alimony through the legal system. She did not come for revenge or punishment, but for compensation. Julia's case might confirm the argument of Estremadoyro that Andean women do not seek punishment or divorce. However, Julia did not seek conciliation either, as Estremadoyro suggests. Rather, she sought safety for herself and her children and hoped for an agreement over alimony. Julia's case also highlights women's partial economic dependency on men, and although Julia did not ask for a divorce from the husband who had abandoned her, she did need an officially registered separation in order to be able to enforce alimony payments.

The lack of access to an effective judicial system that enforces alimony payments and offers protection against violent husbands is a more real problem than champions of conciliation as cultural practice suggest. This is illustrated by the work of Manuela Ramos in Pamplona Alta, Lima. Manuela Ramos has run a women's house there since 1997, the Casa de Bienestar (House of Well-Being), which is staffed by women from the neighborhood.[14] Among other services, fourteen trained *orientadoras legales* (paralegal counselors)

---

13. Personal conversation with Julia in the police station for women, Ayacucho, with the help in translation of Kelly Alanya, December 2002.
14. Women who become paid staff in nonprofessional neighborhood service delivery such as these are selected from activists in women's organizations.

offer women informal legal support in taking severe cases of violence and abuse to court. Because going to court is a time-consuming, expensive, and not always successful process, the Casa de Bienestar established a conciliation and agreements office for less severe cases. However, by their own account, the *orientadores legales* in Pamplona Alta do not intend to reconcile broken marriages. Rather, they seek extrajudicial agreements over child support and visiting hours. The *orientadoras legales* set up a system whereby the ex-partners come to an agreement over weekly child support payments. The counselors draw up a "contract" that both parties must sign. The man hands over his weekly contribution to the counselors, not directly to his ex-wife. The woman can safely pick up the weekly contribution without having to see her ex-husband.[15] This system allows for contributions other than financial and often stipulates foodstuffs. According to the *orientadores legales*, and confirmed by the high demand for these services, this is a positive alternative for women and men who confront irresolvable conflicts. Overall, conciliation in cases of domestic violence—broadly defined to include mediation in conflict and separation—indeed seems to be part of the custom in Andean and migrant families. However, whether this is a consequence of culturally defined preferences, or because legal institutions have traditionally ignored them, remains open to question. Probably both are true: institutional abandonment helps define culturally defined practices.

Return to Democracy: National Plan to Combat Violence Against Women

Just around the corner from the Casa de Bienestar in Pamplona Alta, a special police station for women was founded in 1999 to support the existing nongovernmental services. However, as the transition government of Valentín Paniagua (late 2000 to July 2001) came to an end, the policies and legislation against family violence were insufficient to have a positive impact on the lives of women. Arguably, that transition period confirms the importance of democratization for the implementation of policies against family violence. The Paniagua government rapidly implemented a series of measures in order to speed up democratization, including establishing the Truth and Reconciliation Commission, as well as a special gender team within the commission to focus on the differentiated experiences of women. Given these political changes, the creation of a National Plan to Combat Violence against Women (Plan Nacional contra la Violencia hacia la Mujer)

---

15. Casa de Bienestar, Pamplona Alta, repeated visits during 2001–2002.

was perhaps a logical step for the newly named Ministry of Women and Social Development (MIMDES).[16] The National Plan considered all possible interpretative frameworks for violence against women: discrimination against women and the struggle for equity, human rights and women's rights, public health, and the well-being of the family (PROMUDEH 2001). Recognizing that the visibility of violence in poorer social sectors resulted not necessarily from higher prevalence rates among the poor, but from discriminative justice systems and policing practices and the minimal economic and emotional capital among victims to deal with violence in their families, the National Plan aimed to set up a broad set of services in poorer urban areas.[17] The new Plan included setting up Centros de Emergencia Mujer (Emergency Centers for Women, or CEMs). Each center would include police officers, a psychologist, a prosecutor, a doctor, a lawyer, and a social worker. By 2002, when the majority of the interviews for this chapter were held, thirty-six such centers were in operation throughout the country, eight of them in the poorer neighborhoods in Lima (and none in middle-class Limeño neighborhoods). According to the professionals who worked in the centers, the new program was a big step forward. They felt that they could offer more integrated professional services to women and children, as well as to some men. The steady yearly increases in reports of domestic violence that are registered at the CEMs and the existing women's police stations confirm the need for these services.[18] For example, the police station set up near the Casa de Bienestar in Pamplona Alta was turned into a CEM. Although this meant a doubling of services in the same neighborhood, the number of women relying on the Casa de Bienestar did not diminish; instead, more women in the neighborhood reported violence in the home. However, while these developments were obviously an improvement, expanding access to services does not necessarily change the mechanisms that had caused low

---

16. These changes were introduced under the leadership of human rights lawyer, activist, and feminist Susana Villarán, who was the minister of PROMUDEH, reformed as MIMDES during the transition government.

17. The idea that "the poor" are more violent than the nonpoor has actively been debated. See, e.g., Walby (1990, 133); Scheper-Hughes and Bourgois (2004); Méndez, O'Donnell, and Pinheiro (1999); Goldstein (2003); Moser and McIlwaine (2004). For Peru, see Gonzales de Olarte and Gavilano Llosa (1998, 38.) The latest survey, held in 2005 among 1,046 women in Ayacucho, showed only minor differences between socioeconomic sectors in domestic violence prevalence rates, while in some cases the better off showed higher prevalence (Programa Integral de la Lucha Contra la Violencia Familiar y Sexual 2005).

18. Personal communication with Betsy Flores, Lima, December 2002, and Emma Espinoza, Lima, December 2002. According to Espinoza, the CEM also helps set up agreements concerning separation and child support, similar to the Casa de Bienestar of Manuela Ramos. However, she emphasized that "conciliation" is something different and refers to processes within the family before any state interference, but should not be the goal of the CEMs.

access and poor treatment before, such as prejudices on the part of police officers, justices of the peace, and medical personnel.

From the initial special police station set up in the center of Lima in 1989 onwards, there have been plans to combat the male bias and gender discrimination on the part of police officers with all-female staff. Interestingly, research done in Brazilian police stations (which were the example on which the Peruvian services were based) suggests that prevailing discriminative gender ideologies are as much a part of the world vision of women as of men. According to Sara Nelson, the police stations established in Brazil in 1985, solely staffed by women, had similar problems to the Peruvian ones in relation to law enforcement, resources, and discrimination. The women police officers often undermined victims' denunciations by blaming them for their situation and by suggesting they should tolerate a certain amount of violence in their homes (S. Nelson 1996; see also Hautzinger 2002, Santos 2004). A study of the quality of Peruvian state services against domestic violence published in late 2003 by the feminist organization Flora Tristán came to similar conclusions as those outlined above. Some of the women interviewed in the study did mention a preference for female attendants, but this was not a general opinion. The study also confirms the suspicion that police stations function poorly compared to the CEMs. Twenty-five percent of the women interviewed approved of the police stations, whereas 80 percent approved of the CEMs. This was probably the result of better-trained staff in the CEMs as compared to the traditionally macho environment of police stations. The study's interviewees complained about police officers' indifference, prejudice, rudeness, corruption, and, indeed, the complicity between aggressor and officer. The study also observed a language problem, as, according to its data, a third of the women who attended the police stations spoke a native language as their first language, whereas the attendants in general only wished to speak Spanish. Both the interviewed users and providers in the study complained about the lack of adequate protection mechanisms (Flora Tristán 2003).[19] Thus, to make a special police station or center for battered women a safe and just place, changes in thinking about gender relations among both men and women are necessary, in addition to the recruitment of gender-sensitive staff, adequate training and funding, legislation, and measures to facilitate the protection of victimized women.

Although the post-Fujimori National Plan to Combat Violence Against Women was an important step forward in developing the policies initiated

---

19. The study is based on interviews with users and service providers in twelve Peruvian cities regarding the quality of services such as the CEMs and the special police stations.

during the 1990s, and the CEMs were generally well-received services, funding was (and still is) a continuous problem. The housing of the CEMs and police stations was often poor, insufficient furniture was supplied, computers were rarely available, and often people had to bring their own paper for the typewriters if they wanted their cases to be filed. Electricity and water were not always paid for. Social workers I interviewed in three different cities, including Lima, said that they had paid for several of these basic services themselves. The lack of equipment and the poor working conditions encourage mistrust among women, who may interpret a police officer's request for paper and an accompanying soft drink as an act of corruption ("Aplicación de la ley de protección frente a la violencia familiar 26260" 2003–4). This lack of material support is especially lamentable in the case of the CEMs, which, according to both service providers and users, are a good initiative that has considerably improved support to victimized women, children, and some men (see, e.g., Flora Tristán 2003).

As argued above, these developments—however insufficient—in the area of violence against women, were in great part the result of pressure from civil society, mainly feminist activism since the 1970s (see also Weldon 2002; Waylen 2007). This activism was greatly supported and fed into by the popular women's movement in the urban squatter settlements. In the 1990s, feminist consultants, politicians, and congresswomen worked together to respond to the demands from civil society to reform legislation and design policy to combat violence against women. The Fujimori regime went along with the proposals for its own reasons; perhaps partly out of genuine concern, but, especially considering the self-coup of 1992 and the episode of the president's divorce from his wife, mainly to brush up his image. Feminist scholars and activists who argue that policies against family violence should go hand in hand with the democratization of government overlook the other side of the equation: policies against domestic violence are often pursued under pressure of processes of democratization in civil society. For domestic violence to become an issue for both feminist and grassroots activism, women need to reject existing justifications for violence against women. The high demand for police stations, CEMs, and services provided by NGOs in the area of family violence suggests that tolerance for family violence is steadily diminishing, which, in turn, points to a demand for the democratization of gender relations in families and communities. As I will discuss below, women's participation in grassroots organizations such as *comedores populares, clubes de madres,* and *vaso de leche* committees helped forward this process of decreased tolerance for violence against women and the democratization of family relations.

Negotiating Marriage and Pain

In order to understand what circumstances enable, sustain, and challenge wife beating, we should look at women's experiences with domestic violence and the ways in which they negotiate their marriages. To do so, I look at the personal stories of five women's leaders I met in Ayacucho. Several of the interviewees are women I already introduced in other chapters (although they appear under pseudonyms in this chapter, considering the sensitivity of the topic). Their stories of domestic violence are embedded in their narratives about their lives, which also include recollections about work, marriage, and children, the political violence after 1980, histories of migration, and their experiences as grassroots leaders of women's organizations. This embeddedness is important to note because it indicates the central place these stories have in their memories. Most of the interviews were not specifically about domestic violence, but the issue came up spontaneously. Listening to the stories of women in Ayacucho with regard to domestic violence has, of course, an extra dimension because of the centrality of political violence in recent Ayacuchana history. As research has pointed out, violence against women often intensifies during and after war (Kelly 2000; Pillay 2001; Pankhurst 2003, 2007). Ayacucho's violent history in recent decades has undeniably influenced human relations, forms of conflict resolution, and the incidence of and/or motivations for domestic violence. Since the early 1990s, NGOs, grassroots women's organizations, and some state institutions have been committed to fighting pervasive everyday violence against women in Ayacucho. Slowly, such institutions have started to address the links between wartime violence and peacetime aggression. While I recognize the importance of future research into the links between political and domestic violence, it is beyond the scope of this chapter to address that question (see Boesten 2007, 2008). Rather, I focus on the personal histories of my informants—which are clearly embedded in the violent regional history—in order to look at ways in which the state and women try to combat domestic violence. I selected several personal stories of women for their representativeness and detail to discuss women's personal experiences with violence, fear, and resistance.

Teodomira is a woman of the "older" generation—she was born in 1942—in a community that was once a separate village but is now completely integrated into the city of Ayacucho. Here she married her first love, a neighbor with whom she grew up. Teodomira has been a socially and politically active woman. She was one of the first to found a local *club de madres,* and in 1989 she cofounded the Departmental Federation of Clubes de Madres in Ayacucho (FEDECMA), uniting some eighty thousand women. She fought for peace with marches and meetings and always supported and helped women who had lost family members. Now she feels old and has given up her leadership function in the Federation of Clubes de Madres, but she is still engaged with and active in the community—for example, by organizing her colleagues at the market where she sells the family-produced *artesanía* (handicrafts). Because Teodomira is a strong woman with clear convictions and activist in orientation, it surprised me when I heard that her husband had beaten her heavily for many years. According to Teodomira, her husband started to hit her because he did not like the fact that she went out: "We had already started to organize, but my husband told me, 'where are you going, where will you be going,' he was jealous, 'you are going out with another man, where are you going out every time,' like that he hit me. I let him when he hit me, [as a result] I stopped participating [in activities] for a long time."

Like other women, to minimize her husband's jealousy concerning her participation in the organization, Teodomira constantly emphasized that it was a "mothers'" club that was completely dedicated to the well-being of the family. Just as the motherhood label was politically useful in times of political violence, so it was useful to maintain domestic peace. However, her dedication to the male-headed household did not prevent the occasional violent anger of Teodomira's husband. Thus, she was prepared to stop taking part in activities that could provoke his anger, as she said she would do after an "incident" in 1990. This incident, which occurred the year after the founding of FEDECMA, was a consequence of Teodomira's growing prominence as a women's leader. Teodomira and the women in her movement had actively resisted the political violence in the department of Ayacucho, and now Teodomira had to face her own husband: "And another day in 1990, that was when I had already raised the flag, the national flag, for the first time as the [leader] of my provincial federation of Huamanga,[20] I was given the responsibility for raising the flag. Then my husband beat me up good, good, I had to go to the hospital, that bad. But then the señoras came to my house to talk to my husband, four social assistants came." The collective authority of four social workers forced the husband to explain himself. According to Teodomira, this was his excuse: "And my husband cried and he said, 'No, not my wife, there is a curfew, she shouldn't come home late because they can kill her and who will then take care of the children,' that is what he said to the señoras." Paradoxically, the husband's fear for Teodomira's safety in going out during wartime ended in his beating her so badly that she had to be hospitalized. We can

20. Huamanga is the name used to refer to the city of Ayacucho.

easily condemn these arguments—if he can behave that way toward her, she is not safe from him either and cannot take care of the children—but they made sense to Teodomira. She was prepared to retreat from her position as president of FEDECMA not because of her own fear, but because she thought her husband had given her legitimate reasons for concern. In the end, however, the social workers' explanation to her husband that she "was doing no harm to anyone" with her activities, that she was only helping other mothers, helped her husband change his mind. The emphasis was again put on the fact that Teodomira kept her external activities within the domestic realm, which apparently satisfied her husband. What he was afraid of was likely not that political violence would take his wife away from his children, but that he would lose control over her behavior. Paradoxically, Teodomira's responsibility for her children was perceived as being jeopardized more by the "indecent" behavior that might result from her exposure to the outside world than by the threat of violence, both political and domestic.

In the end, motherhood, helping others, or any other excuse did not protect Teodomira, because her husband did not stop beating her. However, times did change for the next generation: "Now I have my daughter, she is already married, 'An elderly woman, papa, why do you hit my mother,' when he is beating me. So my daughter tells me: 'If it is like that mama, report him, go, let's go, I will take you.'" But Teodomira never reported her husband. She takes pride in the fact that her children defend her now that they are grown up. Arguably, Teodomira told me this story to show me that her daughters would not accept violent behavior in their lives. By narrating her story the way she did, she showed me that the world had changed for the better and that her role in these changes had been significant, because her own daughter is better able to protect herself now that she is married.

When I asked Teodomira if her husband still hit her, she denied it, saying, "No, now we are old." Still, her daughter seemed to encourage Teodomira to denounce her husband: "Now I have my daughter." However, if it is the case that he does not hit her anymore, then she has achieved some measure of peace. Teodomira also claimed that her husband does not know half of the things she does during the day. She has not told him that she has weekly meetings to organize the market men and women. To preserve the domestic peace, she has chosen to keep certain things in her life a secret. Clearly, Teodomira has found some kind of equilibrium in her domestic life, but it is an equilibrium that, after forty-two years of marriage and pain, continues to be negotiated.

Teodomira's story is one of many that show how wife-battering is often motivated by jealousy. Women's stories suggest that men become aggressive because of their fear of losing control over the activities, both sociopolitical and sexual, of their wives. Thus, an important question many women ask themselves when they start a relationship is whether a future husband might be jealous. The term used to refer to such potential wife beaters is "machismo," an attitude that confines and controls women's behavior. One of my informants, Gloria, defined machismo as follows: "The woman has to be in a corner of the house, the woman shouldn't talk like that, with other women; when they talk among women, [the husbands] will say, 'What are they advising each other.'" Gloria's definition suggests that men are afraid of alliances between women that could undermine their powerful position in the family. A further implication, also made in other research, is that women who have large social networks have more chance of being beaten because of husbands' possible anxieties about potential female empowerment (Gonzales de Olarte and Gavilano Llosa 1998, 38; see also Jaquette 1994, 225; Cervone 2002, 184).

Gloria is thirty-five years old and lives in San Miguel, the capital of the province of La Mar in the department of Ayacucho. San Miguel is a small town and in 2002 and 2003 did not provide any special services to combat domestic violence apart from the local authorities such as the justice of the peace. Gloria started her relationship with her current husband when she was fifteen and married four years later following her first pregnancy. When I interviewed her, Gloria was the president of the local *club de madre* of San Miguel. Gloria first told me that her husband hit her because she went out to meetings. But at a certain point in the conversation she said: "Well, I can't say that he became machista when I started in the organization, no. From the moment I lived with him, from the hour that he started looking for me, he always abused me, but I was afraid of him, I thought, maybe that is my obligation, even if he beats me I have to . . . I was a teenager, a girl of fifteen." Gloria conveys several relevant things here. First, she equates "machismo" with the violent character of her husband. Second, although her story initially focused on the abuse in relation to her activities outside the home, she confesses that it actually had nothing to do with her participation in women's organizations. He had beaten her from the very beginning when she was fifteen. So why did she stay with, and even marry, the man who abused her? She says it was because of fear and because she thought it was her obligation to be a good wife "even if he hits me." Gloria did not dare go to the police because "when my husband was here, I did not dare to report him, I was afraid because he was a bad man, he showed it; he had no shame." Gloria was afraid that he would actually kill her, as he had threatened. She did not have another explanation for her husband's violence than his character. He was just a bad, violent, macho man.

So Gloria was afraid of her husband but still participated in the *clubes de madres*, always emphasizing that she did so for the other mothers because they had elected her as president of the local club and she could not let them down. She was afraid and arranged her life just as Teodomira did: she lied to her husband about her activities. Today, by her own account, she has managed to stop the violence and does not have to lie anymore. This is a compelling story: at one point her husband, who of course knew that she was active in *clubes de madres,* made a conciliatory gesture to her by inviting the members of her organization, the *socias,* to their home on New Year's Day. Then, in front of the other women, he beat her up so badly that she had to be taken to the hospital. The doctor in the hospital immediately sent for the chief of the police in order to report the abuse. According to Gloria, this *capitán* received her story with amazement, asking her how it was possible that a strong woman, a leader like Gloria, had lived all those years with domestic violence. Gloria found her position as a community leader undeniably jeopardized by her husband's violence. But what made her really angry about her husband's conduct was his physical aggression *in front of* her *socias:* "So, he beat me up in front of them and *he dishonored me,* that's when I started thinking and I said to myself: that's enough." She felt that this event had undermined the authority she possessed as the president of the *club de madres.* Although her public humiliation was probably a calculated move by her husband in order to teach her a lesson, for Gloria a crucial boundary had been crossed. She states that she became stronger through this event and was able to defend herself better by not taking notice of him (*no hacerle caso*), ignoring his violence, walking away, and physically fighting back. However, she still did not leave him. But fate was kind to Gloria when her husband ended up in jail for drug trafficking.

Women in violent marriages find strategies to do more or less what they believe is right. Some women endure the violence on their own until they end up in the hospital and other people—doctors, nurses, and social workers, but also neighbors, friends, and family members—take notice. Exposure to the outside world seems very important: feelings of solidarity and support can make women stronger in confrontations with their partners and show them that they are not alone; at the same time, feelings of shame and loss of authority toward their peers can push women to action.

Women stay with their violent husbands because they are afraid of them, because they do not know where to go with their children, because (not in Gloria's case, but in many others) their own mothers have endured it and have passed on the message that their daughters should bear the same fate. The story of a young woman, Irma, illustrates this last point. Irma is twenty years old and has two children by her ex-partner. Irma told me that he beat her up constantly but now has left her with the children. When I asked her why she had stayed with him, she said, "for the sake of the children" but also admitted she did not want to be alone. Actually, she said, she went with this man to flee her parents' home, where violence was the only form of communication. Thus, she never told her parents or her sisters about the treatment she received from her husband. She exchanged a very unpleasant family life for an uncertain life with her lover, who gave her two children and many beatings. She did not tell anyone, but also did not go to the police, as she was not yet ready to leave him. But he left her and she had to find a way to survive. Now she can barely support her two children or pay for the apartment she lives in. Her mother helps her, but not in a very loving way, according to Irma, who grimaced when she spoke about her. If Irma has no food, she goes to her mother's place to eat, but must do heavy housework in return. Irma's young life is permeated by violence, and she accepts whichever alternative appears to be least harmful. Because Irma cannot fall back on community structures or even her own family for all the support she needs, she is reliant on the police to protect her and to help her claim alimony payments in order to care for her children. When I met her at the police station, she was there, at her mother's urging, to report that her ex-partner had abandoned her and their children.

Irma did not have the *clubes de madres* to fall back on. As argued in previous chapters, although the outward image of the *clubes de madres* was predominantly based on motherhood, they created all-women groups in which members developed a wide range of activities that defied traditional notions of womanhood. The stories of Gloria and Teodomira showed that their participation in women's organizations created certain circumstances that altered their violent relations with their partners. Other stories show that women encouraged each other not to accept violence, to denounce violent partners, and to learn about their rights as citizens and as women. NGOs, feminist or not, have made good use of the organizational structures the *clubes de madres* have created and have provided courses on a wide range of issues. As a result, *clubes de madres* provide information on women's rights, political participation, reproductive rights, leadership, and self-esteem, which leaders of the *clubes de madres* are expected to transmit to the grassroots. Husbands' fears about their wives "getting ideas" when participating in *clubes de madres* are thus not unfounded.

In the case of Emma, who was an important leader in the Federation of Clubes de Madres in Ayacucho at the time of the interview, conflicts with her husband originated in the very fact that she had ideas at all:

More than anything because of machismo, he did not want me to stand out above other people, he did not want me to be superior to him, because he is a person with a profession so he says that a woman who is not a professional should not excel more than the man. So sometimes we would discuss social problems, sometimes about the people or national problems. But he never agreed with me, he said, "it is not like that, it's like this," so from this, fights sometimes followed, meaning, well, mostly as a result of machismo.

Emma suspects that her husband did not want her to be smart. As in the case of Gloria, Emma considers machismo the main reason why he dismissed her ideas and thus the motivation behind his aggression toward her. Emma was active in women's organizations since the early years of political violence. Together with other mothers, she demanded justice, searched for the disappeared, and tried to protect those who were threatened. These experiences convinced her of the correctness of her social commitment. However, her husband would hit her when she became "too smart" because he wanted to be smarter. Apparently this man, who let Emma participate in public life as much as she wanted, believed that Emma contested his authority as soon as she showed a different opinion than his.

Emma endured the beatings. She did not stop participating in the *clubes de madres*, but was not able to stand up to her husband either. However, during the 1990s something triggered a change of mind:

Despite the fact that I went to more or less all courses since 1990 and I knew my rights very well, very well, but despite this, I was battered. That is why my compañeras *said to me, "listen, Emma, as you give courses, as you are training us about women's rights, about self-esteem, but in the meanwhile you are most abused of all, you are fucked up, your marriage is a disaster. So which rights are you talking about if you do not use them yourself?" That's when I decided; I thought, thanks to my* compañeras *and thanks to some institutions that talked to me, I finally decided to separate.*

Although Emma is, of course, talking to a foreign interviewer with potential institutional money, there is some obvious logic to her story: she gave workshops to the women in the federation with the knowledge she had obtained from various institutions about rights and self-esteem—both typical contemporary feminist concepts. But then, this knowledge did not make Emma divorce her violent husband. Only when her *socias* addressed the issue did she decide that she could not go on with her life as it was. Emma's story—and Gloria's story in a very similar way—shows how empowerment can occur through a combination of strategies: the judiciary that recognizes women's rights, even if the law is not always implemented, the NGO that gives information and training to women, and most importantly, the peers who look after each other and push the boundaries of what is acceptable. After the divorce, Emma went to court to get alimony from her ex-partner, "with a lawsuit and everything."

Women's participation in grassroots organizations often generates conflict over existing power relations within their households, which may lead to violent fights. However, besides some exceptions or temporary withdrawals, most interviewed women persisted in their activism even if that meant enduring increasing violence from their partners or deceiving them about their whereabouts. The stories I examined here show us that the women's organizations do not only trigger anger, but can also lead to solutions. The leaders of the *clubes de madres* developed a sense of right and wrong in relation to domestic violence that led them not to accept it from each other any longer. As they are expected to teach their *socias* not to accept violence in their families, the leaders will have to provide the "good example" if they do not want to lose authority. However, it is also the support women give each other, the knowledge they develop about each other's lives, that—like the consciousness-raising groups of the Western middle classes or the Limeño middle classes during the 1970s—gives women the strength and conviction not to have to live with domestic violence.

Changing One's Own Behavior

The organized women who reject domestic violence and try to convince their peers of its wrongs are not only fighting against the aggressors. They also rebel against the conventions of their social surroundings, where men and women, parents, police officers, and judges do not always see the relevance of a struggle to change gender hierarchies and combat aggressive patriarchal authority. But perhaps even more difficult is the fact that they have to fight against their own assumptions, as Neyla indicated.

Neyla was born in 1960 in San Miguel, La Mar. Her story is a sad story of war, political violence, and forced migration. Neyla started to participate in the *clubes de madres* in the 1980s, when political violence between Shining Path and the army dominated the region. During these years she became a good organizer and a mother of three girls, and she lost three brothers in the war and a husband to divorce. Neyla did not separate because of domestic violence, but because her partner had built up a new life during his time as a refugee in Lima. However, besides the violence of war with which Neyla's family lived, Neyla grew up with domestic violence as well:

In my house, my father is very machista, he is a person who does not tolerate, neither does he know how to admit mistakes, everything he says is perfect, so the one who suffered the most is my mother because my father is like that, he hit her and everything. In the beginning it shocked me, but after that I got used to it. One day my father hit my mother in front of me, I was just getting up and I said to my father, "how is it possible that you talk to her like that" and púa, *what was going to fall on my mother, fell on me. That was the only time when I saw him hit my mum. But she says he has always beaten her. But in front of me, however, no, that was the only time. I suffered violence and abuse and all, well, on my own body, with my aunt. . . . I grew up with an aunt and she hit me, whatever happened, everything was beatings. Despite that she was a teacher, she never knew how to advise me or tell me why this or that was bad; so I lived violence through my own body, didn't I?*

Neyla indicates that what was wrong with this aunt was that she never taught Neyla what was right and wrong, or why. "Everything was beatings," and advice or help in life was not given. Neyla admits that she was the same kind of authoritarian mother to her first daughter after she was born in 1982. When NGOs started to arrive in Ayacucho in the 1990s to support the rebuilding of the war-torn department, Neyla seized her opportunity. As a quick and interested learner, she participated in all the NGO courses that became available. According to her, it was this new information that changed her vision of the world and her attitude towards her daughters:

Two NGOs came to give a workshop about women's rights and the rights of children and adolescents. Well, that was the workshop that made me think, it made me think a lot about how to educate my children, I thought, that's how I should do it. From then on I tried to change my attitude towards my children. Slowly the workshops, I participated in all of them, the workshops have made me a more mature person, I see myself as a woman with rights, I found my self-esteem, but because of that I now have seen how things, how everything, should be.

This last point has made her wonder a lot, because she now sees injustice everywhere around her:

This was exactly what I was talking about with Mrs. Marcela. She said: "before I was a leader I never allowed anyone to talk rudely to me, I went and put that person in her place, and if it was a man I would hit him." . . . But I still saw her solve things violently . . . and I think it is worse; I don't know, but it seems to me that among women we call each other anything and therefore we mistreat each other more. We talk about violence, but among women we abuse each other, that's what I think. I don't know, but I think I assimilated a lot of all this, but now it looks that I am becoming very emotional.

The fact that women amongst each other are not always capable of communicating without physical and verbal abuse makes Neyla feel alone and vulnerable. The lack of immediate change in her daily social relationships, while she absorbed new ideas about authority, makes Neyla uncertain about how to educate her daughters, especially because she has problems with one of them: "Maybe it is a sin that I make it easy on you [the daughter] or maybe I should be like the old parents, hit you. Yes, I mistreated my oldest daughter, well, I hit her a lot; I am not complaining, she is a very responsible person while I educated the other daughter in dialogue, but she is not responsible. Or maybe adolescence is very heavy on her, I don't know" (sighing). Neyla's words give us an idea of the troubles women have with their own education, their private doubts, and the world around them. After all, if they change, then the world has to change with them or they become "very emotional," as Neyla ponders. Nonetheless, the women of grassroots organizations are definitely changing their worlds. They use the support the NGOs give them to expand their knowledge, while they use the courts and other state services to fight violence in their families. Neyla also went to court to obtain alimony after her partner had left her. But most of all, women inform and support each other through their organizations, they disperse the information they receive from workshops to other women, and they help each other to reflect about their lives, even if that is not without difficulties and doubts.

Conclusion

In this chapter, we have seen how male authority over women is often reinforced through violence. Men tell their wives where their "place" is, and especially where it is not. Above all, husbands fear their wives' participation in activities outside the home, probably because such activities might affect their "natural" authority over women through the changing gender relations these activities provoke. The idea of women's responsibility for the family's well-being is often used against those who want to perform other tasks as well. Indeed, women are accused of being "bad mothers" as soon as they participate in women's organizations. Men may view their wives' participation in women's organizations as a direct threat to the established power relations in the household and a motivation for severe domestic conflicts.[21] For men, women's organizations are the embodiment of changing gender relations; it is in the organizations that women learn to read and write, to speak up, to defend themselves, and to negotiate at a political level. After one listens to the stories of leaders of grassroots organizations, such as Teodomira, Gloria, or Emma, the use of their collective representation as organized mothers to legitimize their public activities to their partners, makes sense. Such a strategy also links up to the political use of motherhood as a shield against violence.

The emphasis placed on women's responsibility for the family is also found in state policies against domestic violence. Although the measures followed national and international trends highlighting women's right to a life without violence, initially the Peruvian state—supported by the international financial institutions—sought to protect the structure of the family before the rights of women. Incorporating conciliation as a first and compulsory step after violent domestic conflicts meant that women were supposed to solve their problems within the existing violent, authoritarian, and unequal family structures. Implicitly, this suggests that women's rights were indeed subordinated to family unity, and thus to the authority of men. Moreover, the emphasis on the unity of the family suggests that violence against women is not endemic, but rather, occasional and restricted to certain families perceived to be of a lower class, economically poor and ethnically belonging to the "lower" strata. Such a focus glosses over the relationship between an authoritarian, racist, and sexist culture and the violence with which authority is often enforced.

Given that Peru was still ruled by an authoritarian regime when the first laws were passed, this lack of adequate protection against violence should not surprise us. As we have seen in earlier chapters, the interests of the Fujimori government lay with sending the message to the world that they were guiding Peru into "modernity." Women-friendly policies and legislation were part of this carefully constructed image and seemed less concerned with the actual transformation of social relations. Thus, as Virginia Vargas observes (2002, 213), the rising awareness among women and the actual granting of legal rights "took place within a wider context of minimal respect for citizens' rights." Despite the expansion of formal rights, in practice the exercise of rights was often constrained by the persistent and unaddressed institutional discrimination based on gender,

---

21. The idea of changing gender roles being embedded in larger social transformations that change, but not necessarily increase, motivations for violent spousal conflict is argued by Moore (1994) and Tinsman (1997).

race, and class, reinforcing existing inequalities. In that light, the effectiveness of policies against domestic violence is, like the struggle for women's rights in general, indeed linked to broader measures of democratization and the expansion and consolidation of citizenship. There must be the political will to combat endemic authoritarianism, violence, and inequality, not only at home, but also in institutions and the country at large. The implementation of old plans and new policies by the transition government after the fall of the Fujimori regime in late 2000 further suggests that the development of adequate policies to combat violence against women does indeed go hand in hand with the democratization of government.

Nevertheless, the new policy framework designed after 2001 has not yet solved the problem of pervasive institutional racism and sexism. Existing patterns of gendered authoritarianism and inequality are important components of the persistence of violence against women. We have seen how authorities whose task it is to protect women interpret women's rights as conditioned by factors such as class and ethnicity—they judge women's "worth" according to racist and sexist views. Some authorities actually reinforce images of women as architects of their own misfortune and as responsible for the cohesion of the family no matter what, which leads to a silent confirmation of men's right to dominate women. Police officers, judges, and doctors are still too much part of this gendered authoritarianism to be able to be champions of women's rights and equal citizenship. As a consequence, women have had to rely on themselves and each other in order to change violent family situations. More than actual enforcement, the legislation against domestic violence helps women in their conviction that they are within their rights to resist violence and demand change. The law—whose contents are actively dispersed by both NGOs and the state—gives women a tool in their resistance against authoritarian violence: whereas Teodomira lied to her husband, she was proud to tell me that her daughter would go the police. Thus, legislation and training offered by NGOs support women in a slow but steady process of empowerment that has its roots in women's own networks—just as we saw in the case of food distributions. A recent survey among women in four provinces of Ayacucho showed that women who participated in organizations were *less* likely to suffer domestic violence than those who did not, a result contrary to the earlier cited survey from 1998 carried out by Gonzales de Olarte and Gavilano Llosa.[22] Through their collective action and the experience of some thirty-five years of organizing, women are gaining ground in their fight for women's rights.

---

22. Programa Integral de la Lucha Contra la Violencia Familiar y Sexual (2005) as compared to Gonzales de Olarte and Gavilano Llosa (1998).

However, women's personal struggles against violent authoritarianism also present a tremendous task: because women are responsible for the children, they are also held responsible for changing family communication. As we saw in Neyla's reflection, this is neither an easy nor an automatic process.

6

REVISITING WOMEN

In 2006, I went back to Peru to start a new research project and visit old friends. I visited women I had interviewed in 2000–2003 in Lima and Ayacucho. In Ayacucho, the first thing that caught my eye was a glossy wall poster announcing an event. I looked at it not to find out what was going on in the city, but because the name on the poster sounded familiar: it was Vilma Ortega, long-time president of the Departmental Federation of Clubes de Madres of Ayacucho and one of the women who had played a key role in the fieldwork I carried out for this book. The poster, a homage to her work, included a portrait of her looking pensive while the "masses" cheered her on in the back. The poster urged the public to follow Vilma's example in her struggle for social change and justice, "Hasta la Victoria Final," until the final victory. Such revolutionary language in a city that until recently had been the center of Shining Path activity did not surprise me too much. During my last visit with Vilma in 2003, she made it clear that she had directed the Federation of Clubes de Madres into an alliance with a newly established socialist-nationalist political organization called Inkari. Inkari uses the symbolism and mythology of a precolonial Andeanism and builds on the political thought of early twentieth-century intellectual and hero José Carlos Mariátegui. The political ideology espoused by Inkari refers back to imaginary constructions of what Peru was in the past and should be in the future, continuing a debate that preoccupied intellectuals throughout the twentieth century. Inkari explicitly reinforces the idea of the existence of an Inca communism while also incorporating elements of Marxist-Leninism. Although Inkari seems popular among certain sectors of Ayacuchano society, it did not have any visibility during the 2006 elections and has not found any further evident support beyond Ayacucho and a Limeño migrant community.[1] Nevertheless, for Vilma and several other women's leaders, Inkari seemed to offer new opportunities.

People like Vilma, with a track record of participation in women's organizations, leadership and risk-taking during the war years, and a turbulent personal history, are often ambitious. The women's organization was too small for Vilma, while departmental politics was still too much a man's business, or perhaps a middle-class business. For self-educated women such as Vilma, the top of a women's organization seemed to be the highest public position one could reach. But Vilma was young and single, her children were old enough to take care of themselves, she had won the court battle over alimony from her abusive husband, and her commercial activities gave her the means to make her a living. After some five years of directing the Departmental Federation of Clubes de Madres, Vilma wanted to go into formal politics. Inkari was there, literally around the corner.

The poster highlighting Vilma's dedication to the Federation of Clubes de Madres, the people of Ayacucho, and the "struggle" was actually a commemoration. Vilma, her daughter Kelly Alanya told me later that afternoon, had died in a traffic accident several months before my visit. Many roads in the Andes are bumpy dirt roads that flood during the rainy season and border deadly ravines. Drivers of *micros* (small buses) and long-distance, bigger buses are notorious for their speeding and general recklessness. Buses are often involved in accidents, which are often fatal. Vilma had been traveling the department by bus, as she often did, on her way to meet women's leaders elsewhere, to teach a course, or to discuss issues. She had died immediately, an observer had assured Kelly.

Kelly, a recently graduated anthropologist in her early twenties who had married ten days before her mother's death, was preparing to leave the country when I saw her again. She had taken care of her two younger siblings for six months, but, as the larger family agreed, Kelly should not miss her chance to live a happy, and new, life with her American husband in the north. Kelly's ambitions are not in politics as were her mother's. Although she lived through the war years as a child, saw family members being killed and disappeared, and had firsthand experience of her mother's struggle for life and livelihood, she grew up with far better opportunities than her mother did. Kelly was able to go to university and study anthropology, the discipline of foreigners who come to Peru to observe its culture. Kelly's interest in the struggle of her mother and her contemporaries is framed by this distance created by education. She worked on a project to document

---

1. Inkari had a Web site as of 2006: http://www.inkariperu.com.

Fig. 1 Commemoration poster for Vilma Ortega Quispe, president of the Departmental Federation of Clubes de Madres of Ayacucho.

the history of the Federation of Clubes de Madres, and she went on fieldwork visiting rural communities and learning about her own heritage through the eyes of the participant observer. She also helped me communicate with Quechua-speaking women at the police station for battered women. Instead of fighting for public voice and recognition, Kelly wanted to start her own family, perhaps work as a teacher, and do a masters in anthropology in Washington, DC. When I saw her in April 2006, Kelly was still in shock at her mother's death, and seemed both happy and distressed talking about her. She grumbled about the funeral: people had contested Vilma's leadership before she died, and many women had withdrawn from the Federation of Clubes de Madres because of her political involvement. However, during the funeral they were all there, praising her work, lauding her legacy. For Kelly, this demonstrated people's hypocrisy and, at the same time, represented an affirmation of her mother's reputation as a dedicated *luchadora,* someone who fights for rights and livelihood. However, in reality, Vilma had made enemies among local leaders and was disliked for her authoritarian ways and her political dogmatism. NGOs that had previously worked with the Federation had withdrawn their projects, since NGOs do not like to fund political organizations.

Kelly's observation about the attention attracted by Vilma's funeral has still another dimension. In the Andes, buses tumble down the ravines rather frequently. Such events generally merit an article in the local newspaper, and perhaps a short notice in the national papers. Sometimes a new government starts an infrastructure project and the construction of better roads; often such projects are abandoned halfway. Bigger, Lima-based bus companies have realized that there is a market for "safe" traveling, promising well-paying costumers two drivers on a long-distance route instead of one, and assuring riders about the quality of the bus itself. Most bus companies, however, cannot promise such luxuries. The danger of these mountain routes, and the yearly victims they create, does not seem to generate significant concern among the ruling elites. Of course, such a situation again highlights the differentiated meaning of citizenship in Peru, and even the differentiated value of human life. Nevertheless, Vilma's sudden death was commemorated widely, her funeral was attended by hundreds of people, posters were distributed throughout the town, and a Google search shows that she is remembered and honored on the Web sites of several national organizations and a Yahoo discussion group. The dedication given to Vilma Ortega's memory suggests that she had succeeded in establishing a legitimate and widely respected platform for poor Andean women. Kelly's decision to migrate, carrying a diploma in anthropology in her suitcase, might be the unintended certificate of Vilma's—and her vehicle of success, the Federation of Clubes de Madres'—achievement.[2]

April 2006, when I visited Ayacucho and spoke with Kelly, was also election month. Election posters were everywhere, and candidates visited the main square. It was, as always, a turbulent election between extremes. The visit of candidate Alan García was received with general tension. Hundreds of Special Forces soldiers patrolled the streets of Ayacucho, while young APRA supporters, *Apristas,* were bused in from surrounding provinces. The elderly ladies of ANFASEP, the organization of family members of the disappeared established at the height of political violence in 1983, were not intimidated by the aggressive chanting of the *Apristas,* and staged a brave counterprotest in front of the church. These women accused García of human rights abuses during his previous government (1985–90). It came to a confrontation, and a young worker of a supportive NGO took a beating aimed at the ANFASEP *señoras.*

The other electoral candidate who generated tension and conflict during the 2006 election campaigns was Ollanta Humala. The three Humala brothes, Antauro, Ulises, and Ollanta, all veterans of the Peruvian military, are associated with the ethnonationalist movement called *etnocaceristas.*[3] After a failed, and little supported, uprising against Alberto Fujimori in 2000, the brothers went different ways. Antauro staged a coup attempt in 2005, killing six people, Ulises continued the ethno-nationalist line, and Ollanta was successful in gaining widespread national support and almost winning the national elections of 2006. An ex-army officer with accusations of human rights abuses on his record, Ollanta counted on the support of some 60 percent of Ayacuchanos. With a rigid vision of the world, an authoritarian, populist, charismatic, young, energetic, antipolitical manner, and roots in the mestizo urban middle classes, Ollanta Humala appealed to a large segment of the disappointed people who did not benefit from the expanding export economy that Peru had experienced since the mid-1990s—that is, the majority of Andeans. But Ollanta was the moderate of the family: the political ideas of the imprisoned Antauro, voiced by Ulises, are racist, xenophobic, and offensive to some parts of the population, while correctly nationalist to others.[4]

---

2. For better or worse, migrating out of poverty, especially via such a legitimate way as marriage, is generally perceived as an achievement.

3. The *cacerista* part of the name is a reference to Andrés Avelino Cáceres, a Peruvian war hero from the War of the Pacific (1879–84), which Peru lost to Chile.

4. Jaime Bayly, Peru's favorite enfant terrible of the political interview, interrogated Ulises on his, and Antauro's, public statements. The interview can be seen on YouTube: http://youtube.com/watch?v=flpxKW_NBAA.

Fig. 2   Teodomira de la Cruz runs for congress with Avanza País. Poster hangs on the wall next to the newspapers she sells.

It was with the party of Ulises Humala, Avanza País, that I found one of my other interviewees. Teodomira de la Cruz had been the president of the provincial Federation of Mother Clubs in Ayacucho (FECMA) when I spoke with her in 2001. Like Vilma, Teodomira was ambitious and determined and made enemies among her peers while she was making her way in departmental politics. Like most Ayacuchanas, Teodomira had lived through much hardship during the 1980s and 1990s: she still lived in a house that had visibly been burned down several times, and she had lost several family members. I found her nervous, frightened, and suspicious. When I asked her for a personal interview in 2001, preferably in private, she invited me to her house at six o'clock in the morning, before daybreak. I found her living in one room with her three daughters, where they shared the bed. Teodomira and her daughters made a living by selling newspapers on a street corner. It was at her newspaper stall, looking for her in April 2006, where I saw her election poster as a candidate for Avanza País. Already back in 2001 when I first met her, and despite the fact that the family did not make much money, Teodomira spent as much time as she could in meetings and assemblies. She saw herself as a *luchadora*, someone who always participated and who took leadership positions. Her experiences during the war reflected this. Now, however, she was in need of finding a more public voice beyond the women's organizations. For her, the party of Ulises Humala was it.

Both Vilma and Teodomira were women who had made a career in women's organizations. Being of humble origins, they had not gone through formal higher education but, according to their own stories, grew up in families in which leadership and activism was valued. They were young women when war broke out, and they joined other women in their fight against violence and for life. Both became single mothers caring for several children. After the war, they turned into ambitious leaders whose capacity to lead and bring about positive change was constrained by their gender marginalization and their socioeconomic background. They chose very similar paths to gain a more public voice, deciding to join nationalist political parties that gave them an opportunity to participate. This opportunity was partly created by the Fujimori government's reforms: the 25 percent gender quota stipulated in 1998 for all party lists had greatly increased the number of women in national and local politics. However, for Teodomira and Vilma their place on party lists did not take them to congress: Ulises Humala lost and his party disappeared, and, had Vilma's ambitions not been thwarted by a fatal accident, they might well have been by the dogmatism and parochialism of Inkari. Both women were also constrained by their own politics. Already in 2002, the two women did not speak to each other, greatly jeopardizing the collaboration between the organizations they headed (the provincial and departmental federations of clubes de madres). Vilma brought the departmental federation into Inkari, a path that not all member organizations wanted. As an NGO worker once commented to me in a conversation about the tensions in the women's organizations in Ayacucho, this generation of leaders was as authoritarian as the previous generation had been, but did not generate the matriarchal respect that their predecessors had. Teodora Ayme, founder and matriarch of FEDECMA from the late 1980s to mid-1990s, had expanded and strengthened the organization and had been able to keep the peace through the respect she commanded. Vilma and Teodomira, however, were confronted with a younger generation, a more democratic generation perhaps, and definitely as ambitious, conscious, and involved as they were themselves.

I also returned to the town of San Miguel, province of La Mar, department of Ayacucho. There I found Nelly Mejia, formerly leader of a provincial chapter of the Federation of Clubes de Madres but now retired because of the Federation's alliance with Inkari. Nelly had been a great help during my earlier fieldwork and had introduced me to many men and women in San Miguel. Nelly had also lived through traumatic experiences in the 1980s and succeeded in rebuilding her life again. When I met her in 2006, Nelly lived with her three daughters between Ayacucho and San Miguel, traveling back and forth, a dangerous journey of approximately four hours by public transport along the highland roads. Nelly's experiences and ambitions had led her in a different direction than Vilma's and Teodomira's. Soft-spoken and patient, Nelly listened to the stories of the women who came to see her and advised them on improving their situation. Together with several other ex-Federation leaders in San Miguel, she had set up an office "for the well-being of children, adolescents, and women," DEPROMUNA (Defensoría y Promoción de la Mujer, del Niño y Adolescente). She worked with feminist NGOs based in Ayacucho and facilitated workshops on sexual and reproductive health, on domestic violence, and on women's rights. She also helped women to obtain alimony and the recognition and registration of children (a requirement for obtaining alimony). Nelly did not oppose the persistent male-dominated political culture, but rather, collaborated with male leaders and tried to involve them in her projects. She did not necessarily advise women to leave abusive husbands, either. Rather, Nelly worked within the system and tried to change behavior through improved communication.

The experience of a friend of Nelly's, a woman whose story is told in chapter 5 under the pseudonym Gloria, was less fortunate. Although her violent husband left her alone these days, her adolescent daughter became pregnant. Although Gloria had been a leader in women's organizations for many years and had seen and experienced the difficulties that young women often went through, at that moment in 2006 she could not overcome her anger at her daughter and refused to help her. Her daughter, in Gloria's view, should have known better, just as she herself should not have stayed with an abusive husband for so long. However, having sound knowledge about reproductive health does not necessarily give people the ability (or will) to avoid pregnancy. This ability is further diminished in young women, who often feel more inhibited in negotiating safe sexual relations. Gloria's daughter had behaved as many adolescents in Peru, and indeed everywhere, and was perhaps just unfortunate to become pregnant outside of a more responsible relationship.

Nevertheless, Nelly and Gloria were also aware that adolescents needed better information about sexual and reproductive health. The organization to which Gloria and Nelly now belonged, DEPROMUNA, supported a project that sought to inform adolescents about reproductive health and sexuality, while also aiming to empower both boys and girls in managing their bodily health better. A new series of workshops was set up by the feminist NGO Manuela Ramos that used the same techniques as discussed in chapter 4. Facilitators helped a select group of youngsters in drawing up *autodiagnósticos,* which were aimed at helping them to recognize problems and solutions. As Nelly and Gloria recognized, these workshops were important to improve young people's sexual health. In addition, or perhaps even more important, these workshops helped boys and girls speak up about issues related to their health, their bodies, and their sexuality, something they could not do at school or at home. *Autodiagnósticos* drawn up in early 2006 with youngsters in communities neighboring San Miguel showed that before entering the workshop, at least half of the participants had a basic knowledge about their reproductive bodies that would enable them to avoid pregnancy.[5] Observation in San Miguel, a rural town connected by dirt roads to the rest of the department, also revealed that the Internet now reached seemingly remote areas, with two Internet cafés constantly buzzing with the delight of girls and boys in school uniforms. This, of course, has increased access to information substantially—and generated concern among some parents. Despite this increased connectivity to the wider world, the transcriptions of the *autodiagnósticos* made among rural and periurban youngsters in January 2006 also suggested that participating girls (from ten to fourteen years of age) were extremely shy, to the point of being unable to speak up without covering their mouths with their hands. This shyness was worse among more rural girls than among girls who grew up in more urban settings. The workshops were there to help them to speak up, learn, and reflect on their lives and may have been a good resource for the youngsters whom Nelly and Gloria saw in their daily activities as well.

Revisiting Policies

Although the life stories of Vilma, Teodomira, Nelly, and Gloria are marked by their personalities, the decisions they made throughout their lives, and the circumstances they encountered, they are also intimately linked with the contemporary history of Peru and its changing social structures. All four women were of indigenous descent but had become urbanized to a certain extent—Vilma and Teodomira lived in "human settlements" in the city of Ayacucho, Nelly commuted between her family home in San Miguel and her own home in Ayacucho, while Gloria grew up and lived

---

5. *Autodiagnósticos* prepared in the province of Changallo, Department of Ayacucho, south of San Miguel, in January 2006. Transcriptions were provided by Manuela Ramos Ayacucho.

in the urbanizing provincial town of San Miguel. Vilma and Nelly also traveled regularly to Lima, where they had family and organizational activities, and Nelly traveled to Montreal once, where she attended an international conference for indigenous peoples. Gloria and Teodomira, in turn, were local leaders who traveled to more rural communities, both higher up into the Andes as well as toward the *ceja de selva*, the communities toward the eastern jungle areas. Vilma's daughter Kelly's migration to the United States completes these women's inclusion in the contemporary times of global networking.

This increasing mobility went hand in hand with increased social and political inclusion. Just like many other poor and indigenous or mestiza women living in the margins of the state (Das and Poole 2004), they had learned to speak up in their homes and make claims on the state through their participation in women's organizations and the alliances these organizations formed with NGOs, political parties, and state institutions. Although the food aid policies of the 1980s and particularly the 1990s largely appropriated women's unpaid labor to alleviate poverty on the one hand, and included popular sectors in a corrupt political system on the other, they also contributed to the persistence and legitimization of a myriad of women's organizations in both rural and urban contexts. If anything, these organizations provided a fantastic educational path that included leadership and organizational skills, political skills, and gender awareness. At the same time, the clientelism that was increasingly institutionalized during the 1990s, and the undercurrent of stereotyping and discrimination based on gender, race, and class in both the design and implementation of the food aid policies, were a severe constraint on the democratization of the grassroots women's organizations and contributed to internal conflicts and fragmentation.

The class and gender position of organized women targeted by food aid programs in populated urban areas and their hinterlands was instrumentally used by subsequent governments, but especially the Fujimori regime, which used the rhetoric of women as carers in the community, sacrificing themselves in alleviating poverty. The grassroots organizations themselves also used "motherhood" as a useful justification for public activity in the light of both political and domestic violence. In doing so, participating women gained some autonomy and expanded their agency, even if this was done within a corrupt system. But they were not the most marginalized in a hierarchically divided country. During the 1990s, when an increasingly authoritarian and corrupt government under the leadership of Fujimori and his cronies sought to reduce poverty according to contemporary neoliberal models, poor, indigenous women living in rural and periurban areas were actively targeted to reduce the number of children they had. The design of the program, using a quota system for the regions where the facilities were most lacking and fertility was high, but especially the implementation of the program, revealed how gender, race, and class intersect in the lives of all Peruvians. The targeted women bore the consequences of these inequalities.

The often-violent discrimination against poor indigenous women was also prevalent in the policies designed to combat violence against women. Although the services discussed—police stations, women's centers, conciliation, and later mediation offices—were designed to counter such violence, women often found themselves in situations where either the abuse continued or where the denunciation of a violent partner or husband did not have any consequences at all. Although these institutional abuses and inadequacies were not part of the intention of policy, the design of policy did reflect the discriminative and authoritarian structures of Peruvian society. These structures were hardly challenged as part of the policy; many professionals working for these programs obviously lacked respect for women, poor people, and indigenous people, and were not sufficiently trained in women's issues and gender perspectives. At the same time, resources were not allocated to facilitate less aggressive and corrupt services. The policies stood too much on their own, fragmented from other initiatives in civil society and not addressed at reforming the wider institutions the programs were part of, such as through poverty-reduction strategies, health sector reform, and security sector reform.

This fragmentation of service delivery and policy has fed into, and is arguably furthered by, the interlinked processes of neoliberalization of the political economy and the NGOization of civil society. The interventions of the feminist NGO Manuela Ramos, discussed in chapters 4 and 5, do not stand alone. Peruvian society is part of the global trend NGOs becoming involved in the areas of gender, human rights, education, environment, poverty reduction, and advocacy. Questions of accountability, professionalization, representation, and reach are just some of the widely debated issues. In Peru, the relation between NGOs, the state, and the beneficiary grassroots is not always clear; what is clear is that NGOs have become indispensable for social development, in particular in the area of gender equity.

A return visit to the government facilities that are supposed to address domestic violence in San Miguel and Ayacucho revealed that this sector thrives on the interventions of NGOs. Increasingly, professionals working in this field believe that violence against women and children is high as a consequence of the political conflict of the previous decades. When I was in the region in 2006, psychologists, lawyers, prosecutors, social workers, and grassroots women's leaders such as Nelly were involved in addressing family violence from a postconflict perspective. One NGO, CEPRODEP, set up workshops with Nelly and her group in San Miguel to help men and women to process traumatic experiences and to help couples reflect on their current situation. In addition to partner violence, physical violence against children also seemed to be common and is largely seen as legitimate punishment for disobedience (Programa Integral de la Lucha Contra la Violencia Familiar y Sexual 2005). Denunciations of domestic violence are rising; a 2005 survey in the department of Ayacucho concluded that 54 percent of women had suffered beatings at least once, and 30.7 percent of surveyed women (#1.046) experienced regular beatings from their partners (ibid.). Denunciations of sexual violence against minors are on the rise, and courts are keen to sentence men who sexually abuse children.[6] In line with such trends, there is increased public outcry about such abuse, as revealed by the widespread support for Alan García's electoral proposal to reintroduce the death penalty for child molesters, though the proposal was not enacted. Nevertheless, all this indicates that awareness of the high incidence of intimate violence in Peru has increased.

However, at the same time, a process of resource reallocation has slowly dismantled the discussed National Plan to Combat Violence Against Women. In Ayacucho, the state program was saved with the help of a Belgian cooperation fund, which invested in an Integral Program Against Family and Sexual Violence. This program developed strategies to support women socially and economically by reducing financial dependency, through, for example, helping women to produce artisanal crafts and clothing for sale in Lima and the United States. During my visit in 2006, the program had relocated since 2002 and was now strategically situated in the same building as the government's Centro de Emergencia Mujer. This CEM receives regular visits, despite the continuing lack of resources and the fragmentation of services. The CEM offers psychological support and procedural and legal advice, but has to send women to the police stations and the public prosecutor to make a formal complaint. The services are not integrated, as was the initial aim of the CEMs. The police officers who dealt with domestic violence were the same ones I had met during my visit in 2002. According to the officers, the situation had not improved and resources continued to be cut back, while they received an increasing number of denunciations. And

---

6. According to the workers at the Integral Program against Family and Sexual Violence in Ayacucho, a quarter of all criminal offense convictions in the Ayacucho court of law are for sexual violence against minors.

while in 2002 the unit for women had its own premises, separated from other police units, now it was housed in the same building, which has not improved accessibility. The separated office had the disadvantage of being very open, providing no privacy at all, but the new office required passing front guards and crossing several corridors before finding the correct room. Entering into the power display of men, uniforms, and weapons that this police station offers is not a comforting experience. Although a young female officer was trained to deal with cases of domestic abuse, she was new and had to compete with the established male policemen, who were dismissive of her when I asked to speak to her. Interviewed public prosecutors, CEM personnel, and users were unanimously negative about the police's effectiveness and their lack of sensitivity with regard to family violence.

The police office in San Miguel only had one officer, who was replaced by the state every forty-five days. Although according to Nelly the last two officers had been good and cooperative, the lack of continuity does not help attempts to provide protection for battered women and children. The state had also invested in a DEMUNA, an Office for the Defense of Children and Adolescents. This office, Nelly said, was directed by a psychologist from Arequipa who did not speak Quechua and acted in an authoritarian way, decided arbitrarily how couples should solve their problems. The psychologist's preferred solution was reconciliation achieved by getting spouses to sign agreements, a method that had been largely rejected, as we saw in chapter 5. In response, Nelly and her colleagues set up their own center, DEPROMUNA, where they received approximately three women a day. This was a creative solution and proved popular among users; both men and women respected Nelly, and some women even talked about abuse that they would otherwise keep quiet about, such as sexual coercion in marriage.[7] However, Nelly's work also generated further tension with the DEMUNA in San Miguel. Of course, Nelly is not paid for her work and, in her own words, depends on "small jobs that reach her because people know her." If women need more practical help from DEPROMUNA—documents or house visits, for example—then they have to pay for printing paper or transport costs. This is a less than ideal situation, and again suggests that women are left to their own devices and are given little help to develop strategies to solve problems such as violence in the family.

In this chapter, I will not reevaluate completely the studied programs addressing food distribution, reproductive health, and domestic violence.

---

7. Police and CEM personnel indicated that women do not talk about sexual violence. The police officer whom I asked about marital rape raised his eyebrows in answer.

However, these stories do tell us something about the post-2000 evolution of such policies and the relationship between the state and poor women. The governments that succeeded Fujimori's regime have not adequately addressed the problem of the fragmentation of social programs and the limited accountability of these programs to the targeted population. The minimum of accountability demanded in the national political arena as a result of pressure from civil society has often led to excesses being dealt with through the political process. Since the fall of Fujimori, the enormous corruption in PRONAA, the institution responsible for food distribution, has been under increased scrutiny and continuous reform. However, child malnutrition is still at 30 percent, and women's voluntary work is still key to food aid policies. After the sterilization scandal of the mid-1990s, population policies became more conservative and restrictive again; voluntary sterilization was banished, and women were prevented from adequately managing their fertility and sexuality. Recently, the government of Alan García has revived the debate about women's reproductive rights, and access to contraceptive methods and abortion is on the political agenda again. In the meantime, NGOs provide sex education, gender awareness, and reproductive health workshops to adolescents and adults. Despite increased public attention, interventions against domestic violence are mainly in the hands of community-based organizations and externally funded NGOs. As informants in Ayacucho and San Miguel indicated, many state representatives still actively encourage conciliation between spouses, even when there is evidence of severe physical violence, while CEM personnel face a continuous threat of program discontinuation and a lack of resources. Overall, despite its intentions, the state's investment is inadequate and its laws and institutions are incapable of combating such forms of intimate violence. These observations are supported by a recent UN report that investigated Peru's compliance with the Convention on the Elimination of All Forms of Discrimination Against Women, and a shadow report written by the four most important feminist NGOs in Peru, Manuela Ramos, Flora Tristán, DEMUS, and CLADEM (CEDAW 2007; Flora Tristán 2006). Both reports, unfortunately, suggest that there has been no real improvement since the early 1990s, despite all the government policies and institutions in place to deal with poverty, population growth, violence, and gender discrimination in general. The gap between discourse and practice, or between policy and implementation, continues to obstruct women's full and equal participation in civil life.

At the same time, the personal stories narrated here suggest many new trends. This second generation of women working in grassroots organizations, those who organized the existing groups into federations and networks, found new directions for themselves and for their organizations. By 2006, food distribution was definitely not the central concern of the Ayacuchan federated *clubes de madres,* although many do still support *comedores populares* and work closely with the mothers in the *vaso de leche* groups. But other, more political issues had taken center stage. FEDECMA entered formal politics—albeit supporting a party with few members or supporters—while the original leaders of the provincial Federation of Clubes de Madres in La Mar, San Miguel, set up offices to deal with women's rights more generally. The women in La Mar, including Nelly and Gloria, were also in the process of writing a petition to provincial and local authorities to pay serious attention to women's rights. Women have taken a big step forward and entered a public sphere in which the perception of women as passive recipients and active carers has been superseded: they are proving that they can and want far more than caregiving, and that they are more perceptive and creative than those trapped in the clientelism and disinterest that permeates state programs and institutions. Although this may seem banal, a cliché even, I believe that considering the negative press women's groups have received since the mid 1990s, it is necessary to emphasize these positive outcomes.

Another important question arises: does the increased women's participation at the grassroots also contribute to substantial changes in gender ideology? The participating women are not necessarily self-identified feminists, and women have different opinions about gender and gender equality and how to pursue more equality. For example, Nelly's project in San Miguel aims to change people's attitudes and behaviors, encouraging women and young people to talk about abuse and sexuality and expecting men to accept responsibility for their violence and change their behavior. At the same time, her work does not defy existing structures per se—she counters abuse, not existing gender roles. She has chosen a nonconfrontational strategy of working with both women and men in order to improve communication and general well-being. Other women use similar strategies, such as ex-leaders of *comedores populares* and *clubes de madres* who set up microenterprises involving ex-members of their organizations and strongly collaborate with the men in their families and communities.[8] While such strategies are also potentially transformative, many projects focus less on the politics of challenging gender ideology and more on pacifying gender

---

8. For a detailed analysis of women and microenterprises in popular neighborhoods in Lima, see Ypeij (2006).

relations and improving collaboration between the sexes. To a certain extent, the feminist organization Manuela Ramos works along similar lines. This strategy of consciousness-raising and empowerment without directly confronting gendered roles seems to be in contrast with that followed by women of a more radical feminist disposition, who contest male power and the division of labor between men and women and who celebrate sexual diversity. Such more contentious politics is favored by the feminist organizations Flora Tristán and DEMUS, and by grassroots organizers such as Delia Zamudio, who set up the Refugee Center in San Juan de Lurigancho, and grassroots feminist and activist Rosa Dueñas. A third strategy is favored not only by professional middle-class women, but by grassroots women such as would-be politicians Teodomira de la Cruz and Vilma Ortega, who seek political power and do not necessarily advocate women's rights as a first priority. This tells us, then, that women's organizations were and are very diverse and deploy many different strategies to gain different benefits. All these examples also demonstrate that these strategies generally expand women's agency, even if that sometimes means that women prove to be as corrupt, violent, or authoritarian as men can be.

The ways in which race serves to order Peruvian society hierarchically have been a central theme in this book. They were also central to the lives of Nelly, Vilma, and Teodomira. All three women considered themselves of indigenous descent, and all spoke Quechua as a first language; however, they were "urbanized" women as well. Vilma and Teodomira's membership in ethnonationalist groups could be interpreted as an example of ethnic resistance to *criollo* hegemony, of course. It is more likely, however, that these parties appealed to them because they offered a certain type of populist and localist politics that was not offered by other, Lima-based parties. At the same time, championing Indianness as a political identity can also have its merits: it can help mobilize support and provide opportunities—as in the case of Nelly, who traveled to Canada as an indigenous representative. However, indigenous identity for Nelly, Vilma and Teodomira was, above all, part of daily life, not necessarily an element in a defined political project. Nevertheless, these women's Andean roots have influenced their position in the national hierarchy. Just like gender, ethnicity can thus be a marker of differentiation that negatively influences access to citizenship and the ability to gain a sense of belonging, but it can also serve as basis for solidarity and struggle. As these stories show, these identity markers do not mean that individuals can easily be grouped in homogeneous categories, or that grassroots women have similar desires and ambitions.

The intersecting inequalities of gender, race, and class are fluid and real at the same time; they shape social divisions, but they can likewise shape activism and increase sociopolitical awareness. These pillars of discrimination and identity are reflected in the state's institutions, in civil society and its associations and organizations, and in personal, affective relationships, including those that take place within the family. The fluidity and meaning of gender, race, and class are likewise continuously renegotiated and redefined through the interaction between state, society, and individual. Social policy and legislation certainly contribute to challenging inequalities, but often in a two-steps-forward, one-step-back manner. By examining the workings of social policy and legislation, this book has shown how state institutions reflected the existing racism and sexism prevalent in society, and also how grassroots organizations in alliance with professional and activist organizations were able to influence and use policy and legislation to pressure local representatives of state institutions and even national politics. This book thus demonstrates that the so-called state-society partnership in policy and service delivery (a term characteristic of neoliberal times) is just as conflictive as it is productive. In other words, the disjuncture between the ambitions formulated in policy and their implementation, I have suggested, results from intersecting inequalities prevalent in state institutions and society alike. However, these tensions in policy and practice and the underlying inequalities were also contested and reshaped by the women involved.

REFERENCES

Abel, Christopher, and Colin M. Lewis, eds. 2002. *Exclusion and Engagement: Social policy in Latin America*. London: University of London, Institute of Latin American Studies.
Aguirre, Katie. 1991. "Ni con hambre ni terror nos detendran por la paz" reafirman madres de comedores populares frente a amenzas terroristas. *El Peruano*, September 20. Warmi CD-ROM CENDOC-Mujer.
Alvarez, Julia. 1994. *In the Time of the Butterflies*. Chapel Hill, N.C.: Algonquin Books.
Alvarez, Sonia E. 1997. Contradictions of a "Women's Space" in a Male-Dominated State: The Political Role of the Commissions of the Status of Women in Postauthoritarian Brazil. In *Women, International Development, and Politics: The Bureaucratic Mire*, edited by K. Staudt. Philadelphia: Temple University Press.
———. 1998. Latin American Feminisms "Go Global": Trends of the 1990s and Challenges for the New Millenium. In Alvarez, Dagnino, and Escobar 1998.
Alvarez, Sonia E., Evelina Dagnino, and Arturo Escobar, eds. 1998. *Cultures of Politics, Politics of Culture: Revisioning Latin American Social Movements*. Boulder: Westview Press.
Alvarez, Sonia E., Elisabeth Jay Friedman, Ericka Beckman, Maylei Blackwell, Norma Stoltz Chinchilla, Nathalie Lebon, Marysa Navarro, and Marcela Ríos Tobar. 2003. Encountering Latin American and Caribbean Feminisms. *Signs* 28 (2), http://www.journals.uchicago.edu/doi/pdf/10.1086/342589.
Alvarez Rodrich, Augusto, and Julio Cotler. 1995. *Perú, 1964–1994: Economía, sociedad y política*. Lima: Instituto de Estudios Peruanos.
Anderson, Jeanine. 1998. Peruvian Women and the Peruvian State. In Lycklama à Nijeholt, Vargas, and Wieringa 1998.
Andreas, Carol. 1985. *When Women Rebel: The Rise of Popular Feminism in Peru*. Westport, Conn.: L. Hill.
Aplicación de la ley de protección frente a la violencia familiar 26260. 2003–2004. Fascimile. In *Encuentro de redes y mesas inter-institucionales que trabajan en el tema de violencia familiar en Lima metropolitana*. Villa El Salvador, Villa María del Triunfo.
Appelbaum, Nancy P., Anne S. Macpherson, and Karin Alejandra Rosemblatt. 2003. *Race and Nation in Modern Latin America*. Chapel Hill: University of North Carolina Press.
Aramburú, Carlos E. 2002a. *Derechos humanos y salud: Vinculando perspectivas*. Lima: Flora Tristán, APRODEH, CIES.

———. 2002b. Politics and Reproductive Health: A Dangerous Connection. Paper read at Interregional Seminar on Reproductive Health, Unmet Needs, and Poverty, Bangkok, Thailand.

Aripurnami, Sita. 1997. Reproductive Rights Between Control and Resistance: A Reflection on the Discourse of Population Policy in Indonesia. M.Sc. diss., London School of Economics, London.

Arroyo, Juan. 2002. *La salud peruana en el siglo XXI: Retos y propuestas de política.* Lima: Consorcio de Investigación Económica y Social.

Ballón Echegaray, Eduardo, and Maruja Barrig. 1986. *Movimientos sociales y democracia: La fundación de un nuevo orden.* Lima: DESCO.

Barrantes, Carmen. 1990. Mujeres crean Red Nacional. *Mujer y Sociedad* 10 (32): 30–31.

Barret, Christopher. 1998. Food Aid: Is It Development Assistance, Trade Promotion, Both, or Neither? *American Journal of Agricultural Economics* 80 (3): 566–71.

———. 2001. Does Food Aid Stabilize Food Availability? *Economic Development and Cultural Change* 49 (2): 335–49.

———. 2002. Food Aid and Commercial International Food Trade. Background paper prepared for the Trade and Markets Divisions, Organisation for Economic Co-operation and Development.

Barrig, Maruja. 1986. Democracia emergente: Movimientos de mujeres. In *Movimientos sociales y democracia: La fundación de un nuevo orden*, edited by E. Ballón Echegaray. Lima: DESCO.

———. 1988. *De vecinas a ciudadanas: La mujer en el desarrollo urbano.* Lima: SUMBI.

———. 1994. The Difficult Equilibrium Between Bread and Roses: Women's Organizations and Democracy in Peru. In Jaquette 1994.

———. 1998. Female Leadership, Violence, and Citizenship in Peru. In Jaquette and Wolchik 1998.

———. 2001. *El mundo al revés: Imágenes de la mujer indígena.* Buenos Aires: Consejo Latinoamericano de Ciencias Sociales, Agencia Sueca de Desarrollo Internacional.

———. 2002. La persistencia de la memoria: Feminismo y estado en el Perú de los 90. In *Sociedad civil, esfera pública y democratización en América Latina: Andes y Cono Sur*, edited by A. Panfichi. Lima: Pontificia Universidad Católica del Perú; Mexico City: Fondo de Cultura Económica.

Bebbington, Anthony, Samuel Hickey, and Diana Mitlin. 2008. *Can NGOs Make a Difference? The Challenge of Development Alternatives.* London: Zed Books.

Blondet, Cecilia. 1986. *Muchas vidas construyendo una identidad: Las mujeres pobladoras de un barrio limeño.* Lima: Instituto de Estudios Peruanos.

———. 1991. *Las mujeres y el poder: Una historia de Villa El Salvador.* Lima: Instituto de Estudios Peruanos.

———. 1995. El movimiento de mujeres en el Peru. In Alvarez Rodrich and Cutler 1995.

———. 1996. In No-Man's Land: Poor Women's Organziations and Political Violence in Lima's Neighborhoods. In *Emergences: Women's Struggles for Livelihood in Latin America*, edited by R. A. John Friedmann and Lilian Autler. Berkeley and Los Angeles: University of California Press.

———. 1998. *La emergencia de las mujeres en el poder: Hay cambios?* Lima: Instituto de Estudios Peruanos.

———. 1999. *Las mujeres y la política en la década de Fujimori.* Lima: Instituto de Estudios Peruanos.

———. 2002. *El encanto del Dictador*. Lima: Instituto de Estudios Peruanos.
Blondet, Cecilia, and Carmen Montero Checa. 1995. *Hoy: Menu popular: Comedores en Lima*. Serie Infancia y sociedad 3. Lima: Instituto de Estudios Peruanos, Unicef.
Blondet, Cecilia, Rosa Luisa Esquivel, Carmen Montero Checa, and Carmen Yon Leau. 1994. *La situación de la mujer en el Perú, 1980–1994*. Lima: Instituto de Estudios Peruanos.
Boesten, Jelke. 2007. Marrying the Man Who Raped You: Domesticating War Crimes in Ayacucho, Peru. In Pankhurst 2007.
———. 2008. Narrativas de sexo, violencia y disponibilidad: Raza, género y jerarquías de la violación en Perú. In *Raza, etnicidad y sexualidades: Ciudadanía y multiculturalismo en América Latina*, edited by Fernando Urrea Giraldo, Mara Viveros Vigoya, and Peter Wade. Bogota: Universidad Nacional de Colombia.
Boesten, Jelke, and Paulo Drinot. 2004. The Allure of Eugenics: Peru and the History Without People. Paper read at Economic and Social Research Council Seminar Series, Social Policy, Stability, and Exclusion in Latin America, at the Institute for Latin American Studies, London.
Bondi, Liz, and Nina Laurie. 2005. Working the Spaces of Neoliberalism: Activism, Professionalisation, and Incorporation. *Antipode* 37 (3): 393–401.
Bonfiglio, Giovanni. 1999. *Veinticinco años de debate sobre temas de población en la prensa peruana, 1974–1999*. Lima: Asociación Multidisciplinaria de la Investigación y Docencia en Población, AMIDEP.
Boserup, Ester. 1970. *Woman's Role in Economic Development*. London: Allen and Unwin.
Bourque, Susan, and Kay Warren. 1981. *Women of the Andes: Patriarchy and Social Change in Two Peruvian Towns*. Ann Arbor: University of Michigan Press.
Brah, Avtar, and Ann Phoenix. 2004. Ain't I a Woman? Revisiting Intersectionality. *Journal of International Women's Studies* 5 (3): 75–86.
Bunster, Ximena, and Elsa Chaney. 1985. *Sellers and Servants: Working Women in Lima, Peru*. New York: Praeger.
Burt, Jo-Marie. 1998. Shining Path and the "Decisive Battle" in Lima's Barriadas: The Case of Villa El Salvador. In Stern 1998.
Butler, Judith. 1999. *Gender Trouble: Feminism and the Subversion of Identity*. New York: Routledge.
Cadena, Marisol de la. 1991. "Las mujeres son mas Indias." Etnicidad y género en una comunidad del Cusco. *Revista Andina* 9 (1): 7–29.
———. 2000. *Indigenous Mestizos: The Politics of Race and Culture in Cuzco, 1919–1991*. Durham: Duke University Press.
Canessa, Andrew. 2005. The Indian Within, the Indian Without: Citizenship, Race, and Sex in a Bolivian Hamlet. In *Natives Making Nation: Gender, Indigeneity and the State in the Andes*, edited by A. Canessa. Tucson: University of Arizona Press.
Carrión, Julio. 2006. *The Fujimori Legacy: The Rise of Electoral Authoritarianism in Peru*. University Park: Pennsylvania State University Press.
CEDAW. 2007. Comentarios concluyentes del Comitè para la Eliminaciòn dela Discriminacion contra la Mujer: Peru. Informal Spanish translation by Flora Tristán of United Nations, Concluding Comments of the Committee on the Elimination of Discrimination Against Women: Peru, CEDAW/C/PERU/CO/6.http://www.un.org/womenwatch/daw/cedaw/cedaw25years/content/english/CONCLUDING_COMMENTS/Peru/Peru-CO-6.pdf. Fascimile.

Centro de la Mujer Peruana Flora Tristán. 2000. *Mortalidad materna y aborto inseguro.* Lima: Flora Tristán/DEMUS.

———. 2003. *Violencia familiar y sexual: Diagnostico sobre servicios de atencion.* Lima: Flora Tristán.

———. 2004. *Veinticinco años de feminismo en el Perú.* Lima: Heinrich Böll Stiftung.

———. 2006. *Informe Alternativo al Sexto Informe Periòdico del Estado Peruano al Comitè de la CEDAW.* Flora Tristán, Manuela Ramos, CLADEM, DEMUS 2006.

Centro para la Promoción y Desarrollo Poblacional (CEPRODEP). 1997. *Diagnóstico del desplazamiento en Ayacucho 1993–1997: Heroes sin nombre.* Lima: CEPRODEP.

Cervone, Emma. 2002. Engendering Leadership: Indigenous Women Leaders in the Ecuadorian Andes. In Montoya, Frazier, and Hurtig 2002.

Chaney, Elsa. 1979. *Supermadre: Women in Politics in Latin America.* Austin: University of Texas Press.

Chant, Sylvia H., and Nikki Craske, eds. 2003. *Gender in Latin America.* New Brunswick: Rutgers University Press.

Christiansen, Tanja Katherine. 2004. *Disobedience, Slander, Seduction, and Assault: Women and Men in Cajamarca, Peru, 1862–1900.* Austin: University of Texas Press.

Cisneros, Rosa. 1984. El dolor me vuelve más rebelde. *¡Viva!* 1 (2): 12–13.

Clancy-Smith, Julia Ann, and Frances Gouda. 1998. *Domesticating the Empire: Race, Gender, and Family Life in French and Dutch Colonialism.* Charlottesville: University Press of Virginia.

Clay, E., N. Pillai, and C. Benson. 1998. Food Aid and Food Security in the 1990s: Performance and Effectiveness. In *Overseas Development Institute Working Papers.* London.

Collier, David. 1976. *Squatters and Oligarchs: Authoritarian Rule and Policy Change in Peru.* Baltimore: Johns Hopkins University Press.

———. 1978. *Barriadas y elites: De Odría a Velasco.* Lima: Instituto de Estudios Peruanos.

El Comercio. 1995. El 50 % de la población no debe seguir siendo excluida en el mundo. September 14. Warmi CD-ROM CENDOC-Mujer.

Comisión Especial sobre Actividades de Anticoncepción Quirúrgica Voluntaria. 2002. *Informe Final.* Lima: Ministerio de Salud.

Comisión Nacional de la Mujer Peruana (CONAMUP). 1970. Acuerdos y recomendaciones del primer congreso nacional de la mujer Peruana. Facsimile, Trujillo.

———. 1975. Sintesis informativo y anexos de la Conferencia Mundial del Año Internacional de la Mujer. Facsimile, Lima.

Comité Latinoamericano para la Defensa de los Derechos de la Mujer (CLADEM). 1998. *Silencio y complicidad: Violencia contra las mujeres en los servicios pâublicos de salud en el Perú.* Lima: CLADEM; New York, CRLP.

———. 1999. *Nada personal: Reporte de derechos humanos sobre la aplicación de la anticoncepción quirúrgica en el Perú, 1996–1998.* Lima: CLADEM.

Connelly, Matthew James. 2008. *Fatal Misconception: The Struggle to Control World Population.* Cambridge, Mass.: Belknap Press of Harvard University Press.

Contreras, Carlos. 1982. *La ciudad del mercurio, Huancavelica, 1570–1700.* Lima: Instituto de Estudios Peruanos.

Contreras, Carlos, and Marcos Cueto. 1999. *Historia del Perú contemporáneo.* Lima: Red Para el Desarrollo de las Ciencias Sociales en el Perú.

Coral, Isabel. 1998. Women in War: Impact and Responses. In Stern 1998.
Cotler, Julio. 1992. *Clases, estado y nación en el Perú*. 2nd ed. Lima: Instituto de Estudios Peruanos.
———. 1994. *Política y sociedad en el Perú: Cambios y continuidades*. Lima: Instituto de Estudios Peruanos.
Crabtree, John. 1992. *Peru Under García: An Opportunity Lost*. Pittsburgh: University of Pittsburgh Press.
———. 2006. *Construir instituciones: Democracia, desarrollo y desigualdad en el Perú desde 1980*. Lima: Instituto de Estudios Peruanos.
Crabtree, John, and Jim Thomas. 1998. *Fujimori's Peru: The Political Economy*. London: Institute for Latin American Studies.
Craske, Nikki. 1998. Remasculinization and the Neo-liberal State in Latin America. In *Gender, Politics, and the State*, edited by G. Waylen and V. Randall. London: Routledge.
———. 1999. *Women and Politics in Latin America*. New Brunswick: Rutgers University Press.
———. 2000. *Continuing the Challenge: The Contemporary Latin American Women's Movement(s)*. Liverpool: University of Liverpool, Institute of Latin American Studies.
———. 2003. Gender, Poverty, and Social Movements. In Chant and Craske 2003.
Craske, Nikki, and Maxine Molyneux, eds. 2002. *Gender and the Politics of Rights and Democracy in Latin America*. Houndmills, Basingstoke, Hampshire: Palgrave.
Cueto, Marcos. 1997. *El regreso de las epidemias: Salud y sociedad en el Perú del siglo XX*. Lima: Instituto de Estudios Peruanos.
Cueva Beteta, H., and A. Millán Falconi. 2000. *The Women Food Organizations and Their Relationship with the Government*. Report prepared for the Comparative Regional Project, Civil Society and Democratic Governability in the Andes and the South Region, Ford Foundation and the Social Sciences Department of the Catholic University of Peru, Lima.
Das, Veena, and Deborah Poole. 2004. *Anthropology in the Margins of the State*. Santa Fe: School of American Research Press.
Defensoría del Pueblo. n.d. *La aplicación de la anticoncepción quirúrgica y los derechos reproductivos II*. Informe Defensorial No 27. http://www.defensoria.gob.pe/inform-defensoriales.php.
Degregori, Carlos Iván. 2000. *La década de la antipolítica: Auge y huida de Alberto Fujimori y Vladimiro Montesinos*. Serie Ideología y Política 13. Lima: Instituto de Estudios Peruanos.
Degregori, Carlos Iván, Cecilia Blondet, and Nicolás Lynch. 1986. *Conquistadores de un Nuevo Mundo: De invasores a ciudadanos en San Martín de Porres*. Lima: Instituto de Estudios Peruanos.
Degregori, Carlos Iván, José Coronel, Ponciano del Pino, and Orin Starn. 1996. *Las rondas campesinas y la derrota de Sendero Luminoso*. 2nd ed. Lima: Instituto de Estudios Peruanos.
Degregori, Carlos Iván, et al. 1990. *Tiempos de ira y amor: Nuevos actores para viejos problemas*. Lima: DESCO Centro de Estudios y Promoción del Desarrollo.
Denegri, Francesca. 2000. *Soy señora: Testimonio de Irene Jara*. Lima: Instituto de Estudios Peruanos, Flora Tristán, and El Santo Oficio.
Dietz, Mary G. 1998. Context Is All: Feminism and Theories of Citizenship. In Phillips 1998. Oxford: Oxford University Press.

Dore, Elizabeth, and Maxine Molyneux. 2000. *Hidden Histories of Gender and the State in Latin America*. Durham: Duke University Press.
Drinot, Paulo. 2003. States in Crisis: Peru in Historical Perspective. Paper read at Crisis in the Andes, Managing Regional Order, at Oxford University.
———. 2006. Nation-Building, Racism, and Inequality: Institutional Development in Peru in Historical Perspective. In *Making Institutions Work in Peru: Democracy, Development, and Inequality Since 1980*, edited by John Crabtree. London Institute for the Study of the Americas.
Drogus, Carol Ann, and Hannah W. Stewart-Gambino. 2005. *Activist Faith: Grassroots Women in Democratic Brazil and Chile*. University Park: Pennsylvania State University Press.
Eckstein, Susan, and Manuel A. Garretón Merino. 2001. *Power and Popular Protest: Latin American Social Movements*. Updated and expanded ed. Berkeley and Los Angeles: University of California Press.
Egan, Louise. 2000. Rights and Renewal: Peru's Women Take Their Case to the Courts, the Media, and the Streets. *Ford Foundation Report* 31 (1): 26–28. http://www.fordfound.org/pdfs/impact/ford_reports_winter_2000.pdf.
Ehrlich, Paul R. 1968. *The Population Bomb*. New York: Ballantine Books.
Encuesta Nacional de Demografía y Salud (ENDES). 2005. National Demographic and Health Survey. http://www.inei.gob.pe.
Enloe, Cynthia H. 2000. *Maneuvers: The International Politics of Militarizing Women's Lives*. Berkeley and Los Angeles: University of California Press.
Epstein, Helen. 2008. The Strange History of Birth Control. *New York Review of Books*, August 14, 2008, 57–59.
Escobar, Arturo. 1995. *Encountering Development: The Making and Unmaking of the Third World*. Princeton Studies in Culture/Power/History. Princeton: Princeton University Press.
Espinoza Matos, María Jesús. 2000. *Violencia en la familia en Lima y el Callao: Informe de resultados de la I Encuesta de Hogares sobre Vida Familiar en Lima y el Callao*. Lima: Ediciones del Congreso del Perú.
Estremadoyro, Julieta. 2001. Domestic Violence in Andean Communities of Peru. *Law, Social Justice, and Global Development* 1.
Ewig, Christine. 2006a. Hijacking Global Feminism: Feminists, the Catholic Church, and the Family Planning Debacle in Peru. *Feminist Studies* 32 (3): 632–59.
———. 2006b. Global Processes, Local Consequences: Gender Equity and Health Sector Reform in Peru. *Social Politics* 13 (3): 427–55.
Expreso. 1995. Harán gratis vasectomía y ligadura a las personas de escasos recursos. September 12. Warmi CD-ROM CENDOC-Mujer.
Facultad Latinoamericana de Ciencias Sociales (FLACSO). 1993. *Mujeres Latinoamericanas en cifras: Peru*. Santiago de Chile: FLACSO.
———. 1995. *Latin American Women: Compared Figures*. Santiago de Chile: FLACSO.
Federación de Clubes de Madres de la Provincia de Huamanga (FECMA). 1995–99. *Constancia de apertura de libro de actas de la Federación de Clubes de Madres de la Provincia de Huamanga-FECMA-PH 1995–1999*.
FEMOCCPAALC. n.d. Reseña Historico de Nuestra Organización. Facsimile. Lima.
Ferrando, D. 2001. *Estimación de los niveles de Aborto Inducido en el Perú*. Lima: Pathfinder International, Flora Tristán.
Figueroa, Adolfo. 1998. Income Distribution and Poverty in Peru. In Crabtree and Thomas 1998.

Flores Galindo, Alberto. 1999. *La tradición autoritaria: Violencia y democracia en el Perú.* Lima: SUR Casa de Estudios del Socialismo.
Flores Galindo, Alberto, and Nelson Manrique. 1985. *Violencia y campesinado.* [Lima]: Instituto de Apoyo Agrario.
Fort, A. L. 1989. Investigation of the Social Context of Fertility and Family Planning: A Qualitative Study in Peru. *International Family Planning Perspectives* 15 (3): 88–94.
Francke, M. 1990. Género, clase y etnía: La tenza de la dominación. In Degregori et al. 1990.
Francke, Pedro. 2003. Comedores Populares: Sincerando realidades. *La República*, May 1.
Fujimori, Alberto. 1995. Speech Given Before the Fourth World Conference on Women, September 15, 1995, Beijing, China. Unofficial translation from Spanish original. http://www.un.org/esa/gopher-data/conf/fwcw/conf/gov/950915131946.txt.
Fuller, Norma J. 1993. *Dilemas de la femineidad: Mujeres de clase media en el Perú.* 2nd ed. Lima: Pontificia Universedad Católica del Perú Fondo Editorial.
Fumerton, Mario. 2002. *From Victims to Heroes: Peasant Counter-Rebellion and Civil War in Ayacucho, Peru, 1980–2000.* Amsterdam: Rozenberg.
García, María Elena. 2005. *Making Indigenous Citizens: Identities, Education, and Multicultural Development in Peru.* Stanford: Stanford University Press.
Garcia Naranjo Morales, Aida. 2001. *Vaso de Leche: Memoria de mujeres.* Lima: Centro de Asesoria Laboral del peru.
Goldstein, Donna M. 2003. *Laughter Out of Place: Race, Class, Violence, and Sexuality in a Rio Shantytown.* California Series in Public Anthropology. Berkeley and Los Angeles: University of California Press.
Gonzales de Olarte, Efraín, and Pilar Gavilano Llosa. 1998. *Pobreza y violencia doméstica contra la mujer en Lima Metropolitana.* Lima: Instituto de Estudios Peruanos.
Gow, Peter, and Penelope Harvey. 1994. *Sex and Violence: Issues in Representation and Experience.* London: Routledge.
Graham, Carol. 1991. The APRA Government and the Urban Poor: The PAIT Programme in Lima's Pueblos Jovenes. *Journal of Latin American Studies* 23 (1): 91–130.
Griffin, Philip. 1979. The Impact of Food Aid: Peru, a Case Study. *Food Policy* 4 (1): 46–52.
Grupo Autonomo de Mujeres. 1983. Por un Feminismo Revolucionario. March. Facsimile.
Grupo Impulsor Nacional/CESIP. 2000. *El PRONAA y los comedores populares: Yo te doy, pero si no me apoyas yo te quito.* Lima: CESIP.
Güezmes, Ana, Nancy Palomina, and Miguel Ramos. 2002. *Violencia sexual y física contra las mujeres en el Perú.* Lima: Flora Tristán.
Guzmán, José Miguel, et al., eds. 1996. *The Fertility Transition in Latin America.* International Studies in Demography. Oxford: Clarendon Press.
Guzmán Chaganaquí, Alfredo. 2002. Para mejorar la salud reproductiva. In Arroyo 2002.
Hale, Charles A. 1996. Political Ideas and Ideologies in Latin America, 1870–1930. In *Ideas and Ideologies in Twentieth Century Latin America,* edited by Leslie Bethell. Cambridge: Cambridge University Press.
Harris, Olivia. 1978. Complementarity and Conflict: An Andean View of Women and Men. In *Sex and Age as Principles of Social Differentiation,* edited by J. S. LaFontaine. New York: Academic Press.

Hartmann, Betsy. 1995. *Reproductive Rights and Wrongs: The Global Politics of Population Control*. Rev. ed. Boston: South End Press.
Harvey, Penelope. 1994. Domestic Violence in the Peruvian Andes. In Gow and Harvey 1994.
Hautzinger, S. 2002. Criminalizing Male Violence in Brazil's Women's Police Stations: From Flawed Essentialism to Imagined Communities. *Journal of Gender Studies* 11 (3): 243–51.
Heise, Lori L. 1997. Violence, Sexuality, and Women's Lives. In *The Gender/Sexuality Reader: Culture, History, Political Economy*, edited by R. N. Lancaster and M. Di Leonarda. New York: Routledge.
Held, David. 1989. *Political Theory and the Modern State: Essays on State, Power, and Democracy*. Stanford: Stanford University Press.
Henríquez Ayin, Narda, and Cecilia Reynoso Rendón. 2006. *Cuestiones de género y poder en el conflicto armado en el Perú*. San Borja, Lima, Peru: CONCYTEC.
Herman, Judith Lewis. 1992. *Trauma and Recovery*. New York: Basic Books.
hooks, bell. 1981. *Ain't I a Woman: Black Women and Feminism*. Boston: South End Press.
Hünefeldt, Christine. 2000. *Liberalism in the Bedroom: Quarreling Spouses in Nineteenth-Century Lima*. University Park: Pennsylvania State University Press.
Isbell, Billie Jean. 1979. La otra mitad esencial: Un estudio de complementaridad sexual en los Andes. *Estudios Andinos* 5 (1): 37–56.
Jacobs, Susie M., Ruth Jacobson, and Jen Marchbank. 2000. *States of Conflict: Gender, Violence, and Resistance*. London: Zed Books.
Jaquette, Jane S. 1994. *The Women's Movement in Latin America: Participation and Democracy*. 2nd ed. Boulder: Westview Press.
Jaquette, Jane S., and Kathleen A. Staudt. 1988. Politics, Population, and Gender: A Feminist Analysis of US Population Policy in the Third World. In *The Political Interests of Gender: Developing Theory and Research with a Feminist Face*, edited by Kathleen B. Jones and Anna G. Jónasdóttir. London: Sage.
Jaquette, Jane S., and Sharon L. Wolchik. 1998. *Women and Democracy: Latin America and Central and Eastern Europe*. Baltimore: Johns Hopkins University Press.
Jara, Olga. 1975. Apuebran estatuto de Comisión Nacional de la Mujer Peruana. *La Cronica*, July 18. Warmi CD-ROM CENDOC-Mujer.
Jelin, Elizabeth, J. Ann Zammit, and Marilyn Thomson. 1990. *Women and Social Change in Latin America*. Geneva: United Nations Research Institute for Social Development, Zed Books; London: Zed Books.
Jochamowitz, Luis. 1993. *Ciudadano Fujimori: La construcción de un político*. Serie crónicas contemporáneas. Lima: PEISA.
Johannsen, Julia. 2006. *Operational Poverty Targeting in Peru: Proxy Means Testing with Non-income Indicators*. International Poverty Centre Working Paper No. 30. Brasilia: United Nations Development Programme, International Poverty Centre.
Kabeer, Naila. 1992. *From Fertility Reduction to Reproductive Choice: Gender Perspectives on Family Planning*. Brighton: University of Sussex Institute of Development Studies.
———. 2001. *Reversed Realities: Gender Hierarchies in Development Thought*. London: Verso.
Kaplan, Temma. 1982. Female Consciousness and Collective Action: The Case of Barcelona, 1910–1918. *Signs* 7 (3): 545–66.

Kelly, Liz. 2000. Wars Against Women: Sexual Violence, Sexual Politics, and the Militarised State. In Jacobs, Jacobson, and Marchbank 2000.
Kirk, Robin. 1993. *Grabado en piedra: Las mujeres de Sendero Luminoso*. Lima: Instituto de Estudios Peruanos.
Kisic, Drago. 1998. Privatisation, Investment, and Sustainability. In Crabtree and Thomas 1998.
Klarén, Peter F. 2000. *Peru: Society and Nationhood in the Andes*. New York: Oxford University Press.
Koven, Seth, and Sonya Michel. 1993. *Mothers of a New World: Maternalist Politics and the Origins of Welfare States*. New York: Routledge.
Kruijt, Dirk. 1994. *Revolution by Decree: Peru, 1968–1975*. Thela Latin America Series 1. Amsterdam: Thela.
Lenten, Roelie. 1993. *Cooking Under the Volcanoes: Communal Kitchens in the Southern Peruvian City of Arequipa*. Latin America Studies. Amsterdam: CEDLA.
Lerner, Salomón. 2003. *Discurso de presentación del informe final de la Comisión de la Verdad y Reconciliación 2003*. http://www.cverdad.org.pe.
Leydesdorff, Selma, Luisa Passerini, and Paul Richard Thompson, eds. 1996. *Gender and Memory*. International Yearbook of Oral History and Life Stories 4. Oxford: Oxford University Press.
Lievesley, Geraldine. 1996. Stages of Growth? Women Dealing with the State and Each Other in Peru. In Lievesley and Rai 1996.
Lievesley, Geraldine, and Shirin M. Rai, eds. 1996. *Women and the State: International Perspectives*. London: Taylor and Francis.
Lind, Amy. 2005. *Gendered Paradoxes: Women's Movements, State Restructuring, and Global Development in Ecuador*. University Park: Pennsylvania State University Press.
Loli, Silvia. 2007. *Reporte sobre la vigencia de los derechos humanos de las mujeres en el Peru*. Flora Tristán, 2001. Facsimile.
Lowenthal, A. 1975. *The Peruvian Experiment: Continuity and Change Under Military Rule*. Princeton: Princeton University Press.
Lycklama à Nijeholt, Geertje, Virginia Vargas, and Saskia Wieringa, eds. 1998. *Women's Movements and Public Policy in Europe, Latin America, and the Caribbean*. New York: Garland.
Macaulay, Fiona. 2006. *Gender Politics in Brazil and Chile: The Role of Parties in National and Local Policymaking*. Basingstoke: Palgrave Macmillan.
Makhlouf Obermeyer, Carla. 1999. The Cultural Context of Reproductive Health: Implications for Monitoring the Cairo Agenda. *International Family Planning Perspectives* 25 Suppl. S50–S52, S55.
Mallon, Florencia E. 1983. *The Defense of Community in Peru's Central Highlands: Peasant Struggle and Capitalist Transition, 1860–1940*. Princeton: Princeton University Press.
———. 1995. *Peasant and Nation: The Making of Postcolonial Mexico and Peru*. Berkeley and Los Angeles: University of California Press.
Mamdani, Mahmood. 1972. *The Myth of Population Control: Family, Caste, and Class in an Indian Village*. New York: Monthly Review Press.
Manrique, Nelson. 2002. Violencia política, etnicidad y racismo en el Perú del tiempo de la guerra. In *El tiempo del miedo: La violencia política en el Perú 1980–1996*, edited by N. Manrique. Lima: Fondo Editorial del Congreso del Perú.

Marka. 1979. Manuela Ramos: Hacía un feminismo de Izquierda. September 20. Warmi CD-ROM CENDOC-Mujer.

———. 1984. Protestan por violación de testigo clave de Uchuraccay. December 8. Warmi CD-ROM CENDOC-Mujer.

Matear, Ann. 1999. Gender Relations, Authoritarianism, and Democratization in Chile. *Democratization* 6 (3): 100–17.

Maternowska, M. Catherine. 2006. *Reproducing Inequities: Poverty and the Politics of Population in Haiti.* New Brunswick: Rutgers University Press.

Matos Mar, José. 1984. *Desborde popular y crisis del estado: El nuevo rostro del Perú en la década de 1980.* Perú problema 21. Lima: Instituto de Estudios Peruanos.

McClintock, Cynthia, and Abraham F. Lowenthal. 1983. *The Peruvian Experiment Reconsidered.* Princeton: Princeton University Press.

Meintjes, Sheila, Anu Pillay, and Meredeth Turshen. 2001. *The Aftermath: Women in Post-conflict Transformation.* London: Zed Books.

Méndez, Juan E., Guillermo O'Donnell, and Paulo Sérgio Pinheiro. 1999. *The (Un)rule of Law and the Underprivileged in Latin America.* Notre Dame: University of Notre Dame Press.

Méndez G., Cecilia. 2005. *The Plebeian Republic: The Huanta Rebellion and the Making of the Peruvian state, 1820–1850.* Durham: Duke University Press.

Ministerie van Justitie. 2002. *Privé geweld, publieke zaak.* http://www.huiselijkgeweld.nl.

Ministerio para la Promoción de la Mujer y el Desarrollo Humano (PROMUDEH). 2001. *Plan Nacional Contra la Violencia Hacia la Mujer* 2001.Facsimile.

Molyneux, Maxine. 1985. Mobilisation Without Emancipation? Women's Interests, the State, and Revolution in Nicaragua. *Feminist Studies* 2:227–54.

———. 2000a. State, Gender, and Institutional Change: The Federación de Mujeres Cubanas. In Dore and Molyneux 2000.

———. 2000b. Twentieth-Century State Formations in Latin America. In Dore and Molyneux 2000.

———. 2001. *Women's Movements in International Perspective: Latin America and Beyond.* New York: Palgrave.

Montoya, Rosario, Lessie Jo Frazier, and Janise Hurtig, eds. 2002. *Gender's Place: Feminist Anthropologies of Latin America.* New York: Palgrave Macmillan.

Moore, Henrietta. 1994. The Problem of Explaining Violence in the Social Sciences. In *Sex and Violence: Issues in Representation and Experience,* edited by Penelope Harvey and Peter Gow. London: Routledge.

Morris-Suzuki, T. 2000. For and Against NGOs: The Politics of the Lived World. *New Left Review* 2 (March–April): 63–84.

Moser, Caroline O. N., and Cathy McIlwaine. 2004. *Encounters with Daily Violence in Latin America: Urban Poor Perceptions from Columbia and Guatemala.* New York: Routledge.

Movimiento Manuela Ramos. 1983. La Situación de la Mujer, Collique 1983. 567-ICCO, Utrecht Archives.

———. 1984. Las Manuelas se encuentran III. 567-5250-84 G ICCO, Utrecht Archives.

———. 1997. Plan Estratégico 1998–2000. Lima.

———. 2001. Manuela Ramos en la década de los '90. Facsimile. Lima.

———. n.d. La violencia contra la mujer en cifras. Fascimile. Lima.

Moyano, María-Elena. 1990. Dirigimos o cocinamos el Vaso de Leche? *Pagina Libre*, B4.

Moyano, María Elena, and Diana Miloslavich Túpac. 1993. *María Elena Moyano: En busca de una esperanza*. Lima: Centro de la Mujer Peruana Flora Tristán.
Murdock, Donna F. 2003. Neoliberalism, Gender, and Development: Institutionalizing "Post-Feminism" in Medellin, Colombia. *Women's Studies Quarterly* 31 (3–4): 129–53.
Mujer y Sociedad. 1984. A donde va el feminismo. 4 (8): 27–29.
———. 1987. Violencia sexual y las penas. 7 (12): 2–3.
———. 1989. Reforma del Codigo Penal. 4 (29): 17.
Nair, Sumati, and Preetl Kirbat. 2004. A Decade After Cairo: Women's Health in a Free Market Economy. Corner House Briefing 31. http://www.thecornerhouse.org.uk/pdf/briefing/31cairo.pdf
Navarro, Marysa. 2002. Against *Marianismo*. In Montoya, Frazier, and Hurtig 2002.
Nelson, Diane M. 1999. *A Finger in the Wound: Body Politics in Quincentennial Guatemala*. Berkeley and Los Angeles: University of California Press.
Nelson, Sara. 1996. Constructing and Negotiating Gender in Women's Police Stations in Brazil. *Latin American Perspectives* 23 (1): 131–48.
Nugent, José Guillermo. 1992. El laberinto de la choledad. Serie panel 1. Lima: Fundación Friedrich Ebert.
El Observador. 1984. Guardia civil: De profesion ¿Violador? January 28.
Ojo. 1991. Madres serán heroínas de reconstrucción nacional. May 11. Warmi CD-ROM CENDOC-Mujer.
Oliart, Patricia. 1999. Leer y escribir en un mundo sin letras: Reflexiones sobre la globalización y la educación en la Sierrra rural. In *Cultura y Globalización*, edited by Carlos Iván Degregori and Gonzalo Portocarrero. Lima: Red para el Desarrollo de las Ciencias Sociales en el Perú.
Olthoff, Jacobijn. 2006. *A Dream Denied: Teenage Girls in Migrant Popular Neighbourhoods, Lima, Peru*. Utrecht: Universiteit Utrecht.
Paerregaard, Karsten. 1997. *Linking Separate Worlds: Urban Migrants and Rural Lives in Peru*. New York: Berg.
Palomino, Rocio. 2004. Mujeres populares y sus negociaciones con el estado. los programas alimentarios. In Centro de la Mujer Peruana Flora Tristán 2004.
Pankhurst, Donna. 2003. The "Sex War" and Other Wars: Towards a Feminist Approach to Peace Building. *Development in Practice* 13 (2–3): 154–77.
———. 2007. *Gendered Peace: Women's Struggles for Post-war Justice and Reconciliation*. Routledge/UNRISD Research in Gender and Development 2. New York: Routledge.
Pateman, Carole. 1988. *The Sexual Contract*. Stanford: Stanford University Press.
Perks, Robert, and Alistair Thomson. 1998. *The Oral History Reader*. London: Routledge.
El Peruano. 1996. Madres son el gran soporte de la reconstrucción nacional. May 12. Warmi CD-ROM CENDOC-Mujer.
Petchesky, Rosalind P. 2000. *Reproductive and Sexual Rights: Charting the Course of Transnational Women's NGOs*. UNRISD Occasional Paper 8.
Phillips, Anne. 1998. *Feminism and Politics*. Oxford Readings in Feminism. Oxford: Oxford University Press.
Phoenix, Ann, and Pamela Pattynama,. 2006. Intersectionality. *European Journal of Women's Studies* 13 (3): 187–92.
Pillay, A. 2001. Violence Against Women in the Aftermath. In Meintjes, Pillay, and Turshen 2001.

Poole, Deborah. 2004. Between Threat and Guarantee: Justice and Community on the Margins of the Peruvian State. In Das and Poole 2004.
Poole, Deborah, and Gerardo Rénique. 1992. *Peru: Time of Fear*. London: Latin American Bureau.
Portocarrero, Felipe, Arlette Beltrán, María Elena Romero, and Hanny Cueva. 1998. *Economía y política de los programas gubernamentales de apoyo alimentario en el Perú*. Universidad Pacífico. http://www.idrc.ca/lacro/foro/seminario/portocarrero.
Portugal, Ana María. 1987. Política de población: ¿Nos concierne? ¡Viva! 4 (10): 2–3.
Presidencia de la República, PROMUDEH. n.d. Avanzamos hacia un futuro mejor. Promotional leaflet.
Programa Integral de la Lucho Contra la Violencia Familiar y Sexual. 2005. *Levantamiento de indicadores para la linea de base del Programa Integral de la Lucho Contra la Violencia Familiar y Sexual, Ayacucho*. Ayacucho: Ministerio de la Mujer y Desarrollo Social, Cooperacion Belga al Desarrollo.
Quijano, Aníbal. 1967. *La emergencia del grupo cholo y sus implicancias en la sociedad peruana*. Lima.
———. 1980. *Dominación y cultura: Lo cholo y el conflicto cultural en el Perú*. Lima: Mosca Azul Editores.
Radcliffe, Sarah A., and Sallie Westwood. 1993. *"Viva": Women and Popular Protest in Latin America*. London: Routledge.
Red Nacional de la Promociòn de la Mujer. 2002. *La menarquìa y sus implicaciones en la educaciòn en el Perù*. Ayacucho: Red Nacional de la Promociòn de la Mujer, World Education, USAID.
La República. 1991. ¡Queremos paz, justicia y vida! El grito de las madres que luchan contra el hambre y el terror. September 27. Warmi CD-ROM CENDOC-Mujer.
———. 1995. La Iglesia y el gobierno coinciden en planificación familiar con ética. August 16. Warmi CD-ROM CENDOC-Mujer.
Reynaga Farfán, Gumercinda. 1996. *Cambios en las relaciones familiares campesinas a partir de la violencia política y le nuevo rol de la mujer*. Documento de Trabajo 75. Lima: Instituto de Estudios Peruanos.
Richards, Patricia. 2004. *Pobladoras, Indígenas, and the State: Conflicts over Women's Rights in Chile*. New Brunswick: Rutgers University Press.
Rivera, Cecilia. 1993. *María Marimacha: Los caminos de la identidad femenina*. Lima: Pontificia Universidad Católica del Perú Fondo Editorial.
Rodríguez, Alfredo, Gustavo Riofrío, and Eileen Welsh. 1973. *De invasores a invadidos*. Lima: Desco.
Rousseau, Stéphanie. 2006. Women's Citizenship and Neopopulism: Peru Under the Fujimori Regime. *Latin American Politics and Society* 48 (1): 117–41.
———. 2007. The Politics of Reproductive Health in Peru: Gender and Social Policy in the Global South. *Social Politics* 1–33, http://sp.oxfordjournals.org/cgi/reprint/jxm002v2.pdf.
Ruggeri Laderchi, Caterina. 2001. *Killing Two Birds with the Same Stone? The Effectiveness of Food Transfers on Nutrition and Monetary Poverty*. Queen Elizabeth House Working Paper 74. Oxford University.
Ruggeri Laderchi, Caterina, Ruhi Saith, and Frances Stewart. 2003. *Does It Matter That We Don't Agree on the Definitions of Poverty? A Comparison of Four Approaches*. Queen Elizabeth House Working Paper 107. Oxford University.

Sala, Mariela. 1984. La complicidad de las leyes. ¡Viva! 1 (2): 7–10.
———. 1996. Polemica entre el gobierno y la iglesia, Peru. Facsimile. http://www.fempress.cl (accessed October 2001).
Sánchez-Griñan, Marìa Inès. 2002. Hacia una Politica nutricional en el Peru: Estrategias alimentarias y no alimentarias. In Arroyo 2002.
Sangster, Joan. 2000. Telling Our Stories: Feminist Debates and the Use of Oral History. In Perks and Thompson 1998.
Santos, C. M. 2004. Engendering the Police: Women's Police Stations and Feminism in São Paolo. *Latin American Research Review* 39 (3): 29–55.
Saporta Sternbach, Nancy, Marysa Navarro-Aranguren, Patricia Chuchryk, and Sonia E. Alvarez. 1992. Feminisms in Latin America: From Bogotá to San Bernardo. *Signs* 17 (2): 393–434.
Schady, Norbert. 1999. *Seeking Votes: The Political Economy of Expenditures by the Peruvian Social Fund (FONCODES), 1991–95.* Washington, DC: World Bank Poverty Reduction and Economic Management Network Poverty Division.
Scheper-Hughes, Nancy, and Philippe I. Bourgois. 2004. *Violence in War and Peace: An Anthology.* Malden, Mass.: Blackwell.
Schild, Verónica. 1998. New Subjects of Rights? Women's Movements and the Construction of Citizenship in the "New Democracies." In Alvarez, Dagnino, and Escobar 1998.
———. 2000. "Gender Equity" Without Social Justice: Women's Rights in the Neoliberal Age. *NACLA Report on the Americas* 34 (1): 25–28.
Schmidt, Gregory D. 2006. All the President's Women: Fujimori and Gender Equity in Peruvian Politics. In Carrión 2006.
Schmidt, Gregory D., and Kyle L. Saunders. 2004. Effective Quotas, Relative Party Magnitude, and the Success of Female Candidates: Peruvian Municipal Elections in Comparative Perspective. *Comparative Political Studies* 37 (6): 704–24.
Scott, James C. 1985. *Weapons of the Weak: Everyday Forms of Peasant Resistance.* New Haven: Yale University Press.
———. 1990. *Domination and the Arts of Resistance: Hidden Transcripts.* New Haven: Yale University Press.
Scott, Joan Wallach, ed. 1996. *Feminism and History.* Oxford: Oxford University Press.
Shepard, Bonnie. 2002. *Reproductive Health: Building Women's Citizenship.* Ford Foundation. http://www.drclas.harvard.edu/revista/articles/view/412.
Shore, Cris, and Susan Wright. 1997. *Anthropology of Policy: Critical Perspectives on Governance and Power.* London: Routledge.
Silverblatt, Irene Marsha. 1987. *Moon, Sun, and Witches: Gender Ideologies and Class in Inca and Colonial Peru.* Princeton: Princeton University Press.
Skocpol, Theda. 1992. *Protecting Soldiers and Mothers: The Political Origins of Social Policy in the United States.* Cambridge, Mass.: Belknap Press of Harvard University Press.
Sobo, Elisa J. 1993. Bodies, Kin, and Flow: Family Planning in Rural Jamaica. *Medical Anthropology Quarterly*, n.s. 7 (1): 50–73.
Squires, Judith. 1999. *Gender in Political Theory.* Cambridge: Polity Press; Malden, Mass.: Blackwell.
Starn, Orin. 1999. *Nightwatch: The Making of a Movement in the Peruvian Andes.* Durham: Duke University Press.
Stein, Dorothy. 1997. Population as Politics: A Review Article. *Comparative Studies in Society and History* 39 (3): 593–99.

Stepan, Alfred C. 1978. *The State and Society: Peru in Comparative Perspective*. Princeton: Princeton University Press.
Stern, Steve J., ed. 1998. *Shining and Other Paths: War and Society in Peru, 1980–1995*. Durham: Duke University Press.
Sternberg, Peter. 2000. Challenging Machismo: Promoting Sexual and Reproductive Health with Nicaraguan Men. *Gender and Development* 8 (1): 89–99.
Stokes, Susan Carol. 1995. *Cultures in Conflict: Social Movements and the State in Peru*. Berkeley and Los Angeles: University of California Press.
Stoler, Ann Laura. 1995. *Race and the Education of Desire: Foucault's History of Sexuality and the Colonial Order of Things*. Durham: Duke University Press.
———. 2002. *Carnal Knowledge and Imperial Power: Race and the Intimate in Colonial Rule*. Berkeley and Los Angeles: University of California Press.
Tamayo, Ana María. 2003. Anfasep y la lucha por la memoria de sus desaparecidos (1983–2000). In *Jamás tan cerca arremetió lo lejos: Memoria y violencia política en el Perú*, edited by Carlos Iván Degregori. Lima: Instituto de Estudios Peruanos.
Theidon, Kimberly Susan. 2003. Disarming the Subject: Remembering War and Imagining Citizenship in Peru. *Cultural Critique* 54:67–87.
———. 2004. *Entre prójimos: El conflicto armado interno y la política de la reconciliación en el Perú*. Estudios de la sociedad rural 24. Lima: Instituto de Estudios Peruanos.
Thorp, Rosemary, and Geoffrey Bertram. 1978. *Peru, 1890–1977: Growth and Policy in an Open Economy*. London: Macmillan.
Thurner, Mark. 1997. *From Two Republics to One Divided: Contradictions of Postcolonial Nationmaking in Andean Peru*. Durham: Duke University Press.
Tinsman, Heidi. 1997. Household *Patrones*: Wife-Beating and Sexual Control in Rural Chile, 1964–1988. In *The Gendered Worlds of Latin American Women Workers*, edited by John D. French and Daniel James. Durham: Duke University Press.
La Tortuga. 1987. Comisión Nacional de los Derechos de la Mujer. 20:21–23.
Truth and Reconciliation Commission (TRC). 2002. AT Mujer. Videos of Public Hearings Concerning Gender and Violence, Lima.
———. 2003. *Informe Final*. http://www.cverdad.org.pe.
Urrea Giraldo, Fernando, Mara Viveros Vigoya, and Peter Wade. 2008. *Raza, etnicidad y sexualidades: Ciudadanía y multiculturalismo en América Latina*. Bogota: Universidad Nacional de Colombia.
USAID. n.d. Improved Health, Including Family Planning of High-Risk Populations. Peru: Activity Data Sheet 527-003. http://www.usaid.gov/pubs/cbj2002/lac/pe/527-003.html.
Uvin, Peter. 1992. Regime, Surplus, and Self-Interest: The International Politics of Food Aid. *International Studies Quarterly* 36 (3): 293–312.
Valdez Arroyo, Flor de María. 2006. Justicia para las victimas de violencia sexual en el conflicto armado interno peruano. Paper read at Congreso Internacional de Derechos Humanos, Instituto de Investigaciones Jurídicas de la Universidad Autónoma de México y el Instituto Luso-Americano-Filipino de Derecho Internacional, May 23–26, Mexico City.
Vargas, Virginia. 1991. The Women's Movement in Peru: Streams, Spaces, and Knots. *European Review of Latin American and Carribean Studies* 50 (June): 7–50.
———. 1992. *Cómo cambiar el mundo sin perdernos: El movimiento de mujeres en el Perú y América Latina*. Lima: Ediciones Flora Tristán.

———. 1995. Women's Movement in Peru: Rebellion into Action. In *Subversive Women: Women's Movements in Africa, Asia, Latin America, and the Caribbean*, edited by Saskia Wieringa. New Delhi: Kali for Women.

———. 2002. The Struggle by Latin American Feminisms for Rights and Autonomy. In Craske and Molyneux 2002. Durham: Duke University Press.

———. 2004. Los feminismos peruanos: Breve balance de tres decadas. In Centro de la Mujer Peruana Flora Tristán 2004.

Vargas Llosa, Mario. 1994. *A Fish in the Water: A Memoir*. New York: Farrar, Straus and Giroux.

Vasquez del Aguila, Ernesto. 2006. Invisible Women: Forced Sterilization, Reproductive Rights, and Structural Inequalities in Peru of Fujimori and Toledo. *Estudos e Pesquisas em Psicología* 6 (1): 109–24.

Vavrus, Frances, and Lisa Ann Richey. 2003. Editorial. In Women and Development: Rethinking Policy and Reconceptualizing Practice. Special issue, *Women's Studies Quarterly* 31 (3–4): 6–18.

Vega-Centeno B., Imelda. 1994. *Simbólica y política: Perú 1978–1993*. Lima: Fundación Friedrich Ebert.

Velazco, Jackeline. 1998. *La asistencia alimentaria en los hogares pobres dirigidos por mujeres: Un enfoque microeconomico*. Documento de Trabajo no 152. Lima: Departamento de Economía PUCP.

¡Viva! 1985. Necesidad de una política democrática de población. 1 (4): 22.

Wade, Peter. 2003. Race and Nation in Latin America: An Anthropological View. In Appelbaum, Macpherson, and Rosemblatt 2003.

Walby, Sylvia. 1990. *Theorizing Patriarchy*. Oxford: Blackwell.

Ward, Martha C. 1995. Early Childbearing: What Is the Problem and Who Owns It? In *Conceiving the New World Order: The Global Politics of Reproduction*, edited by Faye D. Ginsburg and Rayana Rapp. Berkeley and Los Angeles: University of California Press.

Waylen, Georgina. 1998. Gender and Governance: Democratic Consolidation and Economic Reform. *Journal of International Development* 10:957–67.

———. 2007. *Engendering Transitions: Women's Mobilization, Institutions, and Gender Outcomes*. Gender and Politics. Oxford: Oxford University Press.

Waylen, Georgina, and Vicky Randall, eds. 1998. *Gender, Politics and the State*. London: Routledge.

Webb, Richard. 1977. *Government Policy and the Distribution of Income in Peru*. Cambridge, Mass.: Harvard University Press.

Weldon, Laurel S. 2002. *Protest, Policy, and the Problem of Violence Against Women: A Cross-National Comparison*. Pittsburgh: University of Pittsburgh Press.

Wieringa, Saskia. 1994. Women's Interests and Empowerment: Gender Planning Reconsidered. *Development and Change* 25 (4): 829–48.

World Health Organization. 2005. WHO Multi-country Study on Women's Health and Violence Against Women. Summary Report of Initial Results on Prevalence, Health Outcomes, and Women's Responses. Geneva: WHO.

Yanez, Ana Maria. 2003. Quotas and Democracy in Peru. Paper read at Interntional IDEA Workshop, Lima.

Yon Leau, Carmen. 2000. *Hablan las mujeres Andinas: Preferencias reproductivas y anticoncepción*. Lima: Manuela Ramos.

Young, Iris Marion. 2001. Polity and Group Difference: A Critique of the Ideal of Universal Citizenship. In Phillips 2001.

Young, Robert J. C. 1995. *Colonial Desire: Hybridity in Theory, Culture, and Race.* London: Routledge.
Ypeij, Annelou. 2006. *Produciendo contra la pobreza: La microempresa vista desde el genero.* Lima: Instituto de Estudios Peruanos.
Yuval-Davis, Nira. 1997. Women, Citizenship, and Difference. *Feminist Review* 57 (Autumn): 4–27.
———. 2006. Intersectionality and Feminist Politics. *European Journal of Women's Studies* 13 (3): 193–209.
Zauzig, Maria-Christine. 2000. *Perú: "Política de población" y derechos humanos: Campañas de esterilización 1996–1998.* Lima: Comisión Alemana Justicia y Paz.

INDEX

activism, x, 6–7, 19, 26, 29, 30, 33, 51–52, 56, 71, 109, 110, 123, 131, 143, 153. *See also* feminist activism
abortion, 11, 78, 80, 90–91, 97, 100, 111, 150
Afro-Peruvian, 8n4, 10
agency, 13, 16, 69, 73, 146, 152
APRA, Political Party, 33, 48, 141
authoritarianism, 2, 11, 16, 18, 31, 32, 87, 109, 135, 136
autonomy
   and feminist organizations, 27, 31
   and grassroots organizations, 7, 45, 49, 51, 58, 64, 72–73
   sexual, 93
   of women, 94, 146
Ayacucho, xii, 1, 3–4, 14–15, 17–18, 46–47, 59, 61–62, 66–68, 74, 80, 84, 89, 107–8, 110, 113, 115, 117–19, 121, 124, 125, 127, 132, 135, 137–39, 141–45, 147–48, 150
   and political violence, 14, 50–52, 55, 124–25
   and women's organizations, xii, 15, 17, 46–47, 51–52, 55–56, 58–59, 63, 71–72, 124–25, 129, 137, 142–43

battered women, 4, 112, 122, 126, 130, 140, 149. *See also* domestic violence
Belaúnde, Fernando, 23, 32–33, 38, 48–49, 111
birth control, 17, 75, 77, 79–80, 93–96, 98–100, 102, 105–6, 109. *See also* reproductive health

Casa de Bienestar, xii, 98n20, 119–21
Centro de Emergencia Mujer (CEM), 121, 148–50
cholificación, 22

citizenship, 4–8, 21, 42, 73, 135, 140, 152
class, xi, 2–8, 10–12, 16, 18, 20–21, 25–30, 32, 34, 36–37, 40, 42–43, 46, 56, 61, 72–73, 77–80, 103, 108, 112, 121, 131, 134–35, 138, 141, 146–47, 152–53. *See also* elites; intersecting inequalities; intersectionality; middle class/es
clientelism, xi, 22, 38, 44–45, 48, 59–60, 64, 70, 72, 109, 146, 151
   definition, 23n3
clubes de madres, 3, 13, 15, 23, 46–47, 49, 50–53, 58–65, 67, 71, 83, 85, 102, 123–25, 127–31, 137–43, 151
comedor popular, x, xi, 3, 23, 27, 38, 45–47, 49–50, 52, 55, 57–58, 60, 62–65, 67–68, 71, 83, 85, 102, 123, 151
Comisión Nacional de la Mujer Peruana (CONAMUP), 25–27, 33
comité de damas, x, 23
conciliation
   in domestic violence cases, 115–20, 134, 147, 149–50
   law on, 115–20
contraception, 94
   contraceptive methods, 3, 79–81, 150
   contraceptives, 15, 76–78, 82, 93–99, 104–5
counterinsurgency, 3, 9, 12, 14, 32, 84, 111
criollo, 8n4, 10, 22, 28, 34, 152

democracy, 9, 34, 41, 107, 109, 113, 120
   democratization, 18, 109, 120, 123, 135, 146
development (social and economic), xi, 2–3, 8, 11, 14, 19–21, 26–27, 29–31, 33n7, 35–40, 42–43, 45, 58, 61, 70, 74n2, 76–77, 79–82, 85, 103, 109, 115, 121, 147
divorce, 1, 115–16, 119, 123, 130–31

domestic violence, 4, 11, 109–11, 114–18, 120–21, 124, 128, 131, 144, 146, 147–51. *See also* battered women; violence
and legislation, 4, 40, 108n3, 115–17, 135
and policies, 2, 108, 122–23, 127, 134–35
double militancy, 27, 29, 31

elites, 2, 22, 140
elitism, 27
emancipation, 2, 8, 19–20, 25–27, 34, 37, 39–40, 42–43, 45, 79
empowerment, 13, 20n1, 21, 27, 36–37, 39, 43, 69, 70, 71, 77, 103, 127, 130, 135, 152
ethnicity, 5, 11–12, 16, 21, 28, 61, 72, 99, 135, 152
ethnic, 6, 10, 22, 108, 111n8, 152

family, ix, x, 2, 4–5, 13, 26, 33, 39, 48, 51–52, 54, 60–62, 69, 80, 84, 88–89, 90n10, 91, 97, 102–4, 107–21, 123, 125, 127–29, 131, 133–36, 138, 140–43, 145–46, 148–49, 153
family planning, 3, 40, 76, 79, 80–81, 83, 92n11, 93, 94, 98, 102, 104–5
Federación de Centrales de Comedores Populares Autogestionarios de Lima y Callao (FECCPALC), 55, 57
Federación de Clubes de Madres de la Provincia de Ayacucho (FECMA), xii, 46–47, 53, 55, 58, 59, 61–68, 142
Federación Departamental de Clubes de Madres de Ayacucho (FEDECMA), xii, 46, 50, 61, 63, 124, 125, 126, 143, 151
Federación de Mujeres Organizadas de Centrales de Comedores Populares Autogestionarios y Afines de Lima y Callao (FEMOCCPAALC), xii, 57n14
feminism, 21–22, 25–27, 30–32
feminist activism, 6, 33, 109–10, 123
feminists, 5, 8, 27–30, 41–42, 60, 94, 105, 112, 151
feministas, 27–29
feminist organizations, 3, 7, 10, 26, 29–31, 33, 55, 77–78, 82, 100, 116, 122, 152
NGOs, 14–15, 20, 29, 31, 41, 75, 77, 81, 83, 99, 101, 144–45, 147, 150
Movement, 17, 20, 29, 31, 39, 78, 82, 100, 112
Flora Tristan, Movimiento de la Mujer Peruana, 30–31, 122, 150, 152
food distribution, 3, 17, 39, 45–46, 59, 71–73, 94, 97, 135, 149–51. *See also* food aid

food aid, 3, 17, 38, 44–46, 48–50, 56–62, 64–73, 109, 146, 150. *See also* food distribution
Fujimori, Alberto, x, xi, 2, 4, 7–9, 17, 19–20, 29, 31, 34–36, 38–42, 46, 48, 57, 59, 60, 64, 69, 71–72, 75, 79–82, 94, 96, 100–101, 103–5, 112–13, 122–23, 134, 135, 141, 143, 146, 150
Fujimoristas, 40–41, 112

García, Alan, 33, 38, 46, 48–49, 79, 141, 148, 150
gender, x, 93, 108, 120, 123, 131, 152
awareness, 146, 150
based violence, 18, 91, 113
consciousness, 13, 150
differentiation, 12, 21, 66, 152
equity, 2, 7, 19, 38–39, 41, 79, 147, 151
and feminism, 30, 33
ideology, 21, 27, 36, 42, 109, 122, 151
inequality, xi, 3, 4–6, 11, 16, 21, 28–29, 43, 61, 72, 73, 99, 103, 117, 122, 134–35, 143, 146, 150, 152
intersection with, 2, 4–5, 8, 16, 19, 28–29, 43, 61, 73, 92n11, 103, 146–47, 152–53
politics, 6, 7, 17, 19, 21, 26–27, 41–42, 111, 143
relations, changing, 27, 133–34
grassroots women's organization, x, xi, 3, 15, 25, 27, 29, 31–32, 37–38, 55–57, 64, 66, 68–69, 71–73, 75, 102, 105, 124, 146. See also *comedor popular*; community kitchen; *clubes de madres*

health care, ix, 8, 34, 36, 75, 77, 79, 81, 83–85, 90, 106
access to, 3, 11, 78
providers, 83, 93–105
reproductive, 3, 11, 17, 75, 78, 105
hierarchy, 13, 59, 69, 73, 89, 116, 152
gender, 12
parameters of, 4
Huancavelica, ix, 4, 10, 14–15, 17, 51, 75, 83–85, 87–88, 90–92, 94–98, 101

indigenous, 22, 42, 66, 98, 108, 117, 145, 152
citizenship, 7
peoples, 39, 115, 146–47
population, 8, 10, 98, 105
women, 28, 74–75, 79–80, 83, 96–98, 103–4, 107, 109, 111, 146–47

intersecting inequalities, xi, 2, 8, 12–13, 17, 27, 76, 98, 147, 152–53
intersectionality, 5. *See also* intersecting inequalities
  of gender, race, and class, 2, 4, 7, 20, 43, 147, 152
  and public health, 92n11

machismo, 36, 127, 130
Manuela Ramos, Movimiento, 10, 15, 30–31, 75, 81, 83, 84–85, 88, 90–91, 94n17, 96, 98–103, 105, 118–19, 121, 145, 147, 150, 152
marianismo, 36
maternalism, 27, 37–38, 43
  maternalist rhetoric, 26, 37, 42, 57, 72
mestizo/a, 8n4, 10, 28, 42, 74, 111, 141, 146
middle class/es, 3, 10, 14, 36, 40, 77–78, 121, 138, 141, 152
  and feminism, 17, 25, 27–28, 42, 56, 112, 131
migrant settlement, ix, 23, 26, 63
  human settlement, 145
  pueblos jovenes, 24, 30, 33, 44, 55, 59, 78, 94
  squatter settlement, ix, 22–24, 123
  urban slums, 17, 22
nation, 4, 8, 24, 36, 38, 40, 60, 73
  -state, 9

neoliberalism, 7, 32, 34, 77
  neoliberal restructuring, 2, 17, 31, 45, 104, 115, 147, 153
  reforms, 83, 103
  and women's bodies, 75, 146
NGOization, 29–32, 147
Nongovernmental Organizations (NGOs), 3, 7, 14–15, 20, 23, 29–33, 41, 48, 50, 55, 57, 60–61, 66, 73, 77, 83, 94, 101–2, 123–24, 129, 132–33, 135, 140, 144, 146, 147, 150

patriarchy, 4, 25
patriarchal relations, 13
population, 8–10, 19–20, 22, 24, 32, 33, 35, 45, 49, 68–70, 75–84, 97–100, 102, 104, 109, 111, 141, 150
  control, 3, 39
  female, 32, 39
  indigenous, 8, 98, 105
  policies, 3, 17, 41, 74–76, 80, 82, 101, 103–4, 109, 150
  program(s), 2, 18, 79, 81–83, 99–100, 104–5

poverty, 9–11, 17, 19, 22, 30, 32, 34–36, 40, 44, 56–57, 61, 70–71, 74–77, 82, 109, 150
  alleviation, 2, 23, 41, 146
  definition, 10n6
  reduction, 3, 39, 45, 64, 70–72, 75, 82, 104, 146–47
  relief, 2, 29, 33, 36, 39, 45–48, 52, 57, 64, 69–72, 109
  reproduction of, 75, 82–83, 104
Programa Nacional de Asistencia Alimentaria (PRONAA), 58–60, 62, 68, 70–71, 150
promotoras, 15, 84–86, 90–91, 96, 98, 101–3
pueblos jovenes. *See* migrant settlement

race, 10, 18, 152–53
  discrimination based on, 146
  intersecting inequalities, xi, 2–5, 7–8, 10, 12, 20–21, 28, 43, 103, 135, 147, 152
  racism, 2–4, 12, 75, 83, 104, 108, 111n8, 135, 153
rape, 8, 11, 111–14, 149
  as weapon of war, 111n8
reproduction (of inequalities), 2, 87
  (Biological), 11, 82–83, 92–93, 95, 104–5
  of poverty. *See* poverty
reproductive health, 3, 4, 15, 17, 75, 77–78, 81, 83–85, 92, 94, 99–100, 102–3, 105, 144, 149–50. *See also* health care
  policies, 76
  services (care), 3, 11, 17, 75, 78, 100, 105, 109

ReproSalud, 83–84, 99–103, 105
resistance, 12, 16, 45, 50, 52, 55–57, 93, 107, 117, 124, 135, 152
rights (civil, political, and social), 4–6, 26, 31, 36, 43, 53, 58–59, 63, 71, 119, 129, 130, 134, 140
  human, 41, 46, 51–52, 75, 81–82, 106, 113–14, 121, 141, 147
  property, 24
  reproductive, 77–79, 100–101, 105, 129, 150
  women's, 1, 2, 7, 17, 25, 33, 37, 39, 41, 42, 77–78, 80–81, 84, 96, 104, 109, 112–13, 116, 121, 129–32, 134–35, 144, 151–52

sexism, 2–4, 12, 75, 83, 108, 111n8, 114, 135, 153
sex education, 80, 88, 150

sexuality, 4n3, 15, 85, 87, 89, 91–92, 102, 104–5, 144–45, 150–51
sexual health, 145
Shining Path, 3, 9, 11, 14, 22, 32, 35, 45, 50–53, 55–57, 65, 84, 111–12, 131, 137
social policy, 3, 20–21, 37, 39, 42–43, 153
squatter settlements. *See* migrant settlement
state, x, xi, 5, 9, 24–26, 29–31, 33, 36–37, 39, 45–46, 48–50, 55, 58–61, 63–65, 67, 72–73, 77–78, 80, 90, 93–94, 98, 100, 102, 104, 108–9, 116, 118, 122, 133–35, 146–50
  agency(ies), 63, 70
  claims on, 7, 55, 57
  institution(s), 62, 66–67, 108, 124, 146, 151, 153
  and nation, 9
  state-society relations, 5–7, 15, 17, 20–21, 109, 153
  and women, 5, 7, 12, 15, 17, 19–20, 42, 124, 150
sterilization, 3, 4, 41, 74, 76, 79–82, 94–97, 100–101, 105, 150

Truth and Reconciliation Commission (TRC), 9, 16, 112, 120

USAID, 17, 48, 76, 81–83, 90, 99–103, 105, 115

Vaso de Leche
  Committees, 3, 44–47, 49, 52, 63–64, 68, 71, 83, 123, 151
  Program, 44, 46–47, 49, 52, 58
Velasco Alvarado, Juan, 8, 22, 24, 25–27, 32–33, 38, 42, 48
violence. *See also* domestic violence
  against women, 4, 16, 18, 88, 91, 102, 107–11, 113–14, 117, 120–21, 123, 133, 135, 147
  as communication, 129, 132–33
  everyday, 4, 9, 117, 124
  legislation against, 42, 113–14, 116, 120, 134
  male, 108, 110, 127
  political, 3, 9, 11–12, 16–17, 22, 32–34, 45, 50–51, 53, 56–57, 72, 109–11, 119, 124–26, 130–31, 141
  resistance against, 50, 52–53, 56, 117, 128–29, 131, 134, 143
  sexual, 11, 92, 111–12, 114–15, 148

"woman question," 19, 21, 25–27, 36–37, 40
women's
  mothering roles, 37, 42, 46–47, 73
  practical and strategic interests, 28–29, 42
  rights. *See* rights

www.ingramcontent.com/pod-product-compliance
Lightning Source LLC
Chambersburg PA
CBHW021406290426
44108CB00010B/412